Connected Parenting

Also Available from Bloomsbury

Critical Perspectives on Language and Kinship in Multilingual Families, Lyn Wright
Discourse and Identity on Facebook, Mariza Georgalou
Social Networks in Language Learning and Language Teaching, edited by Avary Carhill-Poza and Naomi Kurata

Connected Parenting

Digital Discourse and Diverse Family Practices

Jai Mackenzie

BLOOMSBURY ACADEMIC
LONDON • NEW YORK • OXFORD • NEW DELHI • SYDNEY

BLOOMSBURY ACADEMIC
Bloomsbury Publishing Plc
50 Bedford Square, London, WC1B 3DP, UK
1385 Broadway, New York, NY 10018, USA
29 Earlsfort Terrace, Dublin 2, Ireland

BLOOMSBURY, BLOOMSBURY ACADEMIC and the Diana logo are trademarks of Bloomsbury Publishing Plc

First published in Great Britain 2023
Paperback edition published 2024

Copyright © Jai Mackenzie, 2023

Jai Mackenzie has asserted her right under the Copyright, Designs and Patents Act, 1988, to be identified as Author of this work.

For legal purposes the Acknowledgements on p. viii constitute an extension of this copyright page.

Cover design: Tjaša Krivec
Cover image © Getty Images

All rights reserved. No part of this publication may be reproduced or transmitted in any form or by any means, electronic or mechanical, including photocopying, recording, or any information storage or retrieval system, without prior permission in writing from the publishers.

Bloomsbury Publishing Plc does not have any control over, or responsibility for, any third-party websites referred to or in this book. All internet addresses given in this book were correct at the time of going to press. The author and publisher regret any inconvenience caused if addresses have changed or sites have ceased to exist, but can accept no responsibility for any such changes.

A catalogue record for this book is available from the British Library.

A catalog record for this book is available from the Library of Congress.

ISBN: HB: 978-1-3502-6253-9
PB: 978-1-3502-6257-7
ePDF: 978-1-3502-6254-6
eBook: 978-1-3502-6255-3

Typeset by Deanta Global Publishing Services, Chennai, India

To find out more about our authors and books visit www.bloomsbury.com and sign up for our newsletters.

Contents

List of Figures	vi
List of Tables	vii
Acknowledgements	viii
Introduction	1
1 Grounded Theory and Mediated Discourse Analysis	23
2 The Marginalised Families Online Study	39
3 Introducing Collective Connection	65
4 Elaborating Collective Connection	85
5 Introducing Epistemic Connection	107
6 Elaborating Epistemic Connection	137
7 Introducing Affective Connection	159
8 Elaborating Affective Connection	179
9 The Theoretical, Methodological and Practical Implications of Connected Parenting	201
Notes	215
References	217
Index	232

Figures

1	The three core dimensions of connected parenting	3
2	Research design for the Mumsnet Talk study	27
3	Nate using a suction bowl (29.07.2018)	36
4	Jenny's original network diagram	55
5	Jenny's modes of contact diagram	56
6	Jenny's network connections and density diagram	56
7	Jenny's homophily diagram	57
8	Jenny's forms of support diagram	57
9	Lynne's homophily diagram	71
10	Lynne's network connections and density diagram	72
11	Cheryl's homophily diagram	87
12	Cheryl's forms of support diagram	88
13	The Teenage Whisperer homepage (retrieved 04.03.2022)	96
14	'Because that always goes so well' (04.04.2019)	97
15	'Exactly this isn't it' (25.04.2019)	98
16	'Another one that feels like our life' (30.04.2019)	98
17	'The wording the author chose' (07.12.2018)	120
18	Excerpt from a Tes article (07.12.2018)	121
19	'Cried a bit at this' (03.12.2018)	124
20	Excerpt from Sally Donovan's blog post (03.12.2018)	125
21	Jenny's initial retweet-with-comment (06.02.2019)	128
22	Original tweet by @C4Dispatches (05.02.2019)	129
23	Rachael's forms of support diagram	139
24	'A little taste of Friday night' (29.03.2019)	148
25	'A walk in this lovely forest' (15.05.2018)	153
26	Tony's network connections and density diagram	168
27	Peter's modes of contact diagram 1	181
28	Peter's modes of contact diagram 2	181

Tables

1	Participant demographics	16
2	Interview schedule and key questions	43
3	NVivo categories after the initial coding process	47
4	The 'recounting life before children' category	47
5	Numerical overview of participants' combined digital data	50
6	The 'extra-ordinary parenting' category	52
7	The 'building a (virtual) village' category	53
8	Procedure for creating a network diagram	55
9	The 'connected parenting' category	59
10	Types of post in the Parenting Adult Adoptees and New Families groups	93
11	Types of RwC in Jenny's Twitter data	119
12	Rachael's Instagram post types	145
13	Types of post in Tony's UKFR Facebook group data	172
14	Communicative functions in Peter's WhatsApp message sequences	186

Acknowledgements

I am indebted to Lucy Jones and Louise Mullany, who mentored me throughout my time as a British Academy Postdoctoral Fellow at the University of Nottingham. Thank you for always being there to lend a sympathetic ear and sound out ideas, for championing my work and for reading drafts of chapters that appear in this book, as well as related journal articles. Special thanks to Lucy, who I first tentatively approached with an idea for the Marginalised Families Online project at the 2016 IGALA conference in Hong Kong and who has been a huge support ever since.

I'd also like to thank the anonymous reviewers of both the draft manuscript and initial proposal for this book. Your comments have been constructive and insightful, and your enthusiasm for my work gave me the drive to complete this project. Thanks also to Morwenna Scott and Laura Gallon at Bloomsbury, for all your support and advice throughout the preparation, writing and production process. My biggest thanks, of course, must go to the nine parents who generously gave their time and energy to participate in the research on which this book is based. I have learned so much from you and without you this book would not have been possible. Finally, thank you to my husband, Roger, and my children, Hamish and Leo, for keeping me on the straight and narrow.

The images shown in Figures 2, 13, 14, 15, 16, 18, 20 and 22 are reproduced with the permission of the Taylor and Francis Group, Sam Ross at the Teenage Whisperer, Tes, Sally Donovan and Channel 4. All remaining figures are either my own original work or screenshots from my participants' social media, which they have consented to share.

This book is based on research funded by the British Academy and the University of Nottingham (grant number PF2/180026).

Introduction

This book explores the relationship between everyday parenting, family practices and digital media in the lives of networked individuals who have access to an expansive repertoire of tools and technologies for relating to others and doing things in the world. It places social action at the centre of its investigation, considering how parents' actions and practices are constructed, translated and transformed in and through digitally mediated texts, and, in turn, how those mediated actions relate to, and reverberate through, their wider practices, digital networks and social lives. This interwoven relationship between social action, mediated text and family practice is explored through the theorization of *connected parenting* as a collection of practices that involves the construction, negotiation and maintenance of parenting and family practices *through* mediated connections with friends, family members, groups and communities.

This investigation of connected parenting practice draws from my own qualitative research with nine UK-based parents: the *Marginalised Families Online* study. The participants involved in this research constitute a relatively diverse group of parents, whose family structures and practices present a challenge to the limiting social, biological and legal structures that still dominate concepts of 'family' in contemporary UK society. They are all single, and/or lesbian, gay or bisexual, and they each brought children into their lives in non-traditional ways, for example through donor conception, surrogacy, adoption and other non-romantic arrangements. Over the course of eleven months (December 2018–October 2019), each of these participants completed a short questionnaire, took part in three face-to-face interviews and shared selections of their digital media from a range of apps and platforms including Facebook, Twitter, Instagram and WhatsApp. The research design and analytical impetus for this study combine the key principles and processes of constructivist grounded theory (Charmaz, 2014; Corbin & Strauss, 2015) and mediated discourse analysis (Norris & Jones, 2005; Scollon, 1998, 2001).

The concept of connected parenting is borne out of the Marginalised Families Online participants' experiences, their use of digital media and their family practices. The experiences of one participant, Cheryl, usefully illustrate what I mean by connected parenting at this point. Cheryl, a single adoptive parent, relies almost exclusively on other adopters, especially single adopters, for social, emotional and practical support, and connects with these parents primarily through digital media. She is emphatic about the importance of other adoptive parents in her life, claiming that without them, she 'wouldn't have survived' and pointing to multiple occasions when adopters have acted as an extended family network in times of need. For example, Cheryl points to the time her son was arrested, and she was waiting for him at a police station in the middle of the night. Distressed and alone, she reached out to a fellow adoptive parent, who stayed in contact with her throughout the night via mobile messaging and phone calls, helping her to navigate both her interactions with the police and her son. To give a more everyday example, Cheryl also frequently uses a single adopters' Facebook group to ask for advice and second opinions on domestic life decisions such as buying a new car, putting a property on the housing market or choosing a new washing machine. At moments like these, Cheryl both takes action through connecting with others and connects with others through the actions she takes. Her family practices are thus heavily shaped by and intertwined with her connection to a network of adoptive parents.

Through close examination of interview and digital data from the Marginalised Families Online participants, this book identifies three core dimensions of connected parenting:

1. Collective connection
2. Epistemic connection
3. Affective connection

These dimensions are visually represented in Figure 1. In brief, collective connection revolves around the sharing and foregrounding of common experiences and circumstances. It can be realized through a mobile message saying 'I've done that too' when a friend shares a parenting mishap, through shared reference to 'our lives' in posts to a Facebook group of adopters or through a request for others to share 'similar experiences' so that a single parent feels less alone in challenging times. Epistemic connection is practised through the construction and exchange of information and knowledge, for example through positioning a life event as a 'top tip' for other single mothers in an Instagram post, through recommending a tried-and-tested suction bowl to members of a Facebook group who practice 'baby-led weaning' or through rousing tweets that mobilize a community of adoptive parents to challenge established forms of knowledge about children's behaviour. Finally, affective connection involves

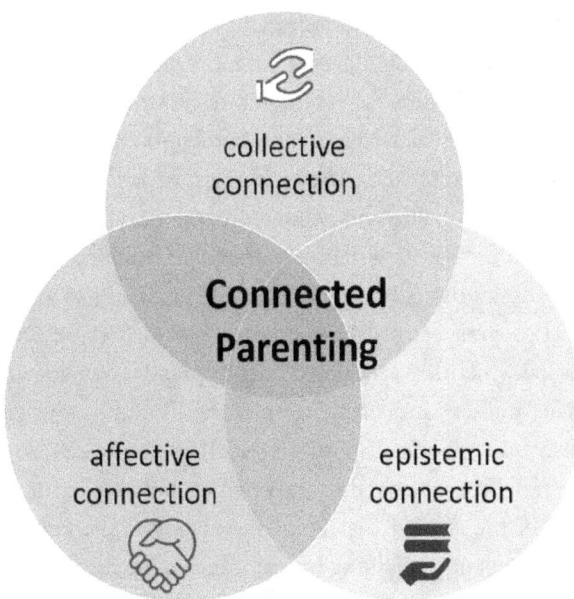

Figure 1 The three core dimensions of connected parenting.

the formation of social ties through the construction and flow of emotions, feelings, moods, dispositions and attitudes, for example in a Facebook post that responds to a group member's cry for help with the words 'I'm sending you love ♥', in a WhatsApp message that commiserates a friend with a 'big hug' or in retweets that recontextualize others' posts through an affective lens, with evaluations such as 'frightening', 'Aaagh!!' or 'love this ♥'. These are all examples shared by the Marginalised Families Online participants, many of which will be examined more closely in the chapters that follow. As the visual illustration of Figure 1 demonstrates, these three dimensions of connected parenting combine and overlap, so that whilst they can be examined individually, they can also be understood as intersecting and complementary components of a larger constellation of practices. Taking influence from Scollon (2001, p. 4), I therefore describe connected parenting as a 'nexus of practice', a concept that will be explained further in Chapter 1.

Through in-depth elaboration of connected parenting practice, this book contributes to scholarly investigations of parenting, family practices and digital media in two key areas. First, its focus on the practices of single and/or lesbian, gay or bisexual parents who brought children into their lives in non-traditional ways provides the foundation for a diverse and expansive exploration of both familial and connective practices. This exploration departs from a continued emphasis on traditional nuclear families and heterosexually coupled mothers, both in a sociocultural/academic context more generally and in studies of parent-to-parent digital interactions and online communities more specifically. Further, my emphasis on social action and family practices facilitates a shift of emphasis away from family structures and roles, which can work to reinforce dominant ideals of family life and gendered parenthood. Instead, I embrace a more nuanced and flexible exploration of the wide-reaching practices that can extend beyond the traditional boundaries of nuclear families and parent–child relationships. This perspective is indebted to Morgan's (1996, 2011) work in family sociology, which has examined family practices as something people 'do', rather than family as something people 'are'. I build on this work through a mediated discourse analytical approach (Norris & Jones, 2005; Scollon, 1998, 2001) which, similarly, centres action and practice in its exploration of discourse and social life. In the section that follows, I elaborate the concept of 'family practices' in more detail, explaining how it informs the research on which this book is based.

This book also continues an emerging trajectory in qualitative sociolinguistic research that situates participants as networked individuals with access to a wide range of mediated technologies and examines their digital media use as it is intertwined with their everyday lives (e.g. Androutsopoulos, 2021; Tagg & Lyons, 2020, 2021b, 2021a). Accordingly, the Marginalised Families Online study is concerned less with the structures and affordances of individual tools and technologies themselves, and more with the ways in which a constellation of connected parenting practices can be constructed and maintained across multiple sites of engagement. Further, whilst this book focuses primarily on parents' use of digital media, it seeks a holistic understanding of their digital media practices as they are integrated in, and overlap with, their everyday social lives, experiences and multi-modal communicative practices. More specifically, it builds on an emerging body of work that explores the complex ways in which parent-to-parent digital interactions and everyday parenting practice intertwine and overlap (e.g. Hanell & Salö, 2017; Lyons, 2020).

These themes and perspectives are examined over nine chapters. This introductory chapter elaborates the concepts of 'family practices' and 'connection', introduces the Marginalised Families Online participants and provides a detailed overview of the book's contents. Chapter 1 outlines the methodological principles and processes that underpin this research, and offers a rationale for my combination of constructivist grounded theory and mediated discourse analysis. Chapter 2 shows how these methods were deployed in practice, including a detailed explication of the research design for the Marginalised Families Online study. In Chapters 3 to 8, I present the empirical findings of this research, with each chapter introducing a different case study that exemplifies a specific dimension of connected parenting. As I will make clear throughout this book, the three key domains of connected parenting rarely operate in isolation. However, in order to fully examine each of these dimensions in depth, I take each one in turn, focusing on the *collective* dimension of connected parenting in Chapters 3 and 4, the *epistemic* dimension in Chapters 5 and 6 and the *affective* dimension in Chapters 7 and 8. In Chapter 9, I reunite these dimensions in a summative examination of connected parenting as a single nexus of practice.

What are family practices?

Family practices, as defined in this book, include repeated actions and exchanges between parents or carers and their children, such as the everyday, mundane actions of changing a nappy, feeding a child or taking them to school, as well as the actions that combine to produce more significant events such as bringing a child into the family, celebrating a birthday or mourning a death. Family practices also, and importantly, include repeated caring and supportive actions that extend beyond the boundaries of the parent–child relationship: to romantic couples, friendship groups, small communities or extended families, for example. Such expansive family practices may include maintaining close, regular contact, checking-in, sharing an embrace or holding hands. This book is titled 'connected *parenting*' because all of the participants who took part in the Marginalised Families Online project are parents, and most (but not all) of the digital interactions they shared relate in some way to the actions and practices they undertake as parents to their children. However, through an emphasis on *family practices*, we will also move beyond the parent–child relationship to consider other family-related actions and practices. In this way, I open the door to an exploration of connected parenting that may be messy and diffuse, but is also open, nuanced, flexible and able to account for the wide range of relationships and encounters that may form part of an individual's 'family life', including those that might be difficult to identify or categorize.

My exploration of connected parenting and diverse family practices brings multidisciplinary perspectives to a discourse analytical project. It owes much to the field of family sociology, especially the work of Gabb (2011), Finch (2007) and Morgan (1996, 2011). Morgan's (1996; 2011) influential work on family practices places *action* and *practice* at the centre of family studies, precipitating a shift of emphasis from the structure of familial roles and relationships to the way relationships, connections and commitments between intimates are realized and maintained by agentive social actors. As part of this shift, the field of family sociology has become more inclusive of non-traditional groups such as same-sex couples, extended kinship groups, close friendships defined as family, blended families and families 'stretched across different households' or even across continents (Finch, 2007, p. 67). Morgan's (1996) exploration of family practices also moves to reinstate links between family and community studies, situating family relationships in the wider context of overlapping familial, kinship, friendship and neighbourly ties. Extending the boundaries of 'family' in this way is particularly important for this book, which seeks to examine parents' family practices as they are constructed, mediated and mobilized through connections with a wide range of social actors.

Morgan's call for practice-based explorations of family life was extremely influential both within and beyond family sociology. However, since Morgan's first (1996) publication, others have worked to re-emphasize the relevance of wider historical and social structures for the constitution of family practices amongst different groups. Finch (2007), Gabb (2011) and Heaphy (2011), for example, note that 'displays' of family practices can take on very different meanings, and have very different consequences, for people who have been marginalized by normative social concepts of the ideal family. As Heaphy (2011, p. 27) explains, white, middle class, heterosexual families have 'historically been the benchmark' for 'successful families', and thus, family displays that fall outside of these narrow margins will always be measured against those norms. He gives the example of lone-parent families, for whom 'the risks of being judged as failing to display family appropriately are especially high', as they come up against 'constructions of feckless mothers, absent fathers and irresponsible single-parent families who 'sponge' on the state' (Heaphy, 2011, p. 27). Considering the simple family practice of holding hands, Gabb (2011) explains how, for same-sex parents, this often taken-for-granted gesture can be fraught with uncertainty and fear around whether it is safe to hold hands in a public place and how a child may be affected by the consequences of this action – or indeed the consequences of withholding it. Some family practices then, as Gabb (2011, p. 55) shows, can have significant emotional consequences, 'both to the individuals involved and to the forms of family that can be displayed'. Taking account of these perspectives, which are particularly relevant for the parents who took part in my research, this book's exploration of connected parenting and family practice will connect the repeated actions and experiences of individual parents with wider social structures and constraints. In the section that follows, I further contextualize this discussion by outlining the social context in which this research took place.

Single, adoptive and LGBT parents

Sociological and psychological research has shown that, in the United Kingdom and the United States, two-parent heterosexual families continue to be positioned as the most 'natural', 'good' and in the 'best interest of the child' (Correia & Broderick, 2009, pp. 243, 245; Golombok, 2015; Malmquist, 2015). Research across the humanities and social sciences has shown that such narrow criteria for morally and normatively 'right' families have marginalized and stigmatized those who do not fit this mould. Same-sex parents, for example, continue to be depicted in the media and popular culture as dangerous, incompetent and damaging for children (Goldberg, 2012; L. Jones, Mills, Paterson, Turner, & Coffey-Glover, 2017). Gay male parents, in particular, often face both homophobic and sexist discrimination, based on persistent beliefs that women are better caregivers than men (Goldberg, 2012; Golombok, 2015), that gay men are not appropriate masculine role models and even that gay men are likely to sexually abuse their children (Gianino, 2008). This research is further examined in my forthcoming work (Mackenzie, in press), which considers how the two gay fathers who participated in the Marginalised Families Online study work to negotiate normativities of gender, sexuality and the family.

Adoptive parents, many of whom are in same-sex couples,[1] also face a good deal of social stigma, prejudice and misunderstanding. Because 'blood' ties are often implicitly favoured over social relatedness, adoption can be perceived as a 'second-best' route to parenthood and family life. Research has shown that adopters often internalize this stigma, resulting in feelings of inadequacy or inauthenticity (Ben-Ari & Weinberg-Kurnik, 2007; Jennings, Mellish, Tasker, Lamb, & Golombok, 2014; Weistra & Luke, 2017). Further, adoptive parents frequently face a number of practical challenges. For example, a 2021 survey of 2,452 adopters and 159 adoptees found that 75 per cent of adoptive families were experiencing challenges (Adoption UK, 2021). The study also showed that 28 per cent of adoptees aged sixteen to twenty-five were not in education, employment or training at the end of 2020, 46 per cent had needed help from mental health services and 53 per cent of parents felt adoptees aged sixteen to twenty-five weren't getting the support they needed.

Together with these social, emotional and practical challenges, adopters often feel that non-adopters have very little understanding of their lives. For example, Weistra and Luke's (2017, p. 237) study with forty-three adoptive parents in the UK and Ireland found that 93 per cent of participants agreed with the statement 'people in society do not understand adoptive families', as well as suggesting that they were portrayed, by the media and by non-adopters, in reductive and polarizing ways: as either 'heroes' or 'desperate'. Weistra and Luke (2017) found that, as a result, adoptive parents were often unwilling to tell non-adopters when things weren't going well at home or to be open about bad experiences; they also felt judged by non-adopters when their children acted out in public. Unsurprisingly, then, many adoptive parents say that they value peer support over and above both professional services and existing family and friends, and therefore work hard to 'surroun[d] themselves with other adoptive parents' (Weistra & Luke, 2017, p. 239; also see Bryan, Flaherty, & Saunders, 2010; Selwyn, Wijedasa, & Meakings, 2014). The close-knit groups that are formed as a result are described by many of Weistra and Luke's (2017) participants as being akin to family.

Single adoptive parents, further, may face additional stigma and social pressure, with research showing that single mothers continue to be vilified as a social threat in UK and US media and health discourse (Mackenzie, 2021; McDermott & Graham, 2005; Salter, 2018). Research has shown that single mothers 'by choice', who often bring children into their lives through adoption or donor conception, frequently work to distinguish themselves from the stigmatized, stereotypical figure of the young, working class, irresponsible single mum. However, they still face an additional set of prejudices around their adoptive status or their use of donor conception. For example, single women who have conceived via donor conception in the UK, who tend to describe themselves as 'solo mums', often face accusations of 'selfishness' for consciously 'depriving' their children of a father, as well as personal conflict around their 'choice' to enter motherhood as a single parent (Ben-Ari & Weinberg-Kurnik, 2007; Golombok, 2015; Mackenzie, 2021; Mendonça, 2018). Research focusing on the experiences of solo mums suggests that these women, like adoptive parents, often form mutually supportive groups who function in much the same way as traditional neighbourhoods, helping solo mums and their children feel like part of 'an associated movement' (Poveda, Jociles, & Rivas, 2014, p. 338; also see Hertz, Jociles, & Rivas, 2016; Malmquist, Björnstam, & Thunholm, 2019). Recent research has suggested that for solo and single adoptive parents, this kind of support, kinship and community is often forged or supplemented through digital networks (e.g. Hertz et al., 2016; J. J. Miller et al., 2019).

Examining family practice through discourse analysis

Sociolinguists and discourse analysts are well placed to disrupt fixed, essentialist and often damaging normative ideals of family life. Indeed, many have begun to do so by exploring the specific dimensions and trajectories of family-related actions and practices, and the ways in which these practices relate to wider social structures and institutions. Sociolinguistic studies of couple and nuclear family interactions, for example, have elaborated one dimension of the relationship between family practices, specifically *interactional practices*, and wider social structures. The early sociolinguistic and conversation analytical studies of Fishman (1978) and Ochs and Taylor (1995), for instance, suggest that mundane, everyday interactions between members of the same household are key to the construction, maintenance, negotiation and transformation of gender roles and norms. More recently, Ellece (2012) and Han (2018) have attended to very different sets of family practices, with Ellece (2012) looking at how women's domestic role as child-bearer and nurturer is maintained through the 'Rutu', a ritual ceremonial fertility chant in South Eastern Botswana, and Han (2018, p. 2) examining talk 'directed to an expected and imagined child in utero', or 'belly talk', within US families. Both authors point to the persistence of family practices that are institutionally and/or culturally prescribed and legitimized, occur at transitional points in the dynamics of a family unit and serve to enact the ties of family and kinship, as well as embodying the roles and responsibilities of parenting. These practices can therefore be seen to represent meaningful ways of both *doing* family and upholding normative ideals around what *makes* a family, spouse or parent, and demonstrate how those roles can be displayed.

Turning to the intersection between family and digital media practices, recent years have seen an acceleration of research interest in the interdisciplinary area of 'motherhood online' (Mackenzie & Zhao, 2021). In our introduction to a special issue on this theme, Zhao and I have argued that discourse analytical approaches are particularly well suited to explorations of 'the interaction between motherhood as a social construct, mothering as social practice, and online discourse as social action' (Mackenzie & Zhao, 2021, p. 2). As evidenced in this special issue, discourse analytical research has been able to critically examine how a wide range of socio-maternal practices and experiences such as infant feeding, maternal regret and postnatal depression can be navigated in and through various digital media such as blogs, online forums, messaging apps and video-sharing platforms. A related strand of research has examined digital media practices within transnational families. Building on research in media and cultural studies that attends to the way digital media practices have impacted, and indeed become part of, family practices and relationships themselves (e.g. Alinejad, 2019; Madianou, 2014; Madianou & Miller, 2012; Wilding, Baldassar, Gamage, Worrell, & Mohamud, 2020), sociolinguistic research in this area has attended to the mediational repertoires of migratory families (e.g. Artamonova & Androutsopoulos, 2020; Lexander & Androutsopoulos, 2021). Some of this work will be further explored in the section that follows, in relation to concepts of *connection* and *intimacy*.

Further, a small but extremely valuable collection of sociolinguistic research has begun to consider how parenting actions and practices can be taken up and recontextualized in parent-to-parent digital interactions. For example, Hanell and Salö's (2017, p. 159) exploration of the Swedish parenting site Familjeliv ('family life') shows how users of this site's discussion forum produce parent-related knowledge in a way that 'enable[s] future actions'. To give a specific example, these authors explain how one contributor's post about their use of certain wipes and creams may be taken up by another as a useful 'knowledge resource', which in turn may affect their own childcare practice and consumer choices. In a UK context, Lyons' (2020) study of a WhatsApp chat group comprised of London-based mums, similarly, shows how the individuals in this group drew on the digital affordances of WhatsApp to create of a pool of parenting knowledge and information, which could be shared, stored and subject to future evaluation, rejection or valorization. For example, Lyons explains how one participant, Monica, presents her experience of tongue-tie, a condition which limits the flexibility of an infant's tongue and makes it difficult to breastfeed. In a series of WhatsApp messages to the group, Monica presents herself as knowledgeable about the condition, whilst positioning health professionals as under-informed, because of their failure to correctly diagnose it. Another member of the group, Lyons (2020) explains, later draws on Monica's experience to both recognize and seek treatment for her own daughter's tongue-tie.

Whilst this book will elaborate and develop aspects of existing sociolinguistic work around family practice and digital media, it also establishes a new trajectory for research in this area. Most notably, it brings the concept of family practices to the fore in the study of intimate relationships and digital media, and examines the complex ways in which digital interactions and family practices intertwine and overlap. Like Hanell and Salö (2017) and Lyons (2020), I seek to trace the trajectories of parents' mediated actions, in terms of the origins of those actions, the ways in which they are mediated and (re)produced, and the future actions they enable. However, I also extend these investigations in several respects: by taking in the affective and collective components of connected parenting alongside its epistemic dimensions, through a more in-depth engagement with participants' broader lives and social networks, and through attention to family practices that go beyond parenting and childcare.

What is connection?

Connection is defined in this book, first and foremost, in terms of shared social ties, affinities or bonds, which can be felt between individuals, between individuals and groups or even between individuals and objects, places or concepts. Connections may be experienced as a spark ignited by shared experiences, feelings or perspectives; as a sense of togetherness precipitated by physical or digital co-presence; as a reaching out from one person to another or as a more vague and sometimes inexplicable sense that a person, thing or place is related to our lives or experiences in important ways. Connections may be fleeting or sustained; they may be triggered by a passing encounter or accrued over time. They may feel significant and intense, or they may be relatively trivial and quickly forgotten. Connections in this sense overlap with related concepts such as affinities, which Mason (2018a, pp. 1–2) describes as 'potent connections that rise up and matter', as 'connective charges and energies' and as 'animated or living connections'. Connection is also closely related to the concept of intimacy: as Jamieson (2011, p. 3) suggests, practices of intimacy often work to 'create and sustain a . . . special quality of close connection', and vice versa. In contemporary cultures and societies, both established and more fleeting connections are often facilitated by and mediated through digital technologies; indeed, the capacity for social connection has frequently been held up as a defining feature of digital and social media (Papacharissi, 2010; van Dijck, 2013).

Social media researchers working across a range of contexts and disciplines have taken particular interest in the modes of intimate connection that can be enabled or enhanced by mobile technologies. For example, Chambers (2013), Ito and Okabe (2005), Jamieson (2011) and Madianou (2016) have examined the role digital media can play in generating new ways of defining and practising intimate connection between romantic, familial and platonic relations. Ito and Okabe (2005, p. 260), in their research with users of Japanese *keitai* (portable device) email, suggest that a special quality of connection can be constructed through regular use of mobile messaging with a small number of close contacts. Examining the continuous stream of mobile messages between a teenage couple, for example, Ito and Okabe (2005, p. 264) show how the pair maintain an 'ongoing background awareness' of one another, despite their parents' efforts to regulate their intimacy. This kind of ongoing contact, which can range from in-depth chat to lightweight updates about their current activities, sustains the young couple's relationship through what Ito and Okabe (2005, p. 264) call 'ambient virtual co-presence'.

Within transnational families, Alinejad (2019) and Madianou (2016) have explored similar instances of ongoing connection through digitally mediated 'co-presence'. For example, in Madianou's (2016, p. 199) ethnographic study of UK-based Filipino migrants' communication within their transnational family groups, she suggests that the constant availability of information about family members' activities, as shared through social media practices, such as updating a status, checking-in to a geographical location and sharing photographs, can open up 'new ways of being together' and 'doing family'. She defines the 'peripheral, yet intense awareness of distant others' that is made possible through social media and digital affordances as 'ambient co-presence', a concept that is very closely related to Ito and Okabe's (2005) 'ambient virtual co-presence' in its emphasis on sustained, 'background' connections that are maintained primarily through digital channels. Madianou (2016, p. 183) suggests that this form of constant connection can have 'powerful emotional consequences' for familial relationships at a distance. Elaborating on the consequences of such digital 'co-presence' for emotional intimacy between transnational families, Alinejad (2019) has introduced the concept of '*careful* co-presence'. This term reflects the discerning selectivity and emotional care involved in families' intimacy-facilitating social media practices (see further discussion in Chapter 7).

Digital media, however, do not facilitate or enable social connection in any straightforward or neutral way. For example, both Chambers (2013) and Papacharissi (2010, pp. 304–5) have suggested that the structure of social networking sites (SNSs) such as Facebook, which centre around the 'public display of social connections', is transforming our very sense of what connection and friendship can mean. By encoding all connections as friendships, Chambers (2013, p. 59) suggests, the 'positive qualities of friendship' such as 'conviviality, equality, choice and mutual disclosure' have been used to validate new modes of relationality, such as the public sharing of intimate and personal experiences, and expression of emotional attachment to others. Chambers' (2013) discussion of the way 'friendship' has been exploited by SNSs to encourage intimate sharing and prolonged engagement has parallels in van Dijck's (2013) critique of the way large online media corporations have exploited 'connectivity' as a marketable resource. For example, van Dijck (2013, p. 12) notes that those operating SNSs and other Web 2.0 applications have been keen to emphasize and celebrate their capacity to enhance human-to-human connections in ways that suggest their technologies 'merely enable or facilitate social activities'. However, such claims deliberately overlook and oversimplify the complex relationship between 'human connectedness' and 'automated connectivity', whereby social media systems do not just facilitate but also engineer and manipulate human connections, 'coding relationships between people, things, and ideas into algorithms' (van Dijck, 2013, p. 12; also see Nieborg & Helmond, 2019).

Further, many explorations of language, digital media, connection and relationships have pointed to the expectation of constant availability that comes with the drive to connect, through mobile-phone technologies in particular (e.g. Baron, 2008; Baym, 2010; Gangneux, 2020; Takahashi, 2014). In Takahashi's (2014) exploration of Japanese young people's use of social media in everyday life, for example, she notes that her interviewees have their phones switched on and available at all times, even while they sleep. Research has suggested that this pressure to be always connected – 'always on' (Baron, 2008) – can have troubling consequences for mobile and internet users. Gangneux (2020, p. 464), for example, found that some people reported feeling overwhelmed by 'anxieties and stress generated by mobile messaging applications, ranging from pressure to be always on, expectations to answer quickly and fears of missing out'. Critical histories of social media, such as those offered by van Dijck (2013) and Nieborg and Helmond (2019), remind us that such constant connectivity is engineered by the social media companies who benefit from online sociality. At the same time, users are by no means powerless. Individuals have the agency to 'control the volume' on their mobile and SMS engagement, for example by blocking people and letting calls go to voicemail (Baron, 2008), putting their phones face-down and using message previews to bypass read receipts (Gangneux, 2020). Further, people operating in polymedia environments are able to make meaningful choices around their media use, through both strategic selection of media as appropriate for their social and emotional purposes (Madianou & Miller, 2012) and strategic *dis*use of particular media, for example by completely abandoning apps that enforce norms of constant availability (see Takahashi, 2014).

This book will acknowledge the structural constraints of digitally mediated connection, attending to the ways in which digital technologies can affect the shape of connections themselves. However, it also adopts a participant-centred perspective that emphasizes the agency of individual parents as they connect with others through family practice and practise family through connection with others. As such, following recent trends in digital media research (e.g. Madianou & Miller, 2012; Papacharissi, 2010; Tagg & Lyons, 2020), I position participants as networked individuals who are able to navigate and manipulate complex and overlapping networks, tools and technologies for a range of social and communicative purposes. This investigation also takes account of participants' broader lives, experiences and social connections as they both intersect with and exist beyond their digital practices. Thus, parents' connections are not presumed to begin and end with their digitally mediated interactions; rather, digital media are treated as components in a much wider network of mediational means through which meaningful connections are constructed and maintained between their friends, families, networks and communities.

The Marginalised Families Online participants

As explained at the beginning of the chapter, this book is based on my research with nine parents who brought children into their lives through adoption, donor conception, surrogacy or non-romantic co-parenting arrangements. This research aimed to explore the role of digital media for parents in diverse family groups, taking account of their broader lives, experiences and social networks. Given these aims, I adopted an in-depth, qualitative approach, working with only nine participants, but interviewing them each three times over the course of eleven months and collecting a range of their digital media. The interviews, which lasted 105 minutes on average, were spaced at four-to-five-month intervals, in order to facilitate the inductive and iterative research process that will be detailed in Chapter 2. Following a long tradition of qualitative, feminist and grounded theory research, the interviewing and data collection process centred participants themselves, prioritizing their comfort, listening to them on their own terms and valuing their unique experience and expertise (see Charmaz, 2014; Mason, 2018b; Mauthner & Doucet, 1998; Oakley, 1981).

My call for participants targeted parents who were single and/or LGBT and who used the internet or mobile technology to connect with others or talk about family life.[2] The call also stated that parents could participate either as individuals or as part of a couple or co-parenting group. Most of the participants who got in touch were single at the time of recruitment, and the coupled or co-parenting individuals decided to participate independently of their partners. Four of the parents were heterosexual, four were lesbian, gay or bisexual and one preferred not to disclose their sexual identity. No transgender parents volunteered to participate. The nine participants who came forward all had unique family circumstances, but also a good deal in common. Table 1 provides an overview of each individual's demographic information, along with their family circumstances and frequently used digital media. Each participant has been given a pseudonym, and some details (such as where they live and how old their children are) have been obscured in order to preserve their anonymity. The details that are given, here and throughout this book, were accurate at the midpoint of data collection (1 May 2019).

As Table 1 shows, all of the participants who took part in the Marginalised Families Online study are cisgender and white, and most identified themselves as British, with the exception of Anna, who migrated to the UK from Scandinavia, and Tony, who was born in the UK but has a French father. Although the call for participants was disseminated across the UK, all participants live in England. At the mid-point in the data collection process (1 May 2019), their children were aged between fifteen months and twenty-three years old. Most of the participants became parents in their late thirties or early forties, with two exceptions who became parents in their twenties (Peter and Lynne). Further, all participants can be described very broadly as financially secure, well-educated and middle class, although these categories simplify the complexity of their histories and circumstances. For example, whilst Rachael and Peter can be categorized with reasonable confidence as affluent and middle class, due to their income, education, profession, home ownership and location, other participants such as Laura and Sarah, whilst they are well-educated professionals, nevertheless live in areas where a large percentage of residents (83 per cent) are identified as skilled working class, working class or not working[3] and which have an above-average rate of unemployment. Laura, further, rents her home and receives state benefits.

These participants were all embedded in complex social networks. They regularly connected with others via at least three different digital platforms, with Facebook, WhatsApp and Twitter being the most widely and frequently used. Further, their conversations and interactions often traversed a range of modes, shifting, for example, between WhatsApp messages, telephone calls and face-to-face meetings, depending on the communicative goals and content. These individuals therefore represent a well-connected group of parents who operate in what Madianou and Miller (2012) call polymedia environments, strategically deploying a range of communicative tools and digital technologies in ways that

Table 1 Participant Demographics

Name, Age	Ethnicity	Location	Gender and sexuality	Relationship status	Occupation	Children	Digital media
Rachael, 40	White British	North-West England	Heterosexual cisgender woman	Single	HR services manager and self-employed company director	One infant daughter conceived through sperm donation and intracytoplasm-ic sperm injections (ICSI)	Instagram, Facebook, WhatsApp, Twitter, blogs, podcasts
Laura, 38	White British	East Midlands	Heterosexual cisgender woman	Single	Homelessness officer	One infant son conceived through sperm donation and intrauterine insemination (IUI)	Facebook, WhatsApp
Sarah, 65	White British	South-East England	Bisexual cisgender woman	Recently coupled, parented as a single mum	Retired (former social worker)	One adult son conceived through sperm donation and intrauterine insemination (IUI)	Email
Cheryl, 49	White British	Central North England	Heterosexual cisgender woman	Single, celibate	Secondary school teacher (part-time)	One adopted adult son	Facebook, Twitter, WhatsApp, blogs

(*Continued*)

Name, Age	Ethnicity	Location	Gender and sexuality	Relationship status	Occupation	Children	Digital media
Anna, 41	White Scandinavian	North-West England	Lesbian cisgender woman	Single (co-parents with ex-wife)	Academic researcher	Two adopted daughters of primary school age	Facebook, WhatsApp
Lynne, 45	White British	Central South England	Cisgender woman (preferred not to disclose her sexuality)	Single, celibate	Full-time parent/carer	Two children, one infant son and one teenage daughter, both adopted	Facebook, WhatsApp, Messenger
Jenny, 45	White British	Central North England	Heterosexual cisgender woman	Recently coupled, parented as a single mum	Education advisor at an adoption charity	Two adopted children of primary school age	Twitter, Facebook, WhatsApp, blogs
Tony, 54	White European	East Midlands	Gay cisgender man	Single (co-parents with lesbian couple)	Self-employed musician and company director	Two sons of secondary school age, conceived through a non-romantic co-parenting arrangement	Facebook, WhatsApp, Messenger
Peter, 29	White British	North-East England	Gay cisgender man	Coupled	Self-employed musician (part-time)	One infant daughter, conceived through egg donation and gestational surrogacy	WhatsApp, Facebook, Instagram

have important implications for their social relationships and family practices. The participants are able to operate confidently in these environments because they have acquired high levels of familiarity, confidence and mastery with digital technologies and systems over many years.

This book's theory of connected parenting is developed through analysis of the interview and digital media data associated with all nine participants involved in the Marginalised Families Online study. From these nine participants, data from six key individuals (Cheryl, Lynne, Rachael, Jenny, Tony and Peter) were selected for closer examination. These parents were chosen because their data was particularly significant in developing a theory of connected parenting and also because they represented participants' diverse demographics and family circumstances, in terms of their age, gender, sexuality, relationship status, the age of their children and the means by which they brought children into their lives. Chapter 2 details the research design for this study, including the ethical considerations involved in the research process. Case studies focused on each of these participants form the substantive empirical findings of this book, which are presented in Chapters 3–8. These chapters offer more detailed introductions to each key participant, before showing how they engage in connected parenting through their social, digital and familial practices.

Chapter summary and overview of the book

This chapter has provided an overview of the book's key aims, concepts and research foundations. In the two chapters that follow, I detail the methodological tools and perspectives that underpin my investigation, explaining how I combined grounded theory and mediated discourse analysis to develop a theory of connected parenting and examine its dimensions through comparative coding and micro-level discourse analysis. Chapter 1 outlines the defining principles and processes of these approaches, explaining what they each bring to my exploration of parenting, families and digital media. Chapter 2 extends this methodological discussion through in-depth explanation of the Marginalised Families Online study's research design, from participant recruitment to theory building. At this point, I detail my use of specific grounded theory principles and processes, such as an iterative research design, coding, comparative analysis, intensive interviewing and memo writing, and highlight the way core ethical principles are woven through the research process. I bring Chapter 2 to a close by explaining how I expanded and elaborated a grounded theory of connected parenting through close analyses that trace social actions and practices through participants' digital discourse.

In Chapters 3 and 4, I introduce *collective connection* as the first dimension of connected parenting, defined here as the construction and mobilization of alignments, affiliations and shared practices through mediated actions and texts. Drawing relevant scholarly literature together with interview and digital data from the Marginalised Families Online project, I first consider, in Chapter 3, how collective connection relates to comparable concepts that are well used in sociolinguistic and social media research, such as alignment, affiliation and collectivization. I then elaborate this dimension through case studies that focus on the experiences of two heterosexual and voluntarily celibate single adoptive parents, Cheryl and Lynne, who both place high value on their connections with other adoptive parents. Chapter 3 goes on to consider how Cheryl constructs and sustains a sense of collective endeavour and experience through her posts to two private Facebook groups for adoptive parents. Chapter 4 elaborates my exploration of collective connection through a second case study. Here, I show how Lynne constitutes and mobilizes shared parenting actions and practices in her interaction with other parents via Meta's *Messenger* app.

The second dimension of connected parenting, *epistemic connection*, is examined in Chapters 5 and 6. This dimension, which involves connecting with others through information sharing and knowledge construction, is explored through case studies that focus on Jenny and Rachael, two heterosexual single women who are very well connected and active members of their social networks. In Chapter 5, I place the spotlight on Jenny, who adopted her two children as a single woman. The chapter shows how Jenny maintains epistemic connections with other adopters through the reiteration of shared knowledge, experiences and perspectives on Twitter, and how she mobilizes these epistemic connections to appeal for collective action and systemic change. Chapter 6 introduces Rachael, a single woman who conceived her infant daughter with the help of donor insemination and in vitro fertilization (IVF). Here, I show how Rachael selects moments from her life as a single parent and recontextualizes them in the form of shareable knowledge, information and advice through her Instagram posts. Together, these chapters offer an in-depth examination of the ways in which parenting and family actions, events and practices can be made tangible and thus knowable. They focus on the transformative processes of decontextualization, entextualization and recontextualization, and the ways in which these processes are mediated by and constructed through digital technologies.

Chapters 7 and 8 examine the final dimension of connected parenting, *affective connection*, which concerns the formation of social ties through the construction and flow of emotions, feelings, moods, dispositions and attitudes. These chapters consider how affective connections can be formed, sustained and mobilized in parents' digital interactions through practices of love, care, intimacy and affection. This dimension of connected parenting is examined, as in the previous chapters, through two case studies. The first, which is presented in Chapter 7, focuses on Tony, a single gay man who co-parents two sons with a lesbian couple. Looking at his online engagement with the UK Fae Revolutionaries, a community of practice that he describes as his 'queer family', I show how Tony mediates affective practices of love, care, intimacy and affection in his posts to their Facebook group, with particular attention to the entextualization of affective actions such as hugs and kisses, as well as caring practices of love, support and healing. The second case study, which is the subject of Chapter 8, focuses on Peter, a partnered gay man who conceived his infant daughter with the assistance of an egg donor and gestational surrogate. Looking at Peter's dyadic interactions with two of his closest friends via the mobile messaging platform *WhatsApp*, I examine the affective practices through which he sustains intimate, caring and affectionate connections.

Chapters 7 and 8 play an important role in expanding the book's discussion of connected parenting beyond a focus on parent–child relationships and parenting practice. Their analyses re-emphasize the relevance of *family practices* in understanding digitally mediated connection, highlighting links and overlaps between the practices of care that can constitute nuclear family groups and those same practices as they operate in other close-knit and supportive groups that are built around care, intimacy and affection, including 'chosen' families, friendship groups and online communities. These chapters' discussion of affective connection therefore points to the relevance of connected parenting beyond parent-focused communities, showing that the concept can also be used to explore a range of mediated relationships and groups.

In Chapter 9, I begin by drawing together the book's empirical findings in a comprehensive appraisal of collective connection, epistemic connection and affective connection as they intersect in the connected parenting nexus of practice. The chapter then discusses some of the book's key contributions and implications. First, I consider what it reveals about new ways of 'doing' family in a digital and networked age. Here, I emphasize the point that connected parenting is not a fixed concept: it can take multiple and varied forms, depending on an individual's history, circumstances and sense of self. I also foreground the socio-emotional benefits of connected parenting, in terms of individuals' access to connections that can be intimate, supportive and sometimes transformational. Despite these optimistic findings, I also suggest that my analysis of connected parenting points to a need for critical caution. For example, I argue that the potentials and possibilities of digital connection can support and sustain a shift of responsibility, from state and institution to individuals and small communities. Further, I suggest that this shift favours those who already have significant resources at their disposal to manage the demands and challenges of raising their families differently, whilst leaving others under-resourced and vulnerable. I then turn to the book's methodological contributions, emphasizing the value of combining grounded theory and mediated discourse analysis in investigations of digital media and family practice, as well as in sociolinguistic research more generally. Finally, I outline the book's implications for institutional family policy, priorities and guidelines. For example, I emphasize the point that over-reliance on digital networks and support may be in danger of masking, but not resolving, problems faced by specific groups such as single adopters and call for better understanding and acknowledgement of the multiple forms family can take, and the diverse family practices they involve.

1

Grounded Theory and Mediated Discourse Analysis

As explained in the previous chapter, this book seeks to understand how family-related actions and practices are constructed, translated and transformed in and through mediated texts, and how mediated actions relate to, and reverberate through, parents' wider practices, digital networks and social lives. This investigation of connected parenting is based on research from the Marginalised Families Online project: a qualitative study with nine UK-based parents in single, same-sex and co-parenting families. Grounded theory philosophies and processes have guided all aspects of this research, from participant recruitment to interviews, digital data collection and analysis. However, grounded theory is not designed for micro-level discourse analysis of the ways in which social actions are mediated through texts and discourse. This study therefore combines grounded theory methods with a discourse analytical approach that *is* well suited to these aims: mediated discourse analysis (MDA). Through an MDA approach, I work to trace the trajectories of parents' mediated actions, in terms of the origins of those actions, the ways in which they are mediated and (re)produced and the future actions they enable. In this chapter I introduce grounded theory and MDA in turn, outlining their origins, principles and analytical tools. I close by summarizing the benefits of this combined methodological approach and explaining what it brings to this book's exploration of parenting, family practices and digital media.

Grounded theory and symbolic interactionism

Grounded theory is a qualitative paradigm that unites theory and method by promoting the development of new theory from the ground up, directly from data (Charmaz, 2014; Corbin & Strauss, 2015; Gibbs, 2002; Strauss & Corbin,

1990). The method was developed by Glaser and Strauss (1967) as an alternative to the positivist tradition in which data was used to test and support pre-existing, 'grand' theories. In many ways, Glaser and Strauss' (1967) approach was not new, but they specified and formalized existing qualitative strategies in a way that was palatable to positivist researchers who demanded procedural rigour, prescriptive techniques and apparent objectivity (Charmaz, 2008, 2014).

In brief, grounded theorists aim to develop explanatory theories that show how people construct meanings and actions in a range of social situations (Charmaz, 2014). The resulting theory, Charmaz (2014) explains, should be both memorable and compelling, offering new viewpoints and making sense of the relationships between multiple and intersecting phenomena. These goals are facilitated by a flexible set of methodological guidelines that continue to be elaborated and adjusted by researchers across the health and social sciences, including coding, intensive interviewing, memo writing and continual comparative analysis (Birks & Mills, 2015; Charmaz, 2014; Corbin & Strauss, 2015). These processes are driven by an inductive and iterative research design that compels researchers to build theory from the ground up, through concurrent and iterative levels of data collection and analysis that inform and focus one another (Charmaz, 2008).

Since Glaser and Strauss' (1967) seminal publication, grounded theorists working in a range of disciplines have sought to develop and extend the theoretical and methodological impetus of this approach (e.g. Charmaz, 2008, 2014; Clarke, 2005; Clarke, Friese, & Washburn, 2018; Corbin & Strauss, 2015; Strauss & Corbin, 1990). Importantly for this book, these developments include the re-animation of grounded theory's roots in symbolic interactionist and pragmatist traditions, drawing on the work of Blumer (1969) and key pragmatist thinkers such as Mead (1934) and Dewey (1929). For symbolic interactionists, *process* and *change* are a fundamental part of human and social life, whilst *stability* is something to be explained (Charmaz, 2014). In grappling with the complex relationship between social action, human agency and the wider social world, symbolic interactionists posit that action and interaction are not wholly determined by social structures, but rather, social structures are interpreted, reproduced and reworked *through* individual and group actions and interactions. Symbolic interactionists thus focus their attention on the practical activities in which people are engaged and how these activities are accomplished (Charmaz, 2014). Influential grounded theorists including Charmaz (2008, 2014), Corbin and Strauss (Corbin & Strauss, 2008, 2015; Strauss & Corbin, 1990) have positioned grounded theory as an ideal methodology for animating symbolic interactionist principles through close attention to actions, and the ways in which they are accomplished, in research data. As I will show in the discussion that follows, there are also several parallels between symbolic interactionism and mediated discourse analysis, which serve as points of connection between two otherwise distinct traditions.

As well as reinvigorating the symbolic interactionist roots of grounded theory, Charmaz, Strauss and Corbin have continued to refine their approaches to grounded theory analysis in line with postmodern perspectives, moving the methodology further away from its positivist origins. Charmaz's (2008, 2014) constructivist approach to grounded theory has been particularly influential in the research design and theory-building process for the Marginalised Families Online study. In her explication of this approach, Charmaz (2008, 2014) insists that grounded theory analyses cannot hope to produce objective accounts of 'truth' or 'reality'. What they can offer, however, are nuanced, socially situated theories based on participants' meanings and actions (also see Clarke, 2005). Both Corbin and Strauss (2015) and Charmaz (2008, 2014) note that this approach to grounded theory research requires a high degree of self-reflection and that researchers should bring themselves into the analysis by acknowledging their own positionality, the ways in which they influence the research process and indeed how the research process influences *them*. As Charmaz (2008, p. 206) explains, constructivist grounded theorists recognize that 'our theoretical analyses are interpretive renderings of a reality, not objective reportings of it'. By adopting a constructivist approach to grounded theory, I therefore ground my analysis in participants' lives, recognize the interpretive nature of my constructions and take a situated approach that emphasizes social action from the outset.

Grounded theory and qualitative research in applied and sociolinguistics

Although grounded theory is widely used across the social sciences, it has been under-utilized in applied, sociolinguistic and discourse analytical research. As Hadley (2017, p. 5) puts it, in the only publication dedicated to grounded theory in linguistic research, 'the focus of the applied linguistics community . . . has unwittingly overlooked one of the most widely used research methodologies in the world'. Whilst some sociolinguistic and discourse analytical studies have drawn on the principles, and some of the key processes, of grounded theory (e.g. Georgalou, 2017; Sunderland, 2000), this work tends not to specify the analytical mechanisms of grounded theory in detail or address the question of how to bridge the gap between thematic and theoretical analyses on the one hand and in-depth discourse analyses on the other. For example, both Sunderland's (2000) study of parentcraft texts and Georgalou's (2017) exploration of discourse and identity on Facebook specify the influence of grounded theory in developing their *inductive* and *iterative* research design. Georgalou (2017, p. 35), for instance, gathered her data 'on an ongoing, recursive basis', and employed iterative and comparative analytical processes, moving between data and theory in order to identify key patterns in the data. Whilst Georgalou's (2017) research process is influenced by grounded theory practices and principles, however, her coding strategies are in many ways more consistent with qualitative thematic coding more broadly, because (a) the codes and categories she developed (such as place, time, profession and education, stance and privacy) are more thematic and static than grounded theory codes that focus on action and process, (b) the coding process does not lead to the development of a core explanatory theory and (c) she embarks on the research process with an 'orienting theory' in place – a set of pre-existing hypotheses, which somewhat contradicts her claim to an inductive research design (Georgalou, 2017, p. 35).

Others have utilized the principles and processes of grounded theory in a more systematic way and begun to show how grounded theory can be combined with linguistic analysis. In my earlier work exploring constructions of motherhood in an online discussion forum (Mackenzie, 2019), for example, I divided the research process into two parts (see Figure 2). The first part, 'data construction', cycled iteratively between observation, data collection, coding and memo writing, leading to the construction of a corpus of fifty discussion threads and a set of codes and categories that captured key meanings, actions and processes across these data. In the second part, 'identifying and analysing discourses', I used these codes as a springboard for the selection and close linguistic analysis of a smaller number of threads. The results of my amalgamated grounded theory/discourse analytical procedures were similar to Sunderland's (2000), in that I did not see the coding process through to the conclusion of a single, unifying theory. Rather, I used grounded theory principles and processes to identify key 'theoretical codes' that led, in combination with micro-linguistic analysis, to the identification of eight discourses. These discourses captured 'key insights about the social norms, expectations and assumptions parents are navigating in a digital age' (Mackenzie, 2019, p. 106).

Hadley's (2015, 2017) work on experiences of teaching English for Academic Purposes (EAP) in neoliberal universities is the most extensive application of

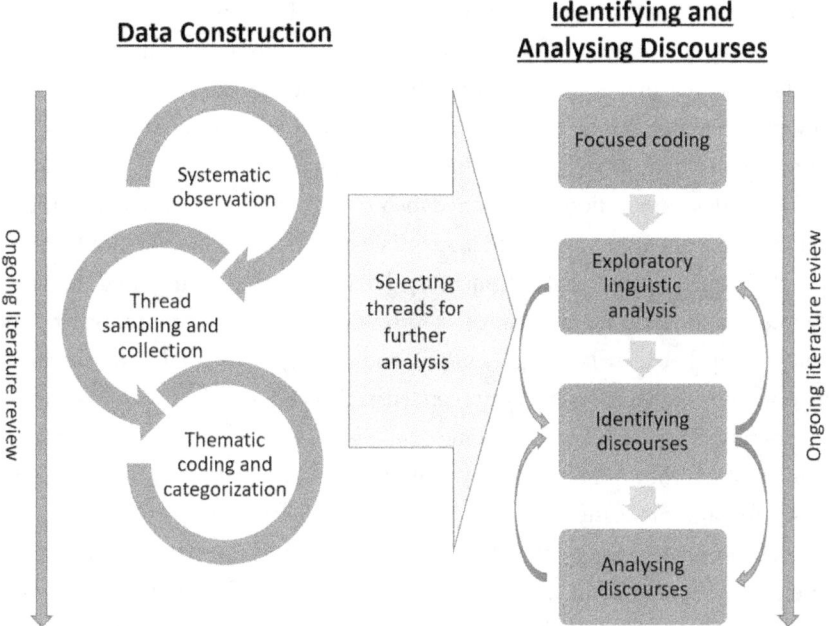

Figure 2 Research design for the Mumsnet Talk study. Research design diagram by Jai Mackenzie, originally published in *Language, Gender and Parenthood Online*, © Jai Mackenzie, 2019. Reproduced with the permission of Taylor and Francis Group, LLC, a division of Informa plc.

grounded theory in language-related research to date. His publications, read in tandem, deal first with the findings of the research itself (Hadley, 2015) and second with a thorough articulation of grounded theory in applied linguistic research (Hadley, 2017). Hadley's (2017) practical guide functions as an introduction to grounded theory for newcomers to the approach. It first introduces the origins, theoretical roots and development of grounded theory, before guiding the reader through the design and research processes of a grounded theory project, from preliminary decisions to the practices of coding, categorizing and memo writing, and finally the dissemination of new theory. Hadley's (2015, 2017) work, however, is not discourse analytical in nature and thus does not involve micro-linguistic scrutiny of data. Rather, his approach involves the kind of broad brushstroke thematic and theoretical analysis that will likely be quite familiar to readers of sociological grounded theories. Whilst his approach is certainly a valuable one, it therefore does not address the question of how grounded theory strategies can bridge the gap between theoretical analyses and in-depth qualitative discourse analysis. In this book, I work to address that gap by advancing theoretical and practical understanding of how grounded theory can be utilized in applied, sociolinguistic and discourse analytical projects. I do so, first, by explicating my systematic application of grounded theory methods from the very outset of the research process and, second, by clarifying the connections, synergies and practical transitions between grounded theory and discourse analyses. The minutiae of this approach are detailed more fully in Chapter 2.

The under-exploration of grounded theory methods in applied, sociolinguistic and discourse analytical research is surprising, since these areas are well-known for their interdisciplinarity, frequently borrowing and combining theories, concepts and tools from a range of disciplines in their explorations of the relationship between language, culture and society. One qualitative, context-driven approach that *has* been more extensively applied in linguistic research is ethnography. In the UK, a tradition of *linguistic* ethnography has been steadily gaining momentum in the last twenty-five years. By uniting ethnographic principles and processes with a sociolinguistic approach to language that gives primacy to context, linguistic ethnographers have considered how actions and interactions are 'embedded in wider social contexts and structures' (Copland & Creese, 2015, p. 13). British linguistic ethnographers such as Rampton (2004), Copland and Creese (2015) and Tusting (2020) trace the development of linguistic ethnography via the work of linguistic anthropologists Dell Hymes and John Gumperz (Gumperz & Hymes, 1972; Hymes, 1962, 1972), as well as pointing to the influence of literacy studies, critical discourse analysis and neo-Vygotskian approaches to language, learning and teaching. What linguistic ethnographers draw from these traditions, Tusting (2020, p. 6) explains, is a sustained interest in 'the relationships between situated action and practices, and macro-level structures and ideologies'. Similarly, the related field of linguistic anthropology, which is rooted in an American anthropological tradition, has worked to produce 'ethnographically grounded accounts of linguistic structures as used by real people in real time and space' (Duranti, 1997, p. 3; also see Enfield, Kockelman, & Sidnell, 2014). Both traditions have a central concern with the way language, along with other communicative resources, is used in people's everyday lives and what this can tell us about the structures, communities and social worlds in which they are embedded.

In recent years, a number of linguistic ethnographers have begun to weave digitally mediated communication into their explorations of cultures, communities and contexts. Most notable in this respect is the TLANG (translation and translanguaging) project, a collaboration that seeks to 'investigate linguistic and cultural transformations in superdiverse wards in four UK cities' (TLANG, 2021). As well as observing and interviewing participants, taking photographs at their workplaces and asking them to audio record interactions with friends and families, some of the TLANG researchers also asked participants to 'select and submit examples of their social media posts and digital messages' (Tagg & Lyons, 2020, p. 11). Tagg and Lyons (2020, 2022) distinguish their approach, which they describe as 'post-digital linguistic ethnography', from relatively well-established ethnographic approaches that tend to centre digital sites, cultures and artefacts, such as virtual ethnography (Hine, 2000), digital ethnography (Varis, 2015) and discourse-centred online ethnography (Androutsopoulos, 2008). This 'blended' perspective, they suggest, 'recognises the conditions of post-digital society, i.e. one in which digital technologies have ceased to be a novel or disruptive influence', instead becoming 'embedded in wider social practices and relationships and intertwined with offline activities and physical contexts' (Tagg & Lyons, 2020, pp. 11–12). The TLANG researchers thus mobilized the adaptability of ethnographic approaches, using them to explore the complexity of their participants' relationships, interactions and language practices without over-emphasizing the relevance of a single specific time, space or context.

This book promotes the application of grounded theory in applied, sociolinguistic and discourse analytical work as an approach which, like ethnography, is highly flexible and adaptable, and can help researchers to ground their analyses in social context. I also argue that grounded theory is particularly well suited to research that includes explorations of digital media as they are embedded in social life. Although ethnographic and anthropological approaches are also well suited to these goals, like all methods they have specific applications and limitations. Most notably, they tend to be based on extended participatory involvement and observation in a particular culture or social setting. Grounded theory, on the other hand, does not require participatory involvement and may thus be a more suitable approach in some interview-based studies or studies based entirely on texts and documentation. Further, grounded theory's explicit emphasis on the development of explanatory theory, and its extensive methodological toolkit for doing so, may be better suited to research that strives to break new ground or prompt transformative change. There is also no reason grounded theory processes cannot be combined with linguistic tools and methods. Indeed, the core tenets of symbolic interactionism that underpin grounded theory practice, namely its emphasis on the ways in which people interpret, reproduce and rework social structures through action and interaction, are highly compatible with applied linguistics, sociolinguistics and discourse analysis, since they pay attention to the dynamic relationship between situated social action, communicative activity and wider social practices.

The Marginalised Families Online study represents a clear example of a combined grounded theory-discourse analytical approach. I used grounded theory strategies to identify participants' situated social actions and to theorize the relationships between these actions, ultimately leading to the grounded theory of *connected parenting* that underpins this book. The in-depth theoretical understanding I gained through grounded theory processes then served as a springboard to a more detailed discourse analysis of specific texts and practices, as in my earlier work with data from Mumsnet (Mackenzie, 2019). This micro-level analysis is therefore rooted not only in the wider context of participants' lives and social contexts but also in robust theory developed through holistic analysis across a full complement of research data. The disparity between grounded theory and discourse analytical methods is in many ways bridged by mediated discourse analysis, which brings an explicit emphasis on social action to discourse analytical research. This approach is examined in the section that follows.

Mediated discourse analysis

As explained in the previous section, grounded theory (especially the iterations that have most significantly influenced this research) animates the symbolic interactionist emphasis on social action and human agency by focusing the analyst's attention on actions, and the ways in which those actions are accomplished, in research data. Mediated discourse analysis (MDA), although it has quite different origins, examines the social world through a similar lens, positioning the mediated social action as its central unit of analysis and seeking to discover how discourse is used to take actions (Norris & Jones, 2005; Scollon, 1998, 2001). Mediated discourse analysts are thus interested in what people *do* in the world, investigating the social, historical and discursive dimensions of a huge range of specific 'doings' such as crossing a busy city street (Scollon & Scollon, 2004), buying a bag of organic brown rice (Scollon, 2007), meeting a friend at a bus stop (Norris, 2004) and handing money to a cashier (Scollon, 2001). Importantly, these actions and practices are always examined in relation to the mediational means through which they are both realized and shaped. In this section, I elaborate the key principles of MDA with an emphasis on how it conceptualizes the relationship between action, discourse, practice and text, and how this kind of analysis can be realized in practice.

MDA is concerned not only with action but also with the complex and multifaceted relationship between discourse and action. 'Discourse' is conceived here in the broad sense of 'language in use' (Gee, 2014), or perhaps more appropriately, 'language in action' (Blommaert, 2005, p. 2). Further, following Blommaert (2005, p. 3), I implement an expanded concept of discourse that includes not just language but 'all forms of meaningful semiotic human activity seen in connection with social, cultural, and historical patterns'. In their introduction to mediated discourse analysis, Jones and Norris (2005a) contend that, through discourse, we can both take action and reproduce action. To explain further, discourse *is* action inasmuch as 'saying something or writing something is a form of *doing* something' – of aligning with others, of bringing a state into being, of challenging oppressive structures and so on (Jones & Norris, 2005a, p. 6). At the same time, actions can be transformed, resemiotized and reconstituted *in* and *through* discourse. Further, as actions are repeated in and through discourse, they may be connected and combined with other actions, and established as recognizable practices (Norris & Jones, 2005).

To complicate matters, MDA (like other discourse analytical approaches) treats actions and practices as intricately connected with systems of power and knowledge, involving 'entrenched beliefs, values and emotions'. Following Bourdieu (1972), MDA explicitly links wider historical and social structures with the repeated, value-laden actions and experiences of the individual, defining practice as 'a historical accumulation of mediated actions within the habitus of social actors' (Jones & Norris, 2005b, p. 97). Thus, action becomes practice through the appropriation and naturalization of repeated actions in the minds and bodies of individuals and groups, which over time become 'part of our sense of who we are, what we know, and how we relate to others' (Jones & Norris, 2005b, p. 98). Further, just as actions may coalesce over time to become practices, practices may become linked over time to form a constellation of practices, which Scollon (2001) describes as the *nexus of practice*. A nexus of practice, Scollon explains, connects specific mediated actions with wider practices, collectives and social structures. Comparing it with the well-known community of practice concept (Lave & Wenger, 1991), Scollon (2001, p. 5) makes the important distinction that a nexus of practice is 'loosely structured', 'unbounded' and 'takes into account that at least most practices . . . can be linked variably to different practices in different sites of engagement and among different participants'. In sum, MDA takes a nuanced, context-sensitive perspective on the complex ways in which actions, practices and socio-historical structures can coalesce in very different ways at specific sites of engagement, through specific mediational means and for specific groups and individuals.

MDA's emphasis on *doing things* in the world extends beyond issues of theory, method and analysis, to the researcher's own action. As Jones and Norris (2005a, p. 11) explain, 'those working in MDA are committed to a project not just of studying social action but of taking social action'. Some of the most memorable examples of social action and activism by MDA analysts come from the work of Scollon and Scollon. For example, in *Nexus Analysis: Discourse and the Emerging Internet,* Scollon and Scollon (2004, p. 143) show how their work exploring discrimination against Alaska Native people in Alaskan court cases has encouraged those participating in the judicial processes to ask new questions of their entrenched actions and practices. For example, a judge was prompted to ask himself 'why must I hold depositions in court?' and 'why must I wear judicial robes in every case?' (Scollon & Scollon, 2004, p. 143). Scollon and Scollon (2004, p. 150) close their book by urging researchers to take action through their analyses, opening up 'the processes of discussion, debate, and interrogation which will ultimately lead to social change'. Their work serves as an important reminder that social problems, injustices and inequalities, however insurmountable they may first appear, are made up of concrete actions, which can be changed. I will return to this point in Chapter 9, where I reflect on this book's implications for social action and transformative change.

Scollon's (2001) examination of a child's crayon as a mediational means for taking action shows how MDA can be operationalized in practice. This example also demonstrates the synergy between mediated discourse analysis and symbolic interactionism, vividly illustrating Blumer's (1969) view that the meanings attributed to an object are bound to practice – what we *do* with that object – rather than assuming the object has intrinsic meanings. In this example, Scollon (2001) shows how crayons are constructed as *mediational means* for taking action through a parent–child interaction in which a two-year-old child holds up three different crayons in succession. The parent responds by (a) talking to the child about the colour of the crayon, (b) asking the child to hand it to her sister and (c) taking the crayon. If we try to understand the nature of the crayon as a mediational object solely by examining it as an isolated entity, Scollon explains, 'we would quickly find that the crayon is an object with specific characteristics', for example it is small enough to be held in the hand, it has a single, bold colour and it readily transfers that colour to other objects (Scollon, 2001, p. 139). However, Scollon argues that we can only truly understand the crayon's function in the social world by looking at how individuals interact with it, talk about it and use it to perform action. In his illustration, for example, the parent assigns a set of *mediated actions* to the crayons, namely 'handing' (the passing of an object from one person's hand to another) and drawing. These actions, Scollon explains, form the *site of engagement* at which the child's action of holding up the crayons intersects with the social practices with which they are known (by the parent) to be associated. Further, he notes, these practices form part of a 'caregiving' nexus of practice, which might also include interacting, cajoling, body care and nurturing.

In his later work, Scollon (2007) uses the concept of 'discourse itineraries' to capture the processes involved in the iterative transformation of text, action and discourse over time, updating his earlier phrase 'cycles of discourse' (Scollon & Scollon, 2004). Scollon (2007) animates the concept of discourse itineraries through his elaboration of the nine processes of resemiotization involved in the constitution of 'a bag of organic brown rice'. Beginning with his purchase of this bag of rice as the *site of engagement,* Scollon shows how an individual action, 'Albert Lundberg plants rice in a certain way in California in 1937', becomes a regular practice over a period of sixty years and is narrativized in the packaging of Lundberg Organic Rice. The processes culminate in 'technologization/ reification', whereby the labelled rice becomes the mediational means for taking future action, namely eating organic rice as both an action and a regular practice (Scollon, 2007, p. 243). Jones (2009, 2020a) has elaborated Scollon's work on discourse itineraries with a particular emphasis on the way actions, when captured and transformed through digital texts and technologies, can be used to perform future actions and, in turn, to sustain ongoing practices.

As Scollon's (2001) discussion of the crayon as mediational means has shown, mediated communication is nothing new. However, digital technologies have brought processes of mediation to the fore, because they are still quite novel and still undergoing rapid processes of change and development. In his exploration of action and text in the digital age, for example, Jones (2009, p. 286) explains how digital technologies have begun to change the ways in which everyday social practices, such as sex, dancing and grocery shopping, are being mediated and thus socially organized. Jones (2020a) elaborates on some of these examples through his ethnographic exploration of the quantified-self movement, which promotes 'self-knowledge through self-tracking'. For example, Jones (2020a) shows how one member's digital practices affect his sense of belonging within the movement and the future actions of other members. This member, Cristian Monterroza, used iPhone apps to track and record every minute of his life, and share these details with others. Jones explains that Monterroza's digitized quantification practices had a significant effect on his own and others' way of looking at the world and relating with others, leading him to 'perceive his location and movements as somehow connected to his well-being', as well as 'helping to make "checking in" a social practice and making Cristian's friends with whom he shares his location feel that they are part of a "community" of location trackers' (Jones, 2020a, p. 204). Another member, Miles Klee, took on a quest to quantify his sex life using apps such as *Love Tracker*. These apps were designed to measure the users' sexual activity, including the duration of their lovemaking. However, Klee found that they were limited in terms of what they could record and measure, and thus not only tracked but also defined and constrained his sexual activity. Unsurprisingly, Klee ultimately gave up the sex tracker apps, complaining that 'technology had transformed me from a considerate lover into a number-crunching monster' (Jones, 2020a, p. 207).

In his explorations of the quantified-self movement, Jones (2009, p. 286, 2020a) employs the concept of *entextualization* to elaborate the specific processes by which actions, when captured and transformed through a range of mediational means, can be used 'to perform future actions, and, ultimately, to sustain social practices and the communities which define themselves through these practices'. This concept of entextualization is a particularly useful one in the analysis of the Marginalised Families Online data. Its utility in mediated discourse analysis, and applications to my own research, will be examined in the section that follows.

Technologies of entextualization

Before I define the concept of entextualization in more detail, it is useful to first consider what is meant by a 'text'. Texts are often the starting point for a mediated discourse analysis and indeed they are the focus for the analyses that are presented in this book. Texts can be conceived as boundaried objects in which action, practice and discourse converge. As such, they are key sites for engagement with the social world and have been described as the 'glue of social life' (Barton & Lee, 2013, p. 27) and the 'building blocks or atoms of shared culture' (Silverstein & Urban, 1996, p. 1). Texts have traditionally been defined, in linguistics, as pieces of written language, although the scale of the text can vary dramatically, from a single-word headline to a whole book (Barton & Lee, 2013, p. 26). However, the concept of text, like discourse, has expanded in recent years to encompass a wider range of semiotic means such as images, videos, audio recordings and memes (Blommaert, 2005). Further, digital technologies have changed both the materiality of texts and the relationships between them. Thus, digital texts now tend to be 'located on a screen', are more easily transmissible than print texts (e.g. through 'forward' or 'repost' functions) and are often dynamically positioned in relation to other texts (e.g. a tweet is situated in-between other tweets in a continual stream of texts) (Barton & Lee, 2013, p. 26). What digital, visual and auditory artefacts share with their written counterparts, however, is their reproducible form. Texts, then, can be defined in a very broad sense as any instance of 'bounded' discourse or social action, which can be taken out of its original context and readily transmitted across time and space – 'decontextualized', 'despatialized' and 'detemporalized', and thus ultimately 'transmitted across social boundaries' (Silverstein & Urban, 1996, p. 1).

The transmission of discourse and social action *through texts* brings us to the concept of entextualization, defined by Bauman and Briggs (1990, p. 73) as 'the process of . . . making a stretch of linguistic production into a unit – a *text* – that can be lifted out of its interactional setting'. Jones (2009, 2020a, p. 206) has modified this definition in a way that is more inclusive of semiotic means beyond language, defining entextualization as 'the primary mechanism through which we *capture* our actions and turn them into texts' (emphasis in the original). For example, a walk in the woods might be entextualized through photographs, videos, a written log of the route, marks on a map to show the path, an audio recording or any combination of these (and other) texts. Jones (2020a, p. 203) argues that these cultural tools, or 'technologies of entextualization', which *mediate* between ourselves and the world around us, are not neutral. As the previous example of Klee's experimentation with sex tracking apps shows, processes of entextualization imbue actions with specific meanings, which inform both how we understand those actions and what we do with them.

Entextualization represents not one but a *series* of processes, involving decontextualization, entextualization and recontextualization. This process can be elaborated through examination of one Marginalised Families Online participant's Facebook post, which is presented in Figure 3. This image–text combination is one of Laura's posts to a private Facebook group for people interested in 'baby-led weaning' (which, in a nutshell, involves allowing young babies to explore and eat soft solid foods with their fingers, rather than giving pureed foods with a spoon). In the written text, Laura captures a series of actions from her daily life – buying a suction bowl and using it to feed her son Nate – and records some of the specific details such as the cost of the bowl and where it came from (the supermarket ASDA). She begins her post with the words 'Nate would like to let you know . . .' and ends with the direct address in Nate's voice

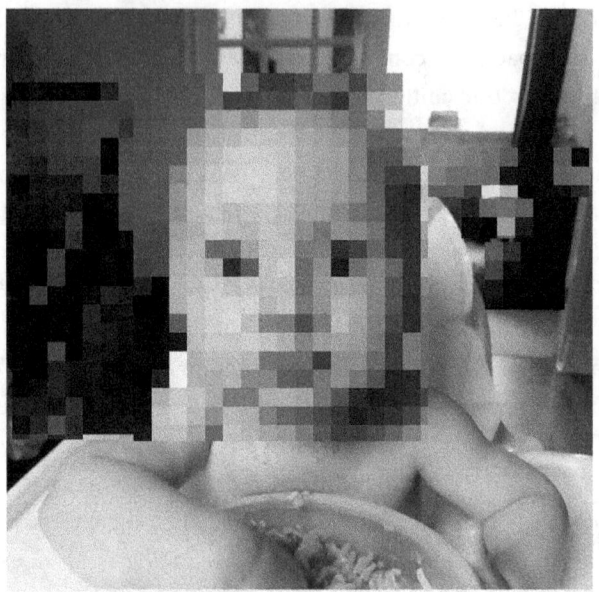

Figure 3 Nate using a suction bowl (29.07.2018).

'why would you need a spoon when you have hands?' The image is a mid-shot photograph of Nate in a high chair, eating pasta with his fingers from one of these bowls and looking straight at the camera to form a 'demand' image that reinforces his position as animator of these words. By positioning Nate as the animator of her message, Laura suggests that Nate himself approves the value of both the bowl and the practice of baby-led weaning. In reproducing a specific set of actions through this image–text combination, Laura *decontextualizes* these actions from their original context and de-centres, or *entextualizes*, them in digital form. Her post may then be viewed by other parents whilst sitting in their living rooms, workplaces, the park and so on. Thus begins the process of *recontextualization*, which involves the 're-centring' of actions and discourse as 'valued texts' (Bauman & Briggs, 1990, p. 77). This process of recontextualization may lead to further actions – for example, members of the baby-led weaning

Facebook group may act on Laura's post by buying their own suction bowls from ASDA.

The example of Laura's Facebook post shows how an MDA approach can be used to investigate the way specific family-related actions and practices – in this case buying and using a new suction bowl – can be mediated through digital 'technologies of entextualisation' (Jones, 2020a, p. 203). Further, it points to the value of such processes in people's everyday lives and parenting practices. In this case, Laura's entextualized actions contribute both to the group's base of useful knowledge resources for taking future actions and to their way of understanding the process of weaning, in line with the baby-led philosophy that unites them. Laura's entextualization, which is 'baby-led' in more ways than one, positions her firmly within this group, as someone who affirms and advocates for baby-led weaning philosophies and practices. Thus, we see how the examination of digital artefacts from a mediated perspective can promote a circular exploration of how knowledge is constructed *through* connection with others, how that knowledge is evaluated and valued, and how co-constructed ways of knowing can shape the quality of connections between people. In Chapter 2, I further explain how the principles of mediated discourse analysis, together with the concept of entextualization, are deployed in micro-level analyses of digital media data from the Marginalised Families Online study.

Chapter summary

This chapter has shown that the principles of grounded theory and mediated discourse analysis, which place social action at the heart of their investigations, are particularly well suited to research that seeks to understand discourse and social action in context, especially research that includes explorations of digital media as they are embedded in social life. Whilst MDA is becoming an increasingly popular method in these areas, grounded theory remains relatively marginal. This chapter, however, has argued for more explicit and systematic utility of grounded theory methods in applied linguistic, sociolinguistic and discourse analytical research. Further, it has illustrated the synergies between grounded theory and MDA, suggesting that their common emphasis on human action and agency, and different but complementary analytical processes, make them fruitful methodological companions. The Marginalised Families Online study represents a compelling case for the combination of these methods. This research shows that a grounded theory research design can form a strong foundation for micro-level mediated discourse analyses that trace social actions through digital texts, whilst situating them in relation to participants' broader networks and family practices. Chapter 2 explains in detail how I combined the principles and processes of grounded theory and mediated discourse analysis for this study.

2

The Marginalised Families Online Study

The previous chapter has outlined the key principles and processes of grounded theory and mediated discourse analysis (MDA) and made a case for combining these approaches. In this chapter, I offer a detailed explanation of the ways in which these methodological components were integrated and mobilized throughout the research process for the Marginalised Families Online study. The chapter will detail the research design from participant recruitment to theory building and analysis, paying particular attention to the way key ethical principles are woven through all aspects of the research. As part of this exploration, I show how specific grounded theory methods such as an iterative research design, coding, intensive interviewing and memo writing were used to identify and theorize the relationship between participants' situated social actions, ultimately leading to the grounded theory of connected parenting that underpins this book. I go on to show how the in-depth theoretical understanding I gained through a grounded theory approach was advanced through mediated discourse analyses of participants' digital media data, which trace social actions through their digital texts, networks and broader family practices.

Research design and ethical considerations

The Marginalised Families Online study adopts the inductive design that is so fundamental to grounded theory research. In other words, it cycles through processes of data collection, analysis and theory building, with each of these processes informing one another (Birks & Mills, 2015; Charmaz, 2008; Schutt, 2012). To facilitate this inductive process, each of the nine participants took part in three rounds of interview and digital data collection, spaced four-to-five-months apart. This allowed time throughout the research process for making connections and comparisons across the data, identifying areas for further exploration and testing early analytical insights against new observations. This inductive design also involved theoretical sampling, whereby data is sampled and collected in ways that focus and feed into the analysis. This process provides opportunities to test the limits of any developing theory and flesh out key concepts and ideas (Birks & Mills, 2015; Gibbs, 2002). The direction of fieldwork and data collection was therefore shaped by developing understandings of the research context, including what was missing, what needed to be further explored or what would drive the analysis and theory building forward. In the sections that follow, these strategies are elaborated in detail, in relation to the interview structure, digital data collection and coding processes for the Marginalised Families Online study.

This research is also underpinned by four key ethical principles, which have been fine-tuned through my engagement with relevant disciplinary guidelines (e.g. AoIR, 2019; BAAL, 2021; ESRC, 2021), the ethical reflections of researchers in the field of language and new media (e.g. Georgakopoulou, 2017; Rüdiger & Dayter, 2017; Tagg, Lyons, Hu, & Rock, 2017) and my own experience of navigating ethical complexities in a range of digital research contexts (e.g. L. Jones, Chałupnik, Mackenzie, & Mullany, 2022; Mackenzie, 2017b, 2019). These principles can be summarized as follows:

1. Maximize benefits and minimize harm;
2. Be attentive to context, including informational norms and participants' needs;
3. Acknowledge and analyse my own positionality as a researcher;
4. Integrate ethical considerations at all stages of the research process.

The guiding ethical principle for the Marginalised Families Online study is to maximize benefits and minimize harm. Thus, as well as following the British Association of Applied Linguistics' (BAAL, 2021, p. 6) call to 'anticipate any harmful effects or disruptions to informants' lives . . . and to mitigate any stress, undue intrusion, and . . . exploitation', I also consider how participants might enjoy and benefit from the research. The second principle acknowledges that ethics is not a 'one-size-fits-all' operation and subsequently advocates an approach that is case-based and attentive to context. Whilst some internet research has judged the appropriateness of online data collection on the basis of whether or not the data is 'public', it is now widely recognized that concepts of 'public' and 'private' digital media are nebulous and changeable, and further, that these categories do not straightforwardly correlate with participants' right to privacy, autonomy and the minimization of harm (Barton & Lee, 2013; Ess, 2007; Mackenzie, 2017b). In response to these challenges, the Association of

Internet Researchers (AoIR, 2019, p. 4) advocates a 'process approach' to internet research, where ethical decisions are made 'from the bottom up', in response to research practice, associated risks and the specific research context. The third ethical principle explicitly foregrounds the role of the researcher in the research process. The importance of acknowledging the researcher's subjective positioning, including the beliefs, experiences and personal circumstances they bring to their research, has been well established across intersecting qualitative (Corbin & Strauss, 2008; Mason, 2018; Schutt, 2012), feminist (Mauthner & Doucet, 1998; Skeggs, 1995; Wilkinson, 1988) and constructivist (Charmaz, 2008, 2014; Clarke, 2005) perspectives. For example, my own position as both a bisexual parent and the daughter of a single lesbian parent significantly affected the ways in which I understood and related to my participants, as well as the development of analytical and theory-building strategies.

The Marginalised Families Online study was designed with the aforementioned ethical principles at the fore and received ethical approval from the Faculty of Arts research ethics committee at the University of Nottingham. However, turning now to the fourth and final principle, it is important to underline the point that the ethical considerations for this study do not begin and end with institutional approval. Rather, following Markham and Buchanan (2015) and the AoIR's (2019) recommendations, I treat ethics as an integral part of the research methodology, evaluating and reflecting on ethical principles throughout the research process, for example in relation to interview design and conduct, analysis and dissemination of results. For this reason, further discussion of ethical considerations is integrated with a detailed explanation of the research process, in the sections that follow.

Participant recruitment

The nine parents who took part in the Marginalised Families Online study were recruited primarily through two charities that were involved with the project's development from its inception: Adoption UK (AUK) and the Donor Conception Network (DCN). These charities agreed to circulate a call for participants (CFP) in October 2018, via communication channels including Twitter, Facebook, websites, mailing lists and newsletters. This CFP targeted parents who were single, and/or LGBT, and who used the internet or mobile technology to connect with others or talk about family life. It also briefly detailed the nature of the project, including the level of commitment that would be required. The CFP was also circulated through a number of smaller LGBT, surrogacy and adoption organizations in England, Scotland and Wales, and via the Marginalised Families Online project's own Twitter account. Most of the project's nine participants received the call via AUK or DCN, although one came via a local LGBT+ organization's newsletter (Tony) and another through a Facebook group (Peter).

Participation in the Marginalised Families Online project required a relatively high level of commitment and a willingness to share personal information. For this reason, I developed a multi-step recruitment process that gave interested parties several opportunities to find out more, ask questions and get to know me as a researcher, before deciding whether to participate. For example, I replied by email to those who made contact after seeing the CFP, attaching a participant information sheet that included details about the aims of the project, participant anonymity, data protection and a rough interview schedule. I also explained my reasons for doing the research, with an emphasis on my own positionality and personal investment in the work. I invited participants to review this information and respond by email if they were still interested. With those who responded, I arranged a brief conversation by telephone or video call. At this stage I also asked participants to complete a short questionnaire, mediated by Qualtrics, so that I could check they met the criteria for the study and gather some demographic information, including their age, gender identity, religion, education and employment status. During the call, I checked that participants had read the information sheet and confirmed key details about the nature of their participation, most notably the commitment to take part in three interviews and to share selections of their digital media.

The final step of the recruitment and informed consent process involved emailing participants with a copy of the consent form, inviting them to read this and ask any questions as necessary. If they were happy to proceed, we arranged our first interview. At the beginning of this interview, I took participants through the consent form again. The document itself included a reminder that they were free to withdraw from the study at any time. It also reiterated the point (made clear in the participant information sheet and email/telephone communication) that they would have full control over what they shared with me, including their digital media, and our spoken interactions (including the option to retrospectively withdraw specific statements or comments made during the interviews). The consent form also made it clear that all of their (interview and digital) data would be anonymized, including the removal of identifying factors. Of the sixteen prospective participants who expressed their interest in the research, eleven proceeded to the preliminary phone call and ten to the first interview. One participant withdrew after the first interview, leaving a total of nine participants who remained for the duration of the study. These participants were introduced in Chapter 1; in-depth explorations relating to six key participants will follow in the case studies of Chapters 3 to 8.

First interviews

The participant interviews took place over eleven months, spaced at four-to-five-month intervals to support an inductive and iterative research process. My interviewing strategy, in line with what Charmaz (2014) calls an 'intensive' style of grounded theory interviewing, relies on a flexible structure and open-ended questioning technique to obtain detailed responses. This approach also gives participants the space to raise (sometimes unexpected) thoughts, issues and experiences, as well as space for me to respond and follow up on these conversations in a spontaneous way (Charmaz, 2014). The flexible and open-ended nature of the intensive interview chimes with a long tradition of qualitative and feminist interviewing strategies that centre participants themselves and emphasize the co-constructed nature of the research and interviewing process. For example, Mauthner and Doucet (1998), Mason (2018b) and Oakley (1981) all underline the importance of prioritizing participants' comfort and autonomy over gathering 'good' data, making space for intimacy and reciprocity in the research process, and allowing participants to decide what *they* feel to be their most relevant experiences and practices. This is achieved through listening to participants on their own terms, valuing their experience and expertise, and relating to them as equals. A summary of the focus, core question and time frame for each set of interviews is represented in Table 2.

Table 2 Interview Schedule and Key Questions

Interview	Time frame	Focus	Core question
1	December 2018–January 2019	Participants' family lives, experiences and support channels	'Tell me about your family'
2	April 2019–May 2019	Participants' use of digital technology to connect with others	'Show me how you use digital media'
3	September 2019–October 2019	How participants conceive their family and support networks; diagrammatic visualization of these networks	'How do you describe your family and support networks?'

The first round of interviews, which took place between December 2018 and January 2019, focused on family lives, experiences and support channels. During the interview planning stages, I centred participants' comfort and convenience, working to fit in with their lives by inviting them to choose an interview time that worked for them and a place where they felt comfortable. Most participants chose to meet in their own home, at a time when they were alone (pre-school children were sometimes present but often sleeping). Each of these interviews was audio recorded and later transcribed. The first interview was the most flexible and participant-centred. Although participants were no doubt guided by what they already knew about the study's focus, I aimed to discover what *they* perceived to be the most relevant detail about their lives and not restrict their explorations with too many focused questions that were based on *my* interests and expectations. I therefore began each of the first interviews, taking influence from Cummings' (2018) grounded theory study of parents' responses to children's trauma,[1] with one central, open question: 'Can you tell me about your family, starting from the point you see as the beginning of your journey?'. With some participants, this was the only pre-prepared question I asked, with the addition of unprepared follow-up, clarification and expansion questions where necessary. With participants who were less verbose, or less comfortable controlling the direction of the conversation, I used pre-prepared reserve questions such as 'can you tell me what it means to you to be an adoptive/LGB/single parent?' and 'where and how have you found support, encouragement and advice in your everyday life?'.

Towards the end of the first interview, some participants agreed that I could start collecting and exploring some of their easily accessible digital media straight away. For example, Rachael, Jenny and Cheryl were all happy for me to collect posts from their public Twitter accounts and blogs. Sarah also added me to her email mailing list for 'solo mums', who conceived via donor conception. Most of the participants' digital media engagement, however, happened in more private domains, and this data was not discussed in detail or collected until the second interview. The process of digital data collection will be further discussed in the section that follows, including detail on sampling criteria, and the ethical considerations involved at this stage.

Memo writing, transcription and QDA software

Immediately after each interview, I wrote a memo. Memos are a form of written record that support a reflexive and systematic approach through the recording of researchers' thoughts, reflections and developing interpretations, the charting of possible sampling strategies and the creation of an audit trail for the research decision-making process (Birks & Mills, 2015; Charmaz, 2014; Corbin & Strauss, 2008; Glaser & Strauss, 1967). These memos included my reflections on the interview, how I shaped the interview talk, anything I didn't ask or wanted to follow up and any relevant contextual detail about the interview setting or the participants' reactions and responses. I also transcribed the interviews verbatim with the help of two research assistants.[2] The first level of transcription did not include pauses, overlaps, pitch or intonation, as sociolinguistic transcriptions often do. It did, however, include any audible non-verbal communication, such as laughter or sighs, and commentary on interruptions, such as a participant leaving the room for two minutes to answer the telephone. Any sections of interview data that I selected for close discourse analysis were later transcribed in full linguistic detail. None of these detailed transcriptions are included in this book, since my primary focus here is the digital data. However, two journal articles that focus exclusively on interview data from this study (Mackenzie, 2021, in press) do include full sociolinguistic transcriptions.

I used qualitative data analysis (QDA) software to store interview transcripts, digital data and memos in a digital project folder, as part of a collection of linked materials. A wide range of software packages, such as NVivo, ATLAS.ti and MAXQDA, are available to support qualitative research processes and facilitate rigorous record-keeping and comparison. As with my previous work exploring constructions of motherhood in the UK online parenting discussion forum Mumsnet Talk (Mackenzie, 2019), for this project I used QSR International's QDA software, NVivo 12. This program allows the researcher to create a project space for their data, with textual, visual and audio data being stored in the 'files' section, memos in the 'notes' section and coded data in the 'nodes' section. Within this digital project space, data can be continually annotated, analysed, adjusted and compared. This software significantly enhances the systematicity and flexibility of grounded theory analytical processes by making it possible not only to create, store and revisit files, codes and memos but also to edit, manage, merge and organize these records as the analytical process develops.

Initial coding and comparative analysis

Coding, a foundational method in grounded theory analyses, involves the attribution of descriptive labels, or 'codes', to individual pieces of data. Codes themselves then become holding spaces for related data, connecting that data with a particular process, concept or idea (Gibbs, 2002). In keeping with constructivist grounded theory's roots in symbolic interactionism and subsequent emphasis on social action, Charmaz (2014, p. 116) emphasizes the importance of coding in a way that reflects actions in the data. Through *coding for action*, I work to avoid the imposition of pre-existing ideas, frames and categories on the data, and by association, the participants, their practices and their worlds. Following Charmaz (2014), I distinguish two broad stages of coding: initial coding, which is detailed in the next paragraph, and focused coding, which is explored later in the chapter.

The initial coding process, which began as soon as the first set of interview and digital data had been collected, involved close, line-by-line, image-by-image or moment-by-moment coding of the data. Corbin and Strauss (2015, p. 110) call this process 'open coding' and advise the researcher to move the process forward by asking questions of the text such as 'who, what, when, where, how, and with what consequences'. Through the initial coding process, I began to construct my first impressions of the processes, actions and practices that participants made relevant in their interviews and digital media data. In keeping with grounded theory principles, at the initial coding stage I sought to leave open multiple possible meanings and interpretations, rather than closing down the analysis or working to produce 'grand' explanatory theories (following Birks & Mills, 2015; Charmaz, 2014; Glaser & Strauss, 1967; Strauss & Corbin, 1990). Nevertheless, I did begin to group related codes within larger categories, so that the list of codes begins to resemble a tree-like structure of superordinate categories and subordinate codes (Bazeley, 2007). For example, most of the participants told me about the processes involved in becoming a parent and the different routes to parenthood they had considered. In coding interview data that related to this theme, I created the category 'preparing for parenthood' to encapsulate more specific codes such as 'believing conception is possible', 'calculating the chances of success', 'doing the research and learning', 'imagining your children' and 'persuading others of your suitability'.

The coding process is intertwined with a second core tenet of grounded theory research: constant comparative analysis. Through the coding process, I continually subjected data to comparison, identifying points of connection between participants' actions, experiences and meanings across a range of contexts and situations. As well as comparing the data itself, I also compared codes and categories. I considered, for example, whether existing codes adequately described new data, whether they should be amended to incorporate slight variations in theme or indeed whether I was observing new processes entirely (see Birks & Mills, 2015). I named, renamed, merged, combined and fractured codes as I made connections and distinctions between different parts of the interview data and modified my understanding of what could be included within a single code or category. This comparative process is far more than a sorting system; it is an analytical process that moves the researcher, inch by inch, towards incisive integration of the data and ultimately, a compelling grounded theory. It is therefore not so much the codes themselves that are important at this stage but the understanding that is gained through continual interrogation of the data and its meanings. After coding the first set of data in full (nine interviews plus some digital media), I had a list of twelve superordinate categories, which each included between three and thirty-two more specific subordinate codes and categories. Table 3 lists all of these superordinate categories, whilst Table 4 shows the subordinate codes and categories grouped under 'recounting life before children' as an illustrative example. The 'number of files' column shows how many files the category/code

Table 3 NVivo Categories after the Initial Coding Process

Superordinate categories	Number of files	Number of references
Negotiating others' views, dominant discourses	25	368
Using fragmented support networks	30	350
Extra-ordinary parenting	34	330
Negotiating identity	41	297
Collectivizing experience	33	199
Being a pioneer	33	161
Making gender relevant	28	156
Being expert, well informed	35	128
Making age relevant	27	121
Collective parenting	22	114
Negotiating relationships	17	85
Recounting life before children	10	63

Table 4 The 'Recounting Life before Children' Category

Recounting life before children's subordinate codes and categories	Number of files	Number of references
Living life to the full	8	36
Having a difficult childhood	3	11
Wanting to make a difference	1	6
Experiences of children and families	1	4
Being open to alternative families and lifestyles	1	3

is used in, whilst the 'number of references' column shows the total number of references coded.

Digital data collection and second interviews

Through the first phase of data collection and coding, I gained a good understanding of participants' family lives, including their routes to parenthood, family circumstances and day-to-day experiences. Most participants had told me a little about their use of digital media, and I had already started to look at some of their social media accounts and websites. However, I had a limited understanding of how the participants used digital media, in terms of what, how and with whom they were communicating, and how digital media was integrated with their everyday lives, practices and relationships. In order to develop a holistic understanding of these parents' digital media practices, I structured the second interview around a virtual 'walk-through' of their digital media engagement. In this interview, I asked participants not just to tell me about their use of digital media, but also to *show* me the different platforms, groups and apps they used on a computer or mobile device. I took a number of steps to protect participants' privacy and autonomy at this stage, as well as that of their wider networks. First, the interviews were not video recorded or screen captured, and I did not collect any digital media data in real time. Second, I asked participants not to repeat any digital content verbatim during the interview, and if this did happen, I erased the detail from the transcript. I also gave participants plenty of notice that I would be asking them to show and talk me through their digital engagement in this interview and explained that they had full control over what they shared.

The second interviews, like the first, were open, flexible and centred around a single question, in this case 'show me how you use digital media'. Looking at participants' digital media on a screen (or screens) provided a clear focal point for these interviews and as a result discussion tended to flow easily. However, as with the first interview, I also prepared several focused reserve questions, with the aim of encouraging participants to elaborate on what they were showing me or prompting them if they weren't sure what to show me. For example, I asked some participants to 'tell me about a digital interaction that was positive, thought-provoking or affirming', or conversely, 'tell me about a digital interaction that was negative, frustrating or upsetting'. Because this was the second meeting with each participant, the schedule included targeted follow-up questions that were different for each participant, based on specific issues, experiences and concepts identified through the coding process.

At the end of the second interview, I began to collect selections of participants' private digital media. At this stage in the data collection process, I relied on participants to choose which data they were happy to share, based on their knowledge of the groups they were part of, and the norms of information sharing in these contexts (see Mackenzie, 2017b; Nissenbaum, 2010, on the importance of informational norms). Many participants, for example, did not want to share message exchanges from WhatsApp or Messenger, or posts to certain Facebook groups that had very strict rules around privacy. Most participants collected the data they *were* happy to share by taking screenshots of their posts or messages and sending them to me via mobile messaging, email or a file hosting service (Dropbox or OneDrive).

Although participants had full control over the digital data they shared, their digital interactions usually involved other people, who had not consented to take part in the research process. Collecting what participants were happy to share was therefore no guarantee of good ethical practice. For this reason, I took two key decisions: first, I asked participants to only share their own words (not replies or responses). This decision had a significant effect on the development of the study, limiting my control over the digital media that was collected, and the nature of the data itself. It also meant that I was not able to examine either the interactional and collaborative dimensions of connected parenting or the practices and structures of participants' wider networks and communities in any detail. However, I would argue, along with researchers who have taken a similar approach (e.g. Tagg & Lyons, 2020; Tagg et al., 2017), that such data selectivity was essential for the ethical viability of the research. Further, this approach helped to foster trusting researcher–participant relationships and empowered participants to take some control of the research process. From a methodological perspective, the limited scope of the data also focused my attention very sharply on the connected parenting practices of my key participants, resulting in a rich and nuanced analysis of these individuals' lives and digital practices.

There were a few exceptions to the general rule that I did not collect participants' interactions with others. First, I collected some tweets and Facebook posts in which participants shared content that they did not produce themselves. In these instances, I only collected shared material if I deemed that (a) it was in the public domain, and (b) the author intended for it to be widely seen and read. For example, in collecting Jenny's and Cheryl's Facebook and Twitter posts, I also collected some articles from websites, blogs and online magazines, and (re) tweets about public issues that were originally written by well-known figures. Even so, I did contact all authors of this secondary material for legal reasons around copyright, and they all agreed to their material being shared in this book. Second, two participants were happy to share selected mobile messages with me: Lynne shared a Messenger exchange between herself and five other friends, and Peter shared chat logs from nine WhatsApp dyads or groups. With these data, Lynne and Peter acted as intermediaries, asking their contacts for informed consent to use the interactions for research purposes, including the completion of a consent form. In general, however, I did not ask participants to mediate this process of informed consent from secondary participants unless they were particularly keen to do so.

I asked participants to collect and send digital data that had been created roughly within a one-year time frame, up to the day before our second interview. Most participants' digital media was therefore created between the period of May 2018 and May 2019. I also employed these parameters when collecting public-domain data myself. However, because two of my participants, Cheryl and Jenny, were prolific users of Twitter, I took the decision to reduce data collection from these accounts to six months, including only tweets posted between 1 October 2018 and 1 April 2019. A numerical overview of the full digital dataset is provided in Table 5.

As noted earlier, participants were informed from the outset that their interview and digital data would be anonymized, and all identifying factors removed or changed. This process went far beyond anonymizing participants' names; pseudonyms were also used for anyone they named in their interview or digital data and for place names. Further, any groups that they used, such as Facebook groups, community groups or organizations, were also given pseudonyms. This was an important part of the anonymization process because these details could

Table 5 Numerical Overview of Participants' Combined Digital Data

Digital medium	Total number	Subtotals
Facebook posts	218	151 posts to private groups
		41 posts to public pages
		26 posts to personal timelines
Tweets	182	N/A
Emails	63	N/A
Instagram posts	48	N/A
Blog posts	24	N/A
WhatsApp chat logs	9	5,183 individual messages
Messenger chat sequence	1	8 individual messages

make it easier not only to identify participants but also to protect the identities of other people and groups involved in their lives. Any photographs included in this data set were anonymized using an app called Skitch, which has a tool for pixellating details beyond recognition. Finally, digital data is often transcribed in this book, allowing me to ensure all identifying details are changed or modified. Where it is possible to do so without compromising participants' anonymity, original screenshots are presented as figures, especially where the layout or images contained in the data are important for their interpretation.

Focused coding

Once each participant's second interviews had been transcribed, and their digital data stored in image files, I again coded both sets of data in the NVivo project space. At this stage I used, modified and adapted pre-existing codes and categories from the initial coding stage, as well as creating new codes and categories where needed. For example, I created three new categories to capture processes and experiences relating specifically to participants' online and digital engagement: 'digital overload', 'documenting and record-keeping' and 'having control and autonomy'. The first two of these categories included almost entirely new codes that were quite specific to digital engagement, such as 'being addicted', 'spending a lot of time online' and 'feeling overwhelmed or triggered' (in the 'digital overload' category), as well as 'filing digital media', 'using digital media to evidence interactions' and 'writing online to record or document experiences' (in the 'documenting and record-keeping' category). By refining and adding to the most useful and significant codes and categories, and testing them against additional data, I intensified and sharpened the analysis at this stage, moving increasingly from *initial* coding to *focused* coding (although as Charmaz (2014) notes, there is not always a clear distinction between the two).

As part of the focused coding process, I also sought to capture and explain participants' actions, practices and experiences in new and compelling ways by developing more 'theoretical codes', which specify the relationship between significant codes and categories (Glaser, 1978, p. 72). For example, I constructed two core theoretical categories around participants' life experiences, support and social networks, and use of digital media. I created the first theoretical category, 'extra-ordinary parenting', in a bid to capture participants' negotiations and explanations of their family circumstances and practices. Many of the subordinate codes within this category focus on participants' redefinition of the boundaries around familial roles and relationships, such as 'negotiating extended family or biological relationships' or 'positioning 'alternative' situations as normative'. Other codes point to families' difficulties and suffering, for example 'finding ways to cope and manage' and 'recognizing children's struggles'. Further, many of the codes in the 'extra-ordinary parenting' category show how participants went to extra-ordinary lengths to both bring children into their lives and give those children the best possible chance in life, for example 'going to extra-ordinary lengths to raise a child' and 'hyper-vigilant parenting'. Conversely, other codes within this category show that participants frequently positioned their families as ordinary and unremarkable, such as 'being very ordinary' and 'backgrounding difference'. With the second theoretical category, 'building a (virtual) village', I attempted to capture and describe the construction and maintenance of supportive relationships and networks, creating codes such as 'maintaining connections', 'negotiating what to share', 'posting to groups you know will be sympathetic' and 'seeking or giving help or advice'. The choice of the term 'village' echoes a phrase I had encountered in several participants' digital media, 'it takes a village to raise a child'. The subordinate codes and categories subsumed under 'extra-ordinary parenting' and 'building a (virtual) village' are shown in Tables 6 and 7.

It is important to note that the theoretical categories I developed at this stage in the research process were incomplete and preliminary. Although they encapsulated some important themes and insights, separating out 'building a (virtual) village' from 'extra-ordinary parenting' also created a somewhat

Table 6 The 'Extra-ordinary Parenting' Category

***Extra-ordinary parenting*'s subordinate codes and categories**	**Number of files**	**Number of references**
Becoming an expert parent	214	1,368
Re-defining the family	128	1,332
Journey to extra-ordinary parenting	89	1,085
Hyper-vigilant parenting	151	1,056
Suffering	136	974
Fulfilling multiple roles	73	263
Being positive	70	207
Collaborative co-parenting	31	181
Commercialization of parenthood and families	58	166
Negotiating relationship	34	107
Maintaining relationships with children	27	91
Counting the costs	29	59
Telling and talking	24	55
Offering an instant, unconditional family	21	49

artificial division between participants' *family* and *digital* practices that I was not able to fully reconcile at this stage. The final interview offered an opportunity to clarify and consolidate this analytical and theory-building process as I moved towards the development of an incisive grounded theory.

Third interviews and network diagrams

I used the third interviews to address specific gaps, problems and questions that had arisen through the developing research process. I did so, first, by introducing the theoretical categories I had established at this stage, 'extra-ordinary parenting' and 'building a (virtual) village'. I asked whether these categories fit participants' experiences and whether there were any other terms or concepts they preferred. This led to some valuable discussion around participants' own concepts of their parenting and family practice, their social and support networks, and their use of digital media. This interview strategy is again influenced by Cummings' (2018, p. 119) research, in which she interviewed her participants several times, and as the interviews progressed, asked questions that would help her to assess and adjust her developing codes and categories. This process helped me to both target important aspects of the developing theory and value participants' expertise and autonomy in describing their own practices.

Table 7 The 'Building a (Virtual) Village' Category

Building a (virtual) village's subordinate codes and categories	Number of files	Number of references
Having control and autonomy	51	1,328
Collectivizing experience	292	1,236
Getting (fragmented) support	89	985
Collective parenting	91	507
Cross-over between groups or spaces	66	337
Maintaining regular contact with people	71	213
Reflecting on participation practices	33	297
Distinguishing from others	53	272
Capitalizing on contacts	49	242
Not getting good support	40	122
Getting reactions from others	34	93
Digital overload	23	80
Competition and conflict	25	64
Documenting and record-keeping	14	33
Concern with children and digital media	14	20
Taking joy in digital practices	7	15

The second component of the third interviews involved the creation of a network diagram, adapted from the well-established sociogram (e.g. Hogan, Carrasco, & Wellman, 2007; Milroy, 1980; Sharma, 2017) as well as the more recently developed mediagram (Lexander & Androutsopoulos, 2021). The sociogram, a tool widely used in sociolinguistics for visualizing social network data, 'represents a set of relations between a given actor (ego) and others (alters)' (Sharma, 2017, p. 395). This diagram tends to deploy an 'ego star' graphic which places the key participant at its centre and sometimes includes concentric circles to represent different levels of closeness to this participant (Hogan et al., 2007). Adapting this popular visualization tool, Lexander and Androutsopoulos' (2021) mediagrams support the documentation and analysis of individual repertoires for mediated interaction. These mediagrams not only deploy the basic 'ego star' structure but also indicate the participant's use of media channels (distinguished by app logos), language choices (distinguished by colour, e.g. red for Norwegian and blue for French) and language modality (distinguished by line style, e.g. continuous lines for written, dotted for spoken and mixed for both).

Taking inspiration from Hogan et al.'s (2007) participant-aided sociograms, I guided participants to create their own network diagrams during the third interview. To support this process, I informed participants in advance about what we would be doing and gave them a pre-prepared example. On the day of the interview, I gave each participant a blank template on A3 paper, which had their name in the middle (the 'ego') and three concentric circles building from this central point. I also gave them an envelope of plain circular stickers and asked them to write the name of a person or group that was important in their family life on each one (the 'alters'). I then asked them to place each alter on the template, positioning them closer to (or further away from) their own name to indicate their closeness and importance. I devised a key to show the usual mode and frequency of contact with the person/group, including the use of parallel lines to indicate connections between linked contacts. I asked participants to keep the detail on the diagrams to a minimum, adding additional details verbally, such as who/what each alter represented and what kind of support they offered. This meant the diagrams did not become too cluttered during the interview process, but I still had a record of additional details. Table 8 shows the questioning and elicitation strategies I used to assist in the creation of these diagrams. Figure 4 shows Jenny's completed diagram, including the key, as an example.

After each interview, I cross-referenced each participant's diagram with their recorded talk and created four separate diagrams using Microsoft PowerPoint. The diagrams I created for Jenny are shown in Figures 5 to 8 as illustrative

Table 8 Procedure for Creating a Network Diagram

Number	Prompt
1	Name 5–10 of your current most significant connections (these can be people, groups, pages or spaces) which meet the following criteria: (a) you share or discover important things; (b) you go to it/them regularly; (c) you go there for help.
2	Explain who they are/ what this is, and how you are connected.
3	Where are they based (geographically)?
4	What is the medium and frequency of your communication with them (see key)?
5	What do you get out of the connection? (a) practical support, (b) emotional support, (c) political engagement, (d) information, (e) contacts/networking, (f) something else?
6	Are there any links between individuals/groups/resources?
7	How much of your knowledge and expertise comes from within/outside of this network?
8	(How) has this diagram changed over the years?
9	What does this diagram represent, and what does that mean to you?

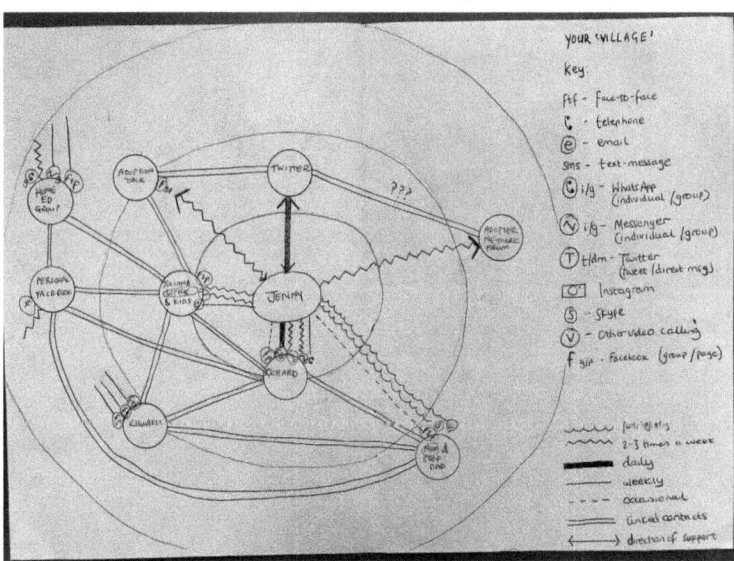

Figure 4 Jenny's original network diagram.

examples. By producing four separate diagrams, I was able to create a clear permanent record of the rather busy and dense originals, as well as separately drawing out the key details that were of most interest to my investigation. First, I created a diagram that exclusively detailed the modes and frequencies of contact between participants and their alters (see Figure 5). This diagram

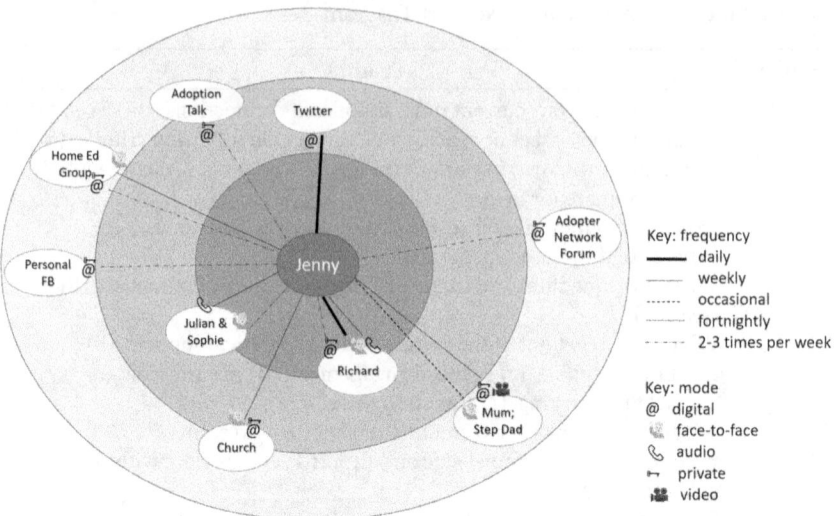

Figure 5 Jenny's modes of contact diagram.

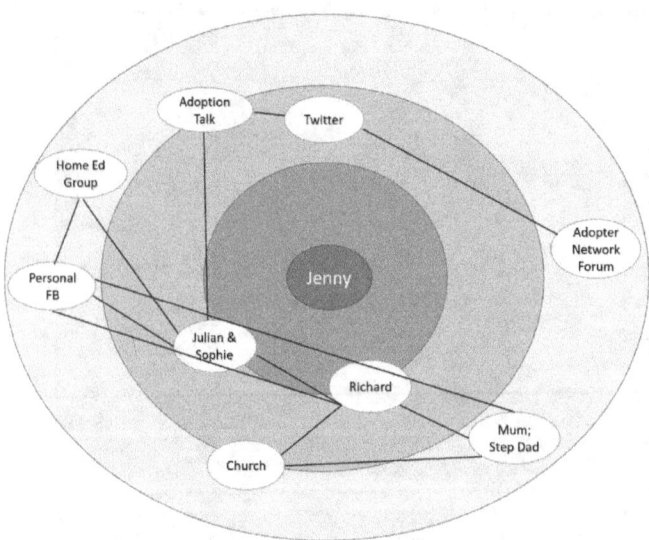

Figure 6 Jenny's network connections and density diagram.

uses line style to distinguish between, for example, daily, weekly and fortnightly contact, and icons to both distinguish between digital, face-to-face, audio or video contact and show whether contact took place in a 'private' sphere (i.e. a locked social media account or messaging within the private space of a mobile phone). The second diagram shows connections between alters using a single

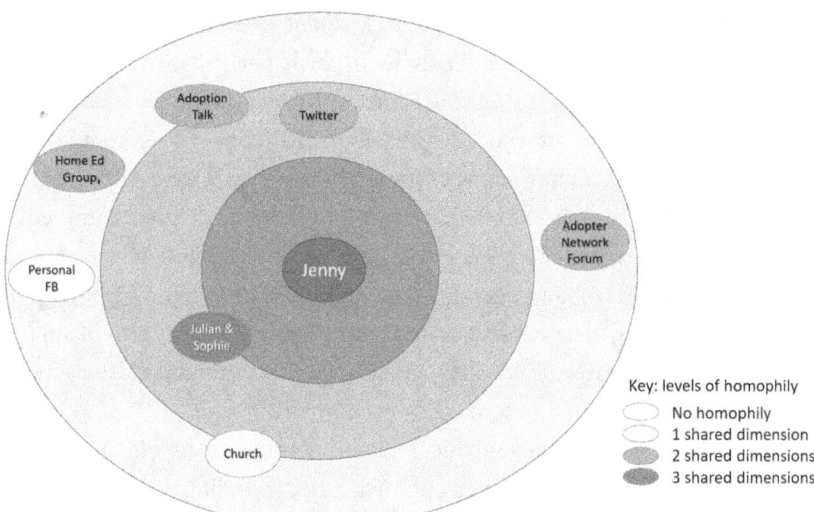

Figure 7 Jenny's homophily diagram.

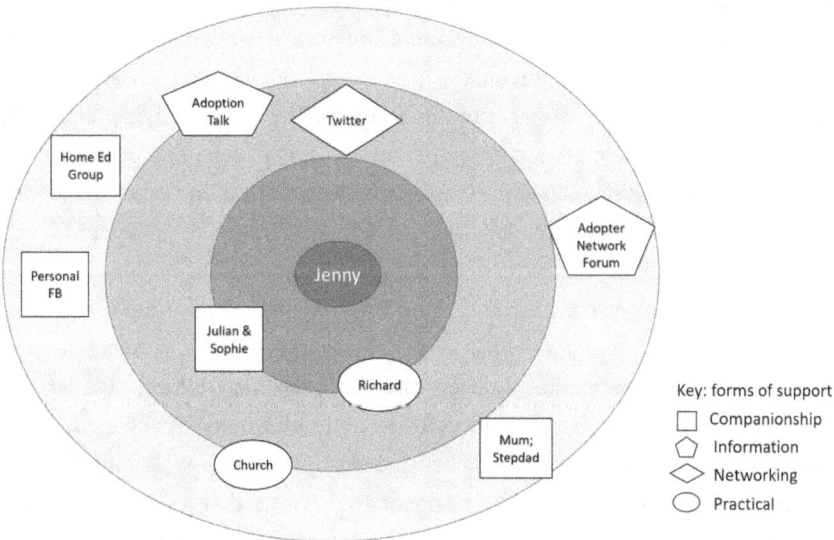

Figure 8 Jenny's forms of support diagram.

bold line (see Figure 6). For example, connecting lines are drawn if alters are friends or members of the same group. This diagram provides an impression at a glance of how dense the network is (i.e. how many alters are connected to one another). In the third diagram, shades of grey are used to show levels of homophily between the participant and their alters – in other words, how much alters have in common with the participant (see Figure 7). The criteria for measuring homophily were different for each participant, depending on the details they foregrounded in describing their own identities, families and experiences, and their connections with others. In Jenny's case, homophily is measured on the basis of how many of the following criteria were shared: parent; adopter; Christian faith; home educator. In the homophily diagrams, immediate family members are excluded, since these are not 'chosen', but 'given', contacts (hence Richard, Mum and Stepdad are excluded from Jenny's homophily diagram in Figure 7). The final diagram illustrates the primary form of support the participant gains from each alter, using shapes to distinguish between each type (see Figure 8).

Creating these network diagrams incurred a number of benefits. First, they helped to capture the complexity of participants' networks, including the importance of different alters, relationships between them, and modes of connection, in a single document. At this stage in the research, I had fragmented the data through the process of coding and reconstructed it around key codes and categories across all nine participants. However, by conducting the analysis in this way I sometimes lost focus on my participants as *individuals*. Creating network diagrams with each participant brought their individual experiences, practices and social networks back to the fore in the final stages of this research. The completed diagrams were also a very useful reference point, in terms of contextualizing specific digital messages or posts in relation to participants' wider networks and practices. A final benefit of this activity was that it helped participants themselves to recognize and engage with the significance of connected parenting practices in their lives. For example, after creating her diagram, Jenny reflected on the important role Twitter had played in opening up a 'whole world' of adoption-relation connections and information that had previously been unavailable to her. Without Twitter, she suggested, 'none of the rest of the adoption related stuff would've happened'. When Cheryl completed her diagram, she became very emotional, explaining that she 'wouldn't have survived' without the supportive network that was mapped out in front of her. These reflections are examined in more detail, in relation to some of Jenny and Cheryl's specific connected parenting practices, in Chapters 4 and 5.

Establishing a grounded theory of connected parenting

The culmination of the initial, focused and theoretical coding processes involved weaving together all codes and categories into a single, core theoretical category: *connected parenting*. A theory of connected parenting contemplates family practices as they are constructed, negotiated and maintained through ties between parents and their networks of friends, family members, groups and communities. In turn, it also theorizes their connections within these networks as they are constructed, negotiated and maintained through their family practices. At the final stage in the coding process, the connected parenting theoretical category included seven subordinate categories, four of which group thematically related practices in the data ('extra-ordinary parenting', 'building a (virtual) village', 'collective parenting' and 'becoming an expert parent') and three of which group semiotic features of the data (under the headings of 'linguistic', 'visual' and 'digital' features). The full complement of subordinate categories is shown in Table 9.

The first two sub-categories of connected parenting, 'extra-ordinary parenting' and 'building a (virtual) village', have been outlined earlier in this chapter. By subsuming these categories under the umbrella of 'connected parenting', I open the door to cross-theorization around the ways in which participants' social connections and digital interactions overlap with, feed into and maintain their parenting and family practices. The third sub-category, 'collective parenting', includes codes that refer quite literally to sharing the care of and responsibility for children, such as 'sharing parental status with biological relatives', 'collaborative co-parenting' and 'sharing or swapping children'. It also includes codes that point more to the kind of support offered (often at a distance) by friends, extended family, groups and communities, such as 'supporting other parents and children', 'being part of a community' and 'being invested in others' lives'. Most participants suggested in their interviews that this kind of collective parenting was contingent on homophily, that is, affiliation on the basis of having similar families, identities or experiences. The importance of homophily in collective parenting practices is expressed

Table 9 The 'Connected Parenting' Category

Connected parenting's subordinate codes and categories	Number of files	Number of references
Becoming an expert parent	251	1,860
Collective parenting	267	2,054
Extra-ordinary parenting	349	5,877
Building a (virtual) village	372	3,294
Linguistic features	215	709
Visual features	94	232
Digital features	138	611

in subordinate codes such as 'connecting with others in the same or similar situation' or 'not having to explain'. Constructing the final thematic category, 'becoming an expert parent', contributed significantly to theory building around parents' self-positioning as *experts*, alongside the construction and negotiation of expertise through practices such as research, reading and engagement with professionals. These practices are captured in codes such as 'being a spokesperson', 'being a mentor to others', 'valuing the views of experts', 'learning on the job', 'looking for balanced and unbiased evidence' and 'being concerned about misinformation'.

There is significant overlap between the four thematic sub-categories of connected parenting, and participants' digital media often illustrates this overlap quite vividly. For example, Anna, a single lesbian adoptive parent, shared a number of posts to Facebook groups in which the dimensions of 'building a (virtual) village', 'extra-ordinary parenting', 'collective parenting' and 'becoming an expert parent' overlap and intersect. Extract 1 shows one of Anna's posts to a group called 'parenting with connection', which brings together parents who follow an empathetic philosophy of parenting that focuses on building a strong parent–child bond. In this post, Anna touches on the impact of her daughter being removed from her birth family, pointing to some of her family's 'extra-ordinary' experiences and practices. The post also shows Anna mobilizing her connections with this online support group to gather a range of experiences and perspectives from people who have a similar parenting philosophy. Passages in this post were therefore also coded to 'building a (virtual) village', 'collective parenting' and 'becoming an expert parent'. The final category, 'becoming an expert parent', is particularly relevant here, as Anna is clearly seeking knowledge and advice from members of this Facebook group.

Extract 1. Anna's Facebook post to a 'parenting with connection' group (14.06.2018)

How & how much do you explain impact of early life trauma to a child who was too young to remember it now?

My AD6 was bit over a year when she was removed from birth family – but her early life has left a big impact on her (dysregulation, anxiety, hyper-alertness, hypersensitivity; very quick to go to flight and terror etc).

We're starting the process of getting help, through an attachment group and possibly some family therapy / something else soon.

She knows she's adopted, she knows her birth parents didn't know how to keep her happy, well and safe, but not much more (I will answer if she has questions but this far that has been enough).

What I'm wondering is how have others navigated explaining to a child that they are different because of how they struggle, or trying to explain the reasons for this – when we're moving forward in getting help for her I wonder if this'll come up somehow – I hope she can learn self-awareness to help her become happier child, teenager and adult eventually, but I'm bit concerned about that it might make her feel bad / different / uncomfortable etc.

Sorry for rambling! I suppose I'm interested to hear if others have had similar situations and how much and how have you shared / explained to your child, and what would be connected way to deal with this. Thank you

👍 3   19 comments

It is worth noting at this point that by introducing me to the 'parenting with connection' philosophy, Anna played quite a significant role in the grounded theory process. Although the philosophies of 'parenting with connection' are markedly different to the theory of connected parenting that is presented in this book, they both revolve around bringing close connections into parenting practice. Exploring this parenting philosophy led me to reflect anew on the relationship between parenting, family practices and digitally mediated connection. In the section that follows, I explain in more detail how I explored and elaborated the dimensions of connected parenting through close discourse analysis of digital media texts such as this.

Discourse analysis

The grounded theory processes that have been described so far form the foundations of the Marginalised Families Online study. In this research process, however, developing a grounded theory of connected parenting does not represent an analytical end point. Rather, it serves as a jumping-off point, from which I hold a magnifying glass to participants' digital media data and situate it in relation to their wider connected parenting practices. In order to closely examine participants' connected parenting practices as they are constructed and maintained through digitally mediated interactions, I undertook six case studies, based on Cheryl, Lynne, Jenny, Rachael, Tony and Peter's interview and digitally mediated data. I selected these participants on the basis of several considerations. First, their interview and digital media data was particularly significant in developing a theory of connected parenting through the first stage grounded theory analysis. Second, these parents represented participants' diversity, in terms of their age (ranging from twenty-nine to fifty-four), gender (male and female), sexuality (heterosexual, gay and unknown), the age of their children (between one and twenty-one), their relationship status and preferences (single, voluntarily celibate, coupled and co-parenting) and the means by which they brought children into their lives (adoption, donor conception, surrogacy and co-parenting). Finally, the diversity of these participants' digitally mediated data allowed me to look at a wide range of digital media platforms and apps, including Facebook (Cheryl and Tony), Messenger (Lynne), Twitter (Jenny) Instagram (Rachael) and WhatsApp (Peter).

When looking at these participants' digitally mediated data from selected platforms, I first examined the form and function of each text, with the aim of capturing general patterns of sharing and engagement in these contexts. I then chose a smaller selection of texts that exemplified salient patterns and practices. With these smaller collections of data, I moved forward to the second, micro-analytical stage of analysis, which drew on the principles and processes of mediated discourse analysis. At this stage, I worked to trace specific actions through participants' digital texts, networks and broader family practices, and consider how they are mediated through digital technologies.

As explained in Chapter 1, mediated discourse analysts position the mediated social action as the central unit of analysis, considering how discourse is used to take actions and how those actions are mediated through a range of tools and technologies. A brief analysis and discussion of Laura's post to a 'baby-led weaning' Facebook group provided an illustration of how this approach is deployed in relation to the Marginalised Families Online project data. Mediated discourse analysts mobilize a range of discourse analytical tools to realize their goals (Scollon, 2001, 2007). For example, *entextualization* (see Chapter 1) is a particularly useful companion concept that is utilized, to different extents, throughout the analytical chapters that follow. The analyses of Chapters 5 and 6, in particular, focus on the ways in which actions, moments, events and practices are made 'tangible' and thus 'knowable' through the transformative processes of decontextualization, entextualization and recontextualization in Jenny's retweets and Rachael's Instagram posts. I also draw on a range of other tools and concepts as appropriate for each case study. For example, Chapter 3 elaborates and develops the concept of 'info-relational sharing' (Fage-Butler & Jensen, 2013) in the examination of Cheryl's posts to a Facebook group. In Chapters 7 and 8, I draw on a relational understanding of affect (e.g. Boler & Davis, 2018; Wetherell, 2012) to examine the way affective actions and practices move through Peter's WhatsApp interactions and Tony's Facebook posts.

Through these micro-level mediated discourse analyses, I further developed my theory of connected parenting through the identification and elaboration of its collective, epistemic and affective dimensions. In doing so, I foregrounded and further interrogated the core categories of 'collective parenting' and 'becoming an expert parent', as well as drawing out a third dimension revolving around *affect*. This final dimension runs through all the core categories and their subordinate codes. Affect is evident, for example, in codes such as 'suffering' (part of the 'extra-ordinary parenting' category), 'being positive' (part of 'building a (virtual) village'), 'feeding each other's misery' (in 'collective parenting') and 'feeling good about helping others' ('becoming an expert parent'). However, it was only through the close analysis of participants' mediated social actions that I was able to identify affective connection as a pervasive element of participants' connected parenting practice and isolate it as a dimension worthy of further investigation in its own right.

Chapter summary

This chapter has outlined the design of the Marginalised Families Online study in detail. It emphasizes the inductive nature of this design, explaining how time has been built into the research process for making connections and comparisons across and between the data, identifying areas for further exploration and testing early analytical insights against new observations. This responsive and flexible development, I explain, works to drive the research forward, continually testing the limits of the developing theory and analysis. Further, I have outlined four key ethical principles that are woven through all aspects of this research design: *maximizing benefits and minimizing harm, attentiveness to context, acknowledging my positionality as a researcher* and *integrating ethical considerations at all stages*. The chapter has also shown how a combined approach that draws on the principles and processes of grounded theory and mediated discourse analysis can be operationalized in practice. For example, I have explained how the grounded theory process of *coding for action* roots the analyses in participants' concrete social actions from the outset, whilst MDA's emphasis on tracing the trajectories of social actions facilitates further scrutiny of the way parents' actions and practices are mediated in specific digital texts, in terms of the origins of those actions, the ways in which they are mediated and (re)produced, and the future actions they enable. Through this approach, the micro-level analyses of digital texts that follow in Chapters 3 to 8 are firmly rooted not only in the wider context of participants' lives and relationships but also in robust theory that is developed through systematic analysis across participants' data.

3

Introducing Collective Connection

The first dimension of connected parenting, *collective connection*, involves the construction, consolidation and mobilization of shared practices and experiences through digitally mediated actions and texts. In this chapter, I begin by situating collective connection in relation to existing scholarship that has theorized the positioning of self in relation to others as a central facet of human identity and interaction, with particular attention to the concepts of alignment, affiliation and collectivization. Further, I explain, digital and social media research has suggested that affiliation around shared values and beliefs has played an important role in shaping digital connections across a range of contexts. I contribute to this interdisciplinary conversation by attending specifically to the digitally mediated collectivization of *action* and *experience*, whereby shared experience and practice are taken as a starting point for the construction of connection and solidarity. In this chapter, I not only point to the socio-emotional benefits of collective connection but also suggest that collective connection forms the foundations for a connected parenting practice that has the potential to reshape contemporary family life in flexible and dynamic ways. In this way, I aim to move beyond the themes of support, solidarity and validation that have dominated existing research with online 'parenting collectives'.

Collective connection is a particularly significant dimension of connected parenting for the single adoptive parents who took part in the Marginalised Families Online study. These parents face a unique set of challenges and often feel they can only be open and honest about their experiences with other adoptive parents. Through a case study that focuses on the digital practices of one single adoptive parent, Lynne, this chapter will show how connections with other adoptive parents can form the foundations for the (re)construction of everyday shared practices, from the simple act of washing nappies to the more complex processes involved in understanding a child's negative behaviours. After introducing Lynne, I focus on her use of Messenger, providing a brief overview of the way she uses this app to draw together ephemeral groups of individuals who share common experiences. The first analytical section examines a sequence of messages that was unfolding on Messenger at the time of our second interview, between Lynne and four other friends. The second analytical strand deals not with digital data itself but with Lynne's interview talk about the way she uses Messenger to connect with close friends. This is the first of two case studies that are used to elaborate the concept of collective connection. The insights of this chapter will be developed in Chapter 4, which introduces a second case study focused on another single adoptive parent, Cheryl. Together, these chapters consider how two single adopters, who each value friendship and community with other adopters very highly, construct collective connections with their peers through the digitally mediated entextualization of actions and practices as *shared experiences*.

Affiliation, collectivization and peer-to-peer solidarity

Practices of alignment, affiliation and collectivization have been extensively theorized through sociolinguistic, discourse analytical and wider social scientific research, especially in relation to theories of group identity. Across this work, the concepts of 'similarity' and 'difference' have often been positioned as the central axis around which group identity relations revolve (Bucholtz & Hall, 2005). For example, Tajfel and Turner's (1979) theory of intergroup conflict explains how individuals position themselves in relation to others through foregrounding similarities between members of an 'in-group' and differences from members of an 'out-group'. Sociolinguists have detailed some of the more nuanced ways in which individuals can be positioned, or position themselves, as certain 'kinds' of people through alignment (or disalignment) with others in written and spoken interaction. For example, Bucholtz and Hall (2005, p. 599) point to interactional processes of *adequation* and *distinction*, whereby perceived similarities and differences between two individuals and groups will either be foregrounded or downplayed, depending on whether the 'immediate project of identity work' involves bringing people closer together (adequation) or moving them further apart (distinction). Van Leeuwen (2008) has specified similar processes of *assimilation and association, differentiation and dissociation*, as strategies for constructing an impression of 'sameness' or 'difference' between individuals and groups in written discourse. Du Bois' (2007) work on positioning and stance focuses on *evaluation* as an interactional resource for the positioning of self through (dis)alignment with others. He captures the relationship between positioning, evaluation and alignment in the 'stance triangle', which elucidates the dual, relational function of evaluation: to position the self, and through that positioning, to (dis)align with others. Overall, these investigations of positioning, relationality and group identity show how constructions of sameness, affiliation and alignment can be achieved through reference to overlapping values, evaluations or identities.

Language and social media scholars, further, have suggested that the drive to affiliate with others who have similar values and beliefs can shape social media connections across a range of contexts, with affordances such as hashtags, likes, digital photography and video being shaped and mobilized in ways that promote group affiliations. For example, Page (2019, p. 91) has shown how, during political, religious, musical and sporting events, creators of Snapchat selfies and videos deploy strategies of 'synthetic collectivization' to construct a group perspective, promoting an idealized construction of the 'Snapchat community' and collective expressions of affect (Page, 2019, p. 91). These strategies include linguistic devices such as the repeated plural pronoun 'we' and relational groups such as 'everyone' and 'all the families', alongside visual devices which 'indirectly position the video creator within a larger group'. In the context of the microblogging platform Twitter, Zappavigna (2014) has shown how tweets using the hashtag #coffee can bring people together around the enjoyment of coffee as a shared value, or as she puts it, a common bond. She conceptualizes coffee as a 'bonding icon', a symbolic resource around which interpersonal meanings ('coffee as solidifying relationships') are foregrounded and ideational meanings ('coffee as a beverage') are backgrounded (Zappavigna, 2014, p. 142). Page (2018, p. 84) has developed this concept of bonding by suggesting that it is a scalar concept – that the subject of evaluation 'can be more or less "bondable"'. For example, in her investigation of Facebook memorial pages for Nelson Mandela and Margaret Thatcher, Page (2018, p. 97) shows how Mandela is represented in ways that promote a shared stance of respect, as in the example of formulaic statements such as 'R.I.P. Madiba', which garnered significant numbers of 'likes'. Thatcher, on the other hand, is often represented in ways that encourage polarized responses, as in the example 'Like if you're glad she's dead, Share if you'll miss her' (Page, 2018, p. 98). Whilst others have theorized Facebook's 'like' button as a tool for bringing diverse individuals together in 'brief moments of focusing' (e.g. Blommaert & Varis, 2015, p. 56), Page's analysis demonstrates that such digital strategies for alignment or 'bonding' will not necessarily induce homogenous responses; indeed, they can be manipulated to do quite the opposite, especially if this results in increased interaction and engagement.

The aforementioned examples pinpoint relatively brief moments of alignment, affiliation and collectivization around a particular object (Zappavigna, 2014), occasion (Page, 2019) or figure (Page, 2018). The collective connections that will be explored in this and the following chapter, however, relate to quite stable dyads and groups, who share more persistent identities, histories and experiences. In these chapters, I am therefore concerned less with the fleeting expression of shared *values, evaluations or beliefs* amongst individuals who are momentarily united by passing and ephemeral affiliations, and more with group members' recourse to the repeated *actions, practices and experiences* that are shared over longer periods of time and across a range of situations. In order to contextualize this exploration of collective connection in relatively stable collectives, I turn now to insights from research that examines online connection within parenting groups and communities.

A wealth of interdisciplinary research with new, expectant and established parents, especially mothers, has emphasized the importance of social media, including discussion forums, messaging apps and Facebook groups, as tools through which parents can find valuable peer support and information (Johnson, 2015; Lyons, 2020; Price et al., 2018; Veazey, 2019; Zhao & Basnyat, 2018). Explorations of discussion forums and blogging communities for mothers, further, have often emphasized the importance of shared experience and solidarity within these groups. For example, Morrison (2011, p. 49) describes 'mommy blogging' communities as a 'set of like others', who offer their members 'group identity as well as emotional release'. Further, Pedersen and Lupton (2018) find that the UK parenting discussion forum Mumsnet Talk provides an important space for mothers to express transgressive views and experiences, and gain reassurance that they are not alone. By discussing their perceived failings and 'ask[ing] others to validate their emotional responses', Pedersen and Lupton (2018, p. 60) explain, Mumsnet users were reassured that 'perhaps others were also feeling the same as them' and 'what they were doing or feeling was right'. Pedersen and Lupton (2018, p. 60) describe the empathic exchanges that followed such calls for validation as 'me too' sharing, a concept that is echoed in Jaworska's (2018) analysis of threads about postnatal depression (PND) within the same forum. Jaworska (2018, p. 29), for example, points to contributors' use of the *confession* and *exemplum* formats, whereby the opening poster's (OP's) confessions triggered 'waves of response stories', with others joining the thread to share similar experiences in the form of exempla. Through these forms of online trouble-telling, Jaworska (2018, p. 29) explains, contributors 'create a sense of solidarity and shared understanding [which] helps validate and "normalise" the turbulent PND experience of the OP'.

Jaworska's (2018) work suggests that being able to connect and share with others who have similar experiences may be particularly valuable for parents who have had marginal, transgressive or otherwise difficult experiences. Research that explores the digital practices of parents to children with conditions such as cystic fibrosis (e.g. Strekalova, 2016), autism (e.g. Blum-Ross & Livingstone, 2017) and congenital heart defects (e.g. Bellander & Nikolaidou, 2017) provide further support for this claim. For example, in Blum-Ross and Livingstone's (2017, p. 7) analysis of interviews with seventeen parent bloggers, they found that parents to children with special educational needs and disabilities felt 'unable to participate in mainstream rituals of parenting' and saw blogging as a way of gaining mutual support from others in similar circumstances. As one of their participants explained, connecting with other parents of autistic children helped her to negotiate various social, health and educational institutions, as well as providing emotional protection for herself and her child, and 'expand[ing] our possibilities' (Blum-Ross & Livingstone, 2017, p. 12). Bellander and Nikolaidou's (2017, p. 5) analysis of parents' online information searching reveals similar findings in relation to parents of children with congenital heart defects. Their work also suggests that parents who shared similar experiences could offer better understanding and support than those who did not. For example, one of their participants, who joined a closed Facebook group to find information and support about her child's condition, explained that she was more open and honest about her feelings and worries in this group than she was with many of her close family and friends, because she was certain that others would relate to her experiences without 'judgment or feelings of pity' (Bellander & Nikolaidou, 2017, p. 15).

These studies of online parenting collectives point to the significant socio-emotional benefits that can be gained from digital connections with others who share common experiences, in terms of support, validation and solidarity. These connections are markedly different from the fleeting affiliations around shared values that have been identified in larger groups and networks, but they are nevertheless constructed and sustained through specific strategies such as emotional reciprocity, or 'me too' sharing, and confessional narratives. In the section that follows, I continue to explore the relevance of peer connection and support for parents who have had marginal or challenging experiences, through a focus on Lynne's experience of collective connection as a single adoptive parent to disabled children.

Introducing Lynne

Collective connection, whilst present in and central to all my participants' digital, parenting and family practices, seems to be a particularly significant dimension of connected parenting for single adoptive parents. The three single adoptive parents who took part in this research (Cheryl, Jenny and Lynne[1]) regularly engaged in parenting actions and practices through connection and collaboration with other parents who they perceived to be raising their children in similar circumstances. They gave advice, shared their own practices and made themselves available to others, present-at-a-distance, during challenging moments, and others did the same for them. This mutual support, they explained, was particularly valuable for single adopters because, first, they faced a unique set of challenges in raising adopted children, and, second, they were often dealing with these challenges as the sole parent. When talking about their most immediate and pressing challenges and concerns during our interviews, most of these participants spoke about the impact of their children's trauma, and the inadequate support they received from institutional networks, most notably social services, the Department for Education (DfE) and Child and Adolescent Mental Health Services (CAMHS). These parents are not alone, as the discussion around family practices in the Introduction to this book has shown.

Cheryl, Lynne and Jenny often positioned themselves as part of a wider community, network or 'tribe' of parents in similar circumstances, including subgroups of adopters such as single adopters, LGBT adopters and adopters of disabled children. They all pointed to the importance of togetherness, of feeling that they are *not alone*, because they are part of a collective who have similar experiences, who 'understand' and can help them through any challenges they might face. The case studies that follow, here and in Chapter 4, show how two of these single adoptive parents, Lynne and Cheryl, construct, sustain and mobilize this sense of togetherness and collective endeavour through their digital practices. Through close examination of these participants' engagement with small-sized and medium-sized groups on the social networking site *Facebook* and the messaging app associated with it, *Messenger*, I consider how parenting and family actions and practices are recontextualized as *shared* actions and practices, as part of a wider practice of collective connection.

This chapter focuses on Lynne, a 45-year-old[2] single adoptive parent who has been a full-time parent and carer of disabled children for most of her adult life. When we first met, Lynne described her role as an adopter and carer to disabled children as a 'calling', to which she 'always knew' she would respond. Her conviction, she explained, is closely tied to her faith as a Christian, her upbringing and her contact with disabled children from a young age. Lynne first applied to foster children at the age of twenty-one, and her first child moved in on a long-term fostering placement when Lynne was twenty-five. She has adopted or been special guardian to four children in total, two of whom died in childhood and currently has two children: Joel, a pre-schooler, and Nadia, a teenager.

As a long-term single foster carer and adopter of disabled children, Lynne has built a robust network that is able to support her and her family. As the network diagram shown in Figure 9 illustrates, a wide range of individuals and groups are situated within this network, including the carers who visit and support Lynne's children at home, the respite care centre Hope Hospice and local community groups such as MOVE (a charity for carers) and Lynne's Church. Lynne's network also includes groups that operate almost exclusively online, for example Facebook groups for parents and carers of children with fetal alcohol spectrum disorder (FASD UK), spina bifida (SB UK), a pureed diet (PD UK) and other special needs (UKSC – UK Special Children). Lynne

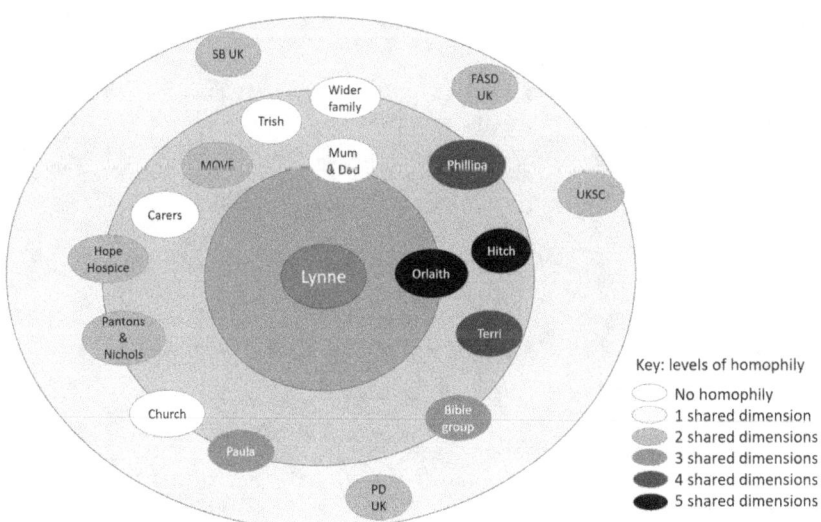

Figure 9 Lynne's homophily diagram.

also has friends with whom she communicates almost exclusively via digital means (mainly instant messaging), for example Trish, Phillipa and Terri. In our interviews, Lynne emphasized the importance of shared experience within this network, noting that she gravitates towards single adoptive parents, especially those who have children with disabilities, because they experience 'exactly the same things'. She describes shared experiences and family structures as a 'shortcut' to friendship, noting that 'it's just easier' to chat with these friends about her day-to-day life because 'I don't have to explain'. With parents of disabled children, Lynne is able to share unconditional, non-judgemental support around the clock; as she explains, these are the people she would turn to 'in the middle of the night'. As shown in Figure 9, Lynne's network exhibits very high levels of homophily, or affiliation with similar others, with many of her 'alters' sharing three, four or five dimensions in common (for further explanation of these diagrams and the criteria for homophily, see Chapter 2). Lynne is also the only participant in this study with contacts who share *five* dimensions of homophily: her friends Orla and Hitch are both Christian single adoptive parents of disabled children.

Lynne's network diagram is the largest and most dense of the nine participants; as shown in Figure 10, the connections between various people and groups in her network are often multiple and complex. For example, three of Lynne's close friends – Hitch, Terri and Orlaith – all know each other. Terri, Orlaith and Phillipa also have at least one Facebook group in common with Lynne. In

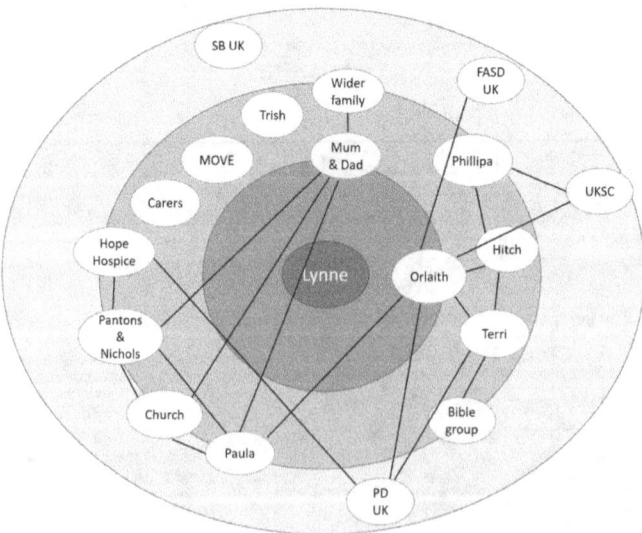

Figure 10 Lynne's network connections and density diagram.

our third interview, after creating her diagram, I asked Lynne how she would describe this network. The metaphors she used, describing it as a 'net' and more specifically a 'safety net', convey both the density of a network with multiple overlaps and interconnections, and its importance in terms of mutual support. As she explains, 'the net . . . holds me and it holds my friend and we hold others . . . it's a safety net . . . it's also the net from the trampoline that can give you the ability to bounce higher.'

The sections that follow explore Lynne's use of Messenger as a particularly significant tool for gaining information, support and social contact from clearly defined groups that are constructed around friendship, common experiences or specific needs. Whilst Lynne is a frequent user of Facebook groups and finds these extremely useful for circulating information and support, she can also become overly invested in strangers' lives, sometimes 'getting very very angry and frustrated' with others' actions and choices or feeling a sense of 'despair' when she is unable to help. At such moments, Lynne suggests, she often turns to Messenger groups, where she can 'just speak to the people that [she wants] to speak to', without having to go through the main Facebook app. Lynne noted, further, that she often uses Messenger to connect specifically with friends and contacts who are *adoptive* parents of children with disabilities, because she feels they are likely to have experiences and issues that biological parents of disabled children may not share. Like many other adoptive and single adoptive parents, then, Lynne particularly values media that help her to connect with homophilous groups of parents, who are perceived to have similar families and experiences.

Messaging apps, Messenger and collective connection

Facebook is part of Meta Platforms Inc., a multinational conglomerate that builds and operates multiple networking services, four of which are extremely well known and widely used around the world at the time of writing: Facebook, Messenger, Instagram and WhatsApp. The Messenger app was initially developed as a simple online text messaging service, facilitating both one-to-one and group communication between Facebook contacts. To this day, Messenger retains the basic function of sending and receiving direct text-based messages to known contacts. However, users can now also forward, 'react' or reply directly to individual messages, as well as sending and receiving various media including emojis, stickers, photos, videos, GIFs and voice messages.

The primary affordances of messaging apps such as Messenger enable relatively private and personalized communication, especially when compared with social networking sites (SNSs) such as Facebook and Instagram, as well as Twitter. Most notably, private messaging interactions need not stray beyond specified contacts, remaining in the personal space of an individual's mobile phone (as explained by Asprey & Tagg, 2019). Further, the targeted communication made possible by mobile messaging apps means that users can directly address specific individuals or bring different combinations of people together at different moments for different purposes. Studies comparing usage of messaging apps and instant messaging versus SNSs have suggested that people use these services very differently as a result. For example, SNSs like Facebook (specifically, its central Timeline interface) are reportedly used as a way of keeping up to date with a social network, broadcasting information to a relatively large audience and having fun. Messaging apps, on the other hand, are used for targeted, private communication between close ties and subsequently afford opportunities to maintain and develop close relationships and share more intimate disclosures (Asprey & Tagg, 2019; Bazarova, 2012; Lyons & Tagg, 2019; Quan-Haase & Young, 2010; Waterloo, Baumgartner, Peter, & Valkenburg, 2018). Other features of messaging apps, such as 'push' notifications that appear on the phone's home screen when locked, the read receipt that signals a message has been read and the 'last seen'/'last active', 'online'/'active now' status that shows when the app was last used, have also been said to foster the development of fast-paced, brief and near-instant message exchanges that can help to sustain intimate relationships at a distance (Asprey & Tagg, 2019; Church & Oliveira, 2013; Ito & Okabe, 2005). However, as discussed in this book's Introduction, the potential for continuous connection can also have negative effects, including pressure to be 'always on' (see Baron, 2008; Gangneux, 2020).

Lynne's use of Messenger

The affordances of Messenger have several specific benefits for Lynne. For example, as noted previously, this app allows her to draw on carefully chosen combinations of Facebook contacts for personalized support with unique situations, away from the busy and sometimes overwhelming activity of Facebook's timeline and groups. Through this app, Lynne is also able to mobilize contacts across the globe who can offer instant help and support 'around the clock'. As she explained in our second interview, Lynne often uses Messenger to connect with international friends she has met online, because 'one of us is always awake when the rest of the local world is asleep'. Lynne also makes the point that mobile messaging affords the possibility for *silent* communication with close contacts, meaning that she can get support even when she cannot move or make a sound. She gives an example of one such situation in our second interview, explaining that 'when we're in hospital and it's not just your child that's sleeping but it's the seven other children in the bay . . . the ability to be in communication with other people and not to be alone whilst also being quiet is really useful'. Mobile messaging in general, and Messenger specifically, is therefore particularly useful and relevant to Lynne as a single parent of disabled children.

Of all the parents who took part in the Marginalised Families Online study, Lynne shared the smallest amount of digital data: just five Facebook posts (each to a different closed group) and one Messenger exchange. This is largely due to Lynne's sense that her digital communication was intensely private, personal and included intimate details about her own and others' children. However, Lynne talked extensively throughout our interviews about the ways in which she created, engaged with and mobilized her support network in digital contexts. This chapter therefore draws on both interview and digital data to explore Lynne's use of Messenger. In the section that follows, I examine a single exchange between five women who are 'all mothers of adopted children with additional needs', except for one member. Some of these women lived in the United Kingdom, some in the United States, and one in Japan, but they all met through Facebook groups. This Messenger chat is a good example of the kind of targeted private group chat described earlier, where the app is used to bring together Facebook contacts from around the world who share similar experiences. As well as using Messenger to create small, targeted groups of Facebook contacts, Lynne also used the app to chat one-to-one with close friends. The second analysis draws on Lynne's interview talk to examine the way she and her best friend construct collective connection through such one-to-one mobile messaging.

Entextualizing actions as shared experience

This section focuses on a sequence of messages between Lynne and four other women who are mothers of children with additional needs: Kimberley, Kristin,

Ellen and Terri. The chat was initiated by Kimberley, who created the group in order to ask a question about putting a nappy through the washing machine. Lynne was added to the group after Kimberley's initial message, so did not have access to this, but she suggested that it would have said something along the lines of 'help I've just put a nappy through the washing machine what do I do'. This messy mistake may be a commonplace experience for parents of babies and toddlers, but it is worth noting that all these women are parents to older disabled children, who may continue using nappies much further into their childhood, perhaps even for their whole lives. Nevertheless, members of the group do not mention or explain their continued use of nappies beyond infanthood. This lack of explanation is the first indication that the group draws on a foundation of shared experience that means they don't need to explain certain actions and events that are out of the ordinary in a broader social context.

Lynne explained in our second interview that this set of messages was 'a very typical conversation that we would have on Messenger' and that pulling different people into short-term groups, to help with specific issues and questions they were all likely to be familiar with, was 'exactly how we use social media' and 'extremely useful' to them all. The sequence is reproduced in full in Extract 2.

Extract 2. 'I was thinking you . . . would understand' (15.05.2019)[3]

Message 1: Kimberley

Kristin Jameson South I was thinking you, **Lynne Collins** (yes, I know you use the washable ones), **Terri Amanda Richardson**, and **Ellen Frankfield** would understand. 4 hours later, I think I have my washer and laundry room clean of the fuzz. 😂😂

Message 2: Kristin
I use washable pads in his wheelchair and washable waterproof sheets just to avoid the mess of cleaning up "fuzz".

Message 3: Kristin
Nasty mess! Glad you have it cleaned up!

Message 4: Ellen
😧☹️☹️😱

Oh my soul… they DO make such a mess! The only thing that makes a worse mess is when a diaper gets pitched in with the laundry.

Message 5: Kimberley
Done that too.

Message 6: Kristin
I've washed the occasional diaper, as well… wasn't sure if I wanted to admit it in fear that the washer would start sending out subliminal messages to "feed me" and another diaper would hear the call…
[1 'laughing' reaction]

Message 7: Terri
Oh dear! I usually just put the washing machine on a quick wash after cleaning the filter and wiping the door clean. Then clean the filter again. It mostly clears it.

Message 8: Lynne
Been there! Oh dear!

Hoovering our (*sic*) the lint trap helps. And if any nicer clothing got caught up in it, and you can't get rid of the fuzz, sticky tape wrapped around your hand and dab dab dabbing at it helps.

In this message sequence, Kimberley entextualizes a series of actions related to putting a nappy through the washing machine, complaining about the messy 'fuzz' she's been left with and asking for help with the situation. In response to Kimberley's message, two members offer help by sharing their own similar experiences. For example, Terri (message 7) explains what actions she takes to deal with the same situation: 'I usually just put the washing machine on a quick clean . . .', and Lynne (message 8) offers the ameliorative actions of 'hoovering our the (*sic*) lint trap helps', as well as 'sticky tape wrapped around your hand and dab dab dabbing at it helps'. On this level, the group messaging sequence constitutes an example of *epistemic connection* between members, whereby they share the actions they take to deal with a specific problem, and in doing so, negotiate and construct a useful set of shared knowledge resources. Participants may draw on these resources in the future: for example, after reading these messages, Kimberley may reproduce Lynne's actions of hoovering her lint trap and dabbing at her ruined laundry with sticky tape, to further tidy up the mess.

Kimberley positions her initial message not only as a request for specific help and advice but also as an invitation to share collective experiences. She signals this collective dimension when she tags each of the group members in her opening message and indicates a presumption of empathy with the words, 'I was thinking you . . . would understand.' Both Terri and Lynne's messages respond to this invitation by confirming that they have indeed put a nappy through the washing machine themselves. Terri's use of the first-person pronoun 'I' positions her explicitly as the agent of this process, and Lynne's use of the unmodified verb 'helps' in simple present tense indicates that her advice is based on repeated personal experience (rather than, for example, 'could help', which would suggest her advice was speculative). Further, Terri's use of the modifier 'usually' makes it clear that she has been in this situation several times. In this way, Terri and Lynne not only entextualize their ameliorative actions as useful knowledge but also affirm that Kimberley's nappy mishap is a *collective* experience, which they can all understand and relate to. Thus, both epistemic and collective dimensions of connected parenting can be seen to intersect in this sequence.

Other messages respond solely to the collective dimension of Kimberley's request. For example, Kristin and Ellen's messages both relate similar experiences without offering the kind of reproducible action-as-knowledge we see in Terri and Lynne's messages. In message 2, for example, Kristin entextualizes the actions of '[using] washable pads in his wheelchair and washable waterproof sheets', and in message 4, Ellen relates 'when a diaper gets pitched in with the laundry'. In message 6, Kristin confesses to '[washing] the occasional diaper as well'. In these examples, Kristin and Ellen echo the actions of other group members, without proposing any future action. Further, both Kristin and Ellen mirror the language Kimberley uses to describe the mess in message 1. 'Fuzz' is not necessarily a descriptor everyone would understand,[4] but Kristen uses the term to relate her own experience in message 2 where she echoes Kimberley's claim that this kind of mess takes a lot of effort to clean up. Kristen's next message, which follows on immediately from her first, again echoes Kimberley's complaint, this time capturing it neatly in the phrase 'Nasty mess!' The term 'mess' is then adopted by Ellen in message 4, where she writes 'oh my soul . . . they DO make such a mess!'. In message 5, Kimberley simply states 'done that too'. Lynne, similarly, uses the deictic expression 'been there' in message 8. This sequence therefore illustrates a reciprocal cycle of shared action, whereby Ellen first echoes Kimberley's experience and follows up with an example of something she's done that made an even 'worse mess', and then Kimberley, in turn, notes that she has 'done that too'. Through these echoes and repetitions, these parents' actions are collectivized, and in turn, group members are able to commiserate with Kimberley, as well as validating her dismay at having made such a mess of her laundry and finding it so difficult to clear up.

The deictic and mirroring devices used throughout this sequence are comparable with the kind of 'me too' sharing found in both Jaworska (2018) and Pedersen and Lupton's (2018) studies of Mumsnet Talk discussions about postnatal depression and transgressive experiences, respectively. In line with the findings of these studies, members of Lynne's Messenger group likely gain a sense of validation, reassurance and solidarity through reciprocal sharing. Further, by mirroring one another's actions, this group can be said to entextualize those actions as *shared experiences* that are already circulating within the group's repertoire of family practices. Members' recourse to this shared repertoire serves as a foundation for the group's collective connection. This is a connection forged not just through shared values but through shared action. The group mobilizes this collective connection to consolidate a sense that, despite their unusual circumstances, they are not alone: they are part of a collective of parents who share in similar everyday parenting and family practices.

Micro-entextualizations of shared action and experience

Lynne explained on several occasions during our interviews that having friends who 'get it' on hand at all times is extremely important to her, especially as a single parent to disabled children who often finds it difficult to arrange face-to-face meetings. As noted previously, Lynne describes this kind of shared experience as a 'shortcut' to friendship, because she feels there is so much that she doesn't have to explain to people with similar families, such as the reasons behind her children's behaviour, her parenting practices and strategies or her feelings about different experiences and events, which may be out of the ordinary in a wider social context. The analysis of the previous section has begun to explore the ways in which this shared experience and understanding is constructed and mobilized in one of Lynne's group Messenger chats, and to theorize the relevance of this practice in relation to the concept of collective connection. In this section, I further explore the ways in which Lynne works to construct and mobilize shared experience and collective parenting practice through her interactions with a very close friend via Messenger. This analysis will focus on Lynne's explanation of these interactions in our second interview, since Lynne did not share this Messenger data with me directly.

In our second interview, whilst Lynne was telling me about her use of digital media, she emphasized the importance of her closest friends, with whom she tended to connect face-to-face, on the telephone, or via Messenger, on a regular basis. She spent a good deal of time talking about her 'very best friend' Orlaith, with whom she had daily contact via mobile messaging. When creating her network diagram in our third interview, Orlaith was the only friend that Lynne positioned in the inner ring of her network, indicating the significant role she plays in her life, equalled only by her parents. This section focuses on Lynne's discussion of Messenger exchanges relating to the recent behaviour of Orlaith's daughter. These exchanges refer to personal details around Orlaith's family life and practices, including some of her daughter's negative behaviour and photographs of her home. In order to understand and contextualize these exchanges, it is useful to look first at the way Lynne describes Orlaith's situation for the benefit of an outsider – me – who does not know Orlaith and is not an adopter *or* a parent of a child with additional needs. Her explanation from our second interview is therefore provided in Extract 3. Here, Lynne explains that Orlaith's family recently had builders in the house, and because of the trauma Orlaith's daughter had experienced as a young child, she was finding this particularly unsettling, and her behaviour was becoming increasingly negative and rude.

Extract 3. Orlaith and her daughter

1. they've got builders in at the moment and her daughter who is eight has made massive
2. keep out signs for her bedroom and you know touch this on pain of death signs for
3. absolutely everything erm yeah and you know w it's funny and it's it's sort've so typically
4. eight but actually it's also I know and I get it that it's coming from the trauma that she's
5. experienced before she was adopted this is really massively unsettling her that you
6. know it's only going to be a tiny change to their house but actually it feels like the
7. world's falling apart so she's trying desperately to cling onto the bit of her room that
8. she you know the bit of her life that she can control which is her bedroom and it's
9. coming out in deeply deeply massively majorly rude signs

Lynne's explanation for the behaviour of Orlaith's daughter is detailed and nuanced. Whilst noting that her creation of rude signs is in some ways 'funny' and 'typical' (line 3) of an eight-year-old, Lynne also emphasizes the seriousness of the child's mental state, pointing to her 'trauma' (line 4), the 'unsettling' (line 5) nature of the events in her house and her feeling that 'the world's falling apart' (lines 6–7). Lynne deploys strings of intensifying modifiers to underline the extreme nature of the daughter's feelings and actions, such as '*really massively* unsettling' (line 5), 'trying *desperately*' (line 7), and '*deeply deeply massively majorly* rude' (line 9). She juxtaposes these extreme reactions with the comparatively 'tiny' (line 6) changes that are happening in her life, but nevertheless notes that the reaction is completely understandable, using the language of solidarity that is extremely common across the adoptive parents' interviews when she says 'I know and I get it' (line 4). By contrast, when detailing her Messenger exchanges with Orlaith, Lynne suggests that the two of them have no need to deploy the same complex, nuanced explanations. Extract 4, which represents the interview talk immediately following Extract 3, reproduces Lynne's discussion of these exchanges.

Extract 4. 'We can ping'
(interviewer interjections in square brackets)

1. she's been sending me photographs of all the different signs that she keeps finding
2. hidden round the house and it's (laughs) yeah it's that and she can show those to other
3. people but if they're not in that adoption community [mmm] they won't get the fear
4. behind that they'll either see just a very rude child or aha isn't she funny [yeah] and it's
5. knowing that all three of those are together [and I presume she doesn't explicitly say
6. that to you] no this is it it's a shortcut [mmm] I know that and she knows that I know
7. that [mmm] in the same way that you know I'll post her something that Nadia's said and
8. she gets it [mmm] completely the you know yes it's the the insult that you know sh the
9. insult and the funniness and the yeah the fear that's come from underneath [mmm] all
10. of that and yeah [all rolled into one] exactly yeah and I don't have to explain that to her
11. [mmhmm] so it's just a shortcut I can just go oh that and she goes oh yes this erm [yeah]
12. you know we can ping

By comparison with the explanation that is produced for my benefit (Extract 3), in Extract 4 Lynne suggests that Orlaith can entextualize her daughter's behaviour in its full complexity in visual form, by 'sending me photographs of all the different signs that she keeps finding hidden round the house' (lines 1–2). The sharing of photographs between these friends can be described as micro-entextualizations, because they translate a complex set of actions, experiences and meanings in a condensed form. As Lynne puts it, to these close friends, a single photograph can capture 'the insult and the funniness and . . . the fear that's come from underneath' (lines 8–9). Such micro-entextualizations rely on shared knowledge, understanding and experience for their meaning. As Lynne herself explains, if Orlaith sent those same photographs to people 'not in that adoption community' (line 3), they would not be able to unpack the same complex set of meanings; they would likely not 'get the fear behind that' but would instead 'either see just a very rude child or aha isn't she funny' (lines 3–4). Because of Lynne and Orlaith's shared experiences of adopting children with additional needs, however, they are able to use technologies of entextualization, in this case digital photography, to construct communicative 'shortcut[s]' (line 6), which signal shared, unspoken experiences and reference points.

Between lines 11 and 12, Lynne's words encapsulate the nature of the communicative flow between her and Orlaith when they deploy such 'shortcuts' in their Messenger exchanges: 'I can just go *oh that* and she goes *oh yes this*.' The deictic pronouns 'that' and 'this' capture their communication of complex chains of actions, events and experiences through condensed expressions and digital resources, which can again be described as a form of micro-entextualization. Lynne's repeated use of deixis between lines 10 and 12, by comparison with the long explanation of Extract 3, very vividly illustrates her claim that she '[doesn't] have to explain' herself to friends who have families like hers, because they just 'ge[t] it'. As well as the deictic pronouns 'this' and 'that', Lynne also uses the word 'ping' to capture the rapid exchange of semantically loaded entextualizations via Messenger (line 12). The word conjures an image of brief, ping-pong style exchanges ('that . . . this . . . ping') and can also be seen as a form of micro-entextualization.

The word 'ping' also carries an additional layer of meaning, as a metonymic representation of the sound Lynne's phone makes when she receives a message. Indeed, Lynne uses this word throughout our interviews, as well as 'buzz', when she is talking about receiving messages on her phone. For example, in our third interview, when Lynne's phone vibrated as we were talking, she looked at the screen and said 'sorry . . . it pinged it buzzed'. These words mimic a mobile phone's aural and haptic notifications: if the sound is turned on, some message notifications make a noise somewhat like 'ping', but if the phone is set to silent, the phone will just vibrate, making a sound (and sensation) something like 'buzz'. Lynne also uses the word 'buzz' when introducing her friend Orlaith in our second interview, noting that 'she's buzzing in my pocket at the moment (laughs) cos she's always buzzing . . . we tend to text each other multiple times every day'. Lynne's use of 'buzz' in this example gives agency to Orlaith rather than the phone, which is the device actually doing the 'buzzing'. A more literal way of relaying her experience of receiving this message would be 'the phone is buzzing in my pocket' or 'my phone is always buzzing'. However, Lynne's words conjure an image of Orlaith *herself* being 'in [Lynne's] pocket', making her presence felt both physically (through vibration) and auditorily (through a 'buzzing' or 'pinging' sound) even though she is geographically distant. These uses of 'ping' and 'buzz' can be described as multi-layered aural and haptic metonymies, whereby the sound, and/or sensation, of a message notification on a mobile phone represents both the quick-fire communication between friends that it enables and a sense of close friends being present-at-a-distance.

The analysis of this section has shown that Lynne's interactions with a close friend who has similar circumstances and experiences can rely almost exclusively on shared knowledge and understanding, with minimal detail or explanation. It points to the significance of micro-entextualizations as a digital resource for consolidating and mobilizing this shared experience, and in turn, shaping collective connections between close contacts. The analysis has also highlighted the significance of aural and haptic metonymies for phone sounds as a way of bringing Lynne's experience of these collective connections to life. Specifically, the metonymic terms 'ping' and 'buzz' communicate not only the concise and rapid nature of Messenger exchanges that are underpinned by collective connection but also the sense of physical togetherness that Lynne gains through her ability to exchange regular messages with close friends. Building on the previous section, this analysis shows how parents' access to personal details about one another's family lives and practices can form the foundation for highly intimate collective connections, which can be easily mobilized in times of need. Further, the analysis of Lynne's interview talk about her friendship and digital communication with Orlaith suggests that their lives and practices are fundamentally intertwined: they are constantly available to one another, intimately acquainted with the details of one another's lives and able to communicate through minimal expressions and micro-entextualizations. Through collective connection, they are therefore able to undertake their parenting and family practice as a collective, rather than as individual single parents.

Chapter summary

This chapter has introduced collective connection as the construction, consolidation and mobilization of shared practices and experiences through digitally mediated actions and texts. After contextualizing the concept in relation to existing theories of affiliation, collectivization and peer-to-peer solidarity, the chapter examines collective connection through a case study that focuses on the way one participant, Lynne, uses Facebook Messenger to connect and affiliate with other adopters of children with additional needs. The first analysis of a Messenger sequence between Lynne and four other friends shows how group members use mirroring devices to entextualize and affirm individual parenting actions as *collective practices*. The second analytical section focuses on Lynne's interview talk about her Messenger exchanges with a very close friend. Here, I elaborate the concept of micro-entextualization to describe a condensed form of bounded action that relies on shared knowledge, experience and understanding for its meaning, functioning as a communicative 'shortcut'. Such micro-entextualizations can take any 'small' linguistic, digital, graphical or visual form that is able to capture a complex set of meanings: short phrases, emojis, gifs or, as we have seen in the earlier analysis, photographs, deictic pronouns and the metonymic term 'ping'. Together, these analyses show how micro-entextualizations can signal collective connection between individuals and groups, as well as pointing to Lynne's use of aural and haptic metonymies to explain her experience of these connections. The most significant implication of this chapter's analyses is that through collective connection, parents like Lynne can experience and undertake their parenting and family practice as a collective. This point will be further examined and elaborated in the chapter that follows.

4

Elaborating Collective Connection

In Chapter 3, I suggested that *collective connection* is a particularly significant dimension of connected parenting for the single adopters who took part in the Marginalised Families Online study. I presented a case study that focused on Lynne's use of Messenger to sustain and mobilize shared actions, practices and experiences amongst her peers, and argued that these practices of collective connection allow them to consolidate and mobilize a reassuring sense of togetherness, understanding and shared endeavour.

In this chapter, I build on the groundwork laid in Chapter 3 through a second case study that focuses on the digital practices of another single adopter: Cheryl. As with the previous case study, this chapter will consider how Cheryl constructs and mobilizes collective connections with her fellow adoptive parents, this time through posts to two relatively small, closed Facebook groups whose members are all adoptive parents: *New Families* (NF) and *Parenting Adult Adoptees* (PAA). After briefly introducing both Cheryl and the nature of Facebook groups, I provide a brief overview of her practices in this context. The substantive analysis of this chapter explores Cheryl's two most common types of group post, looking first at her info-relational sharing within *New Families*, where she recontextualizes content from a teen parenting website. I then analyse Cheryl's collective venting practice in her posts to *Parenting Adult Adoptees*, this time considering how she entextualizes some of her *own* actions and experiences within the group. These analyses expand and elaborate the previous chapter's discussion of micro-entextualization as a strategy for consolidating and mobilizing shared experience and practice. They also serve to further illustrate how, through digitally mediated connections, parents can experience their family lives, and undertake their family practices, as a collective.

Introducing Cheryl

Cheryl is a 49-year-old single heterosexual adopter who works part-time as a secondary school teacher. In our first interview, Cheryl positioned single motherhood as her first-choice route to parenthood, explaining that 'it's just far easier on your own', and 'I wanted to be a mum more than I wanted to be a wife or a partner'. Cheryl adopted her son Keir when he was of primary school age, and he is now a young adult. She explained in our interviews that Keir had struggled with learning difficulties and poor mental health throughout his life, and in his teens had often turned to cannabis as a form of self-medication. This led to a spiral of negative consequences, including criminal behaviour, aggression and vandalism. At the age of eighteen, when both Cheryl and Keir felt they could no longer cope living under the same roof, Keir moved into nearby supported living. In 2017, Cheryl set up a blog in order to document her experience of parenting an adult adoptee, a subject that she suggests is discussed far less frequently than parenting adopted children generally. She also has an extensive online support network of adoptive parents, and her engagement with these groups and individuals is mostly mediated through Facebook groups, instant messaging apps and Twitter.

Throughout our interviews, Cheryl talked about her need for a supportive community of adopters who understand the challenges she faces and would never judge her (or her son). She frequently uses the language of understanding, homophily and affiliation to explain why this support is so important to her. Cheryl notes, for example, that she values having others who've 'been there'; who understand her experiences without her having to explain them in detail or revisit difficult memories. As Cheryl puts it: 'the best people to support you are the people who've been through it ... just someone going I understand how that feels.' Non-adoptive parents and families, she felt, just wouldn't understand situations such as a teenager wetting the bed, getting in trouble with the police or using drugs; they would 'be appalled', or 'judge you', whereas an adopter would 'get it'. The network diagram Cheryl created in our final interview provides a visual illustration of the significant role adopters play in her life. Indeed, the 'homophily' diagram shown in Figure 11 reveals that beyond her immediate family members (mum, dad and auntie), *all* the individuals and groups in Cheryl's network are connected with adoption in some way (see Chapter 2 for a detailed discussion of participants' network diagrams). Those with two shared dimensions are all adoptive parents, and those with three shared dimensions are also *single* adoptive parents, or parents of adopted *adults*. For example, Lane (the only friend in Cheryl's closest circle) is

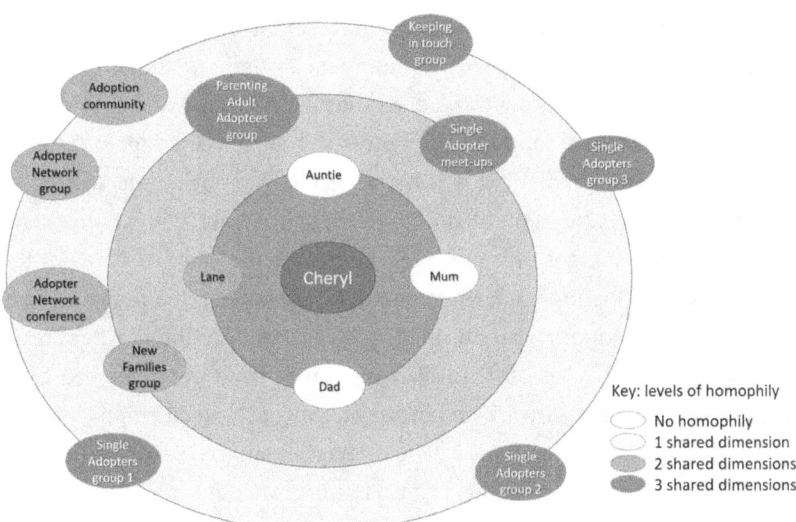

Figure 11 Cheryl's homophily diagram.

also a single adopter, and many of the groups she belongs to are specifically for single adopters or parents of adopted adults.

Despite their consistent presence in her life with Keir, professionals and support services are notably absent from Cheryl's diagram. Indeed, after completing this diagram she noted, pointedly, that there weren't any professionals on it because they had not been able to provide her with anything near the level of support she had received from other adoptive parents. Throughout our interviews, Cheryl expressed a general lack of trust in the professionals and support services she had come across, suggesting that she and other adopters very rarely received adequate support from educational, health, social and adoption services. Indeed, she suggested that *she* was 'the one telling professionals' what her son's problems are, where they stem from and how to best support him. This lack of faith in professionals is echoed in my interviews with Jenny, another single adopter who has had contact with a range of educational and mental health services in a bid to access the support her son needs. Jenny ultimately gave up on state schools and decided to home-school her son, and speaks scathingly of the support she received from Child and Adolescent Mental Health Services (CAMHS). In our first interview, for example, she echoed Cheryl's claim that she knew much more than the professionals in this domain, and that their advice was often unhelpful and patronizing.

Throughout our interviews, Cheryl talked about the extra-ordinary steps adopters would take to support one another, around the clock and in any circumstances. Whilst she acknowledged that in an 'ideal world', professionals should be a key source of support for adopters, she suggests the support is just not there, and when it is, professionals 'just don't get it, they don't understand'. As an anecdotal example, Cheryl pointed to the time she was stuck in a police station all night after her son got in trouble. As she puts it, professionals 'are not there at three o'clock in the morning when you've just come out of a police station . . . whereas another adoptive parent might go yeah I've been there'. After creating her network diagram, with the finished version in front of us, I asked Cheryl what kind of value this network had in her life. She responded emphatically, her voice breaking, that without it, she 'wouldn't have managed'; she 'wouldn't have survived'. The wide range of support Cheryl gains from other adopters, including information and networking, as well as social, emotional and practical support, is illustrated visually in Figure 12, Cheryl's 'forms of support' diagram.

Cheryl is a member of several closed Facebook groups for adopters, including New Families, Parenting Adult Adoptees, Single Adopters (3), Adopter Network and Keeping in Touch. In our first interview, Cheryl explained that she often shared more negative and personal disclosures about her relationship with her son in these groups, especially the PAA group. By contrast, she said she would never mention any of their difficulties on Twitter or her main Facebook page,

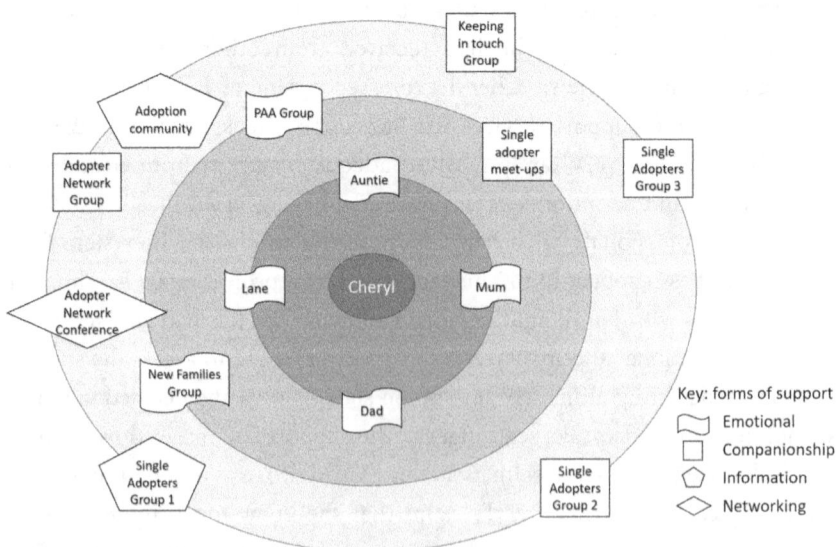

Figure 12 Cheryl's forms of support diagram.

because she didn't want her son to be exposed or shamed. As she explains in relation to the Parenting Adult Adoptees group: 'this is a sounding off board where people can put stuff and nobody's gonna go *stop being miserable*'. Other adoptive parent participants made similar points about the benefits of Facebook groups. For example, Jenny noted in our second interview that she was much more likely to share specific, negative and potentially distressing details of her family life, such as her son's occasionally violent and destructive behaviour, within a secret Facebook group for adopters. Conversely, she would never share details like this with certain family members or close friends who weren't adopters themselves. Cheryl also noted in our first interview that belonging to several Facebook groups for adopters could be problematic at times and that her own well-being sometimes suffered as a result of her constant connection with, and investment in, others' lives. For example, she sometimes felt 'too available' to others and would repeatedly check her phone, wondering 'is everyone all right'. Despite these potential drawbacks, Cheryl suggests that ultimately, Facebook groups are extremely valuable to her, as 'safe spaces' where she can be open and honest about what's happening in her life without fear of judgement.

Facebook, Facebook groups and collective connection

As noted in Chapter 3, Facebook is part of Meta Platforms Inc., which operates multiple interconnected global networking services. Facebook is the company's flagship and most popular social networking service, with roughly 2.9 billion monthly active users as of late 2021 (Statista, 2022a). This social media platform is based around 'friending', a system of reciprocal following where the user invites people to be their friends by either searching named individuals or importing contact lists (e.g. from a mobile phone or email account). Within Facebook's central interface, the timeline, users can interact with friends through their posts, which may include written text, photos, videos and hyperlinks. Users can also tag friends in their posts, add a feeling or 'check in' to a particular location. Facebook posts then appear on friends' timelines, who can respond by reacting (e.g. with 'like', 'love', 'haha', 'wow', 'sad', 'angry' or 'care'), commenting or sharing (if the post is set to 'public'). In turn, users can see and interact with friends' posts on their own timelines.

Facebook affords multiple opportunities for users to circulate others' content on their timelines. The 'share' function, for example, allows users to reproduce content directly, with clear attribution. As with other digital recontextualization practices, such as Twitter's 'retweet' function, Facebook users can reproduce others' content with or without comment. They can also share content from other sources, such as websites, blogs or other social networking sites, by inserting hyperlinks (or, alternatively, screenshots) into the main body of their posts. Again, users can either share hyperlinks directly, without comment, or they can express a stance on the recontextualized material by adding their own content to the post. Thus, as with other recontextualization practices, the sharing-with-comment and hyperlink-with-comment functions both have the potential to change the original text, imbuing it with the new author's perspective (see Gruber, 2017, on retweets and evaluative stance on Twitter). The main difference between sharing hyperlinks and sharing posts is that with hyperlinks, the original content producer is not notified, and so there is less opportunity to engage in direct dialogue.

Facebook has been the subject of a good deal of academic research: Nieborg and Helmond (2019, p. 198) have even claimed that 'half of social media scholarship' focuses on this platform. This work has attended, amongst other things, to the role of the Facebook profile in constructing identities (e.g. Lambert, 2013, 2016; Taylor, Falconer, & Snowdon, 2014), status updates and their attendant comments and reactions (e.g. Bolander & Locher, 2015; Page, 2010; West, 2013), as well as the processes and politics of 'friending' (Ellison, Steinfield, & Lampe, 2007; Lee, Moore, Park, & Park, 2012; McLaughlin & Vitak, 2011; Tong, Heide, Langwell, & Walther, 2008). Looking across this work, it is clear that Facebook cannot be reduced to a single function or interface. Indeed, Facebook has been described as a complex infrastructure that includes a range of technological, social and commercial tools and practices, each of which performs distinct but interrelated roles and can be used in different ways by different groups at different times (Lambert, 2013; Nieborg & Helmond, 2019). This complexity can make it difficult to characterize Facebook or reduce it to a specific function. As Bucher (2021, p. 4) puts it, 'Facebook *is* Facebook.'

Facebook *groups* are interlinked with the main Facebook profile and timeline, in that membership of public groups will be displayed on the user's profile, and all group posts will be displayed on the user's main timeline (depending on an individual's settings). However, the nature of group engagement is also quite distinctive because groups usually revolve around *homophily* (affiliation with similar others) rather than *existing relationships*. For example, Facebook group members may come together around a hobby, such as 'Gardening Hints and Tips' and 'Knitting Network'; an identity or set of experiences, such as 'Parents of Transgender/Non-Binary Kids' and 'Gay Geeks'; or a mixture of the two, for example 'Women with Campervans' and 'LGBTQ+ Gamers'.[1] Gaining admission to a group depends on its privacy settings: public groups are accessible to all, whilst individuals wishing to join a closed group must first be approved by an administrator. A secret group cannot be found using Facebook's search function; no one can see that the group exists except for its members, who must be invited to join by an existing administrator. Once a new member has joined a group, they can share posts with its members, see others' posts and interact with them in much the same way as friends' posts to their timelines, through reactions and comments.

Research focusing on people's use of Facebook groups, especially closed groups that provide peer support, has tended to emphasize the positive gains of group engagement, including emotional support, advice and information, and a sense of belonging (Bellander & Nikolaidou, 2017; Pounds, Hunt, & Koteyko, 2018). Pounds et al.'s (2018, p. 35) study of empathy in a Facebook-based support group for people with type 2 diabetes emphasizes the importance of homophily in facilitating these gains, noting that group members' similar life experiences provide 'the ideal conditions for both expression and perception of empathy'. Pounds et al. (2018, p. 42) also note that group members need not actively engage with the group in order to receive these benefits, pointing out that many users derive encouragement just 'from knowing that other members are going through similar difficult experiences'. Research focusing on Facebook groups for parents, such as those mentioned in Chapter 3 (i.e. Bellander & Nikolaidou, 2017), has revealed similar findings. The emphasis on homophily and mutual understanding in these studies echoes the words of single adoptive parents like Cheryl and Jenny, who point to the benefits of friendship, community and solidarity between adoptive parents. In the analysis that follows, I reiterate claims around the importance of support and validation that are emphasized throughout existing work in this area. However, I also move beyond these themes, elaborating Chapter 3's discussion of how collective connection can transform experiences of family life and parenting practice.

Cheryl's use of Facebook groups

This chapter focuses on Cheryl's use of the two closed Facebook groups that she suggests are most important in her life: New Families (NF) and Parenting Adult Adoptees (PAA). Both groups are relatively small, and their members are all adoptive parents. The NF group is an offshoot of a larger LGBT parenting group (even though Cheryl herself is heterosexual), which Cheryl was invited to join by a fellow single adopter and close friend, Lane. Cheryl set up the PAA group with her friend Ian, a coupled gay man who is also a parent of adopted adults and who she met through the charity Adopter Network. She therefore knows everyone in the PAA group and has met most of them in person. In our interviews, Cheryl explained that she and Ian set up the group 'so we had somewhere safe to talk', noting that they have tried to keep the group very private and exclusive, being 'a bit careful who joins it'. These are both groups in which Cheryl feels able to be open and honest about what's happening in her life, her parenting practice and her feelings. Although she is a member of several other groups, Cheryl explained that she wasn't completely open in all of them because she didn't want to frighten parents of younger children with some of the more troubling details around her family life. In the NF and PAA groups, however, most members had older children, so this was less of a concern. She also noted that these groups had a culture of listening and supporting without judgement or advice-giving. Indeed, she explained that the PAA group description explicitly included the phrase 'we all know how to parent so we don't need advice we just need someone to listen'.

The NF group, at the time of interviewing, had eighty-four members, which is relatively small compared to many Facebook groups but relatively large compared to Cheryl's other groups, most of which had under fifty members. The PAA group is much smaller, with only twenty members, and this membership is distinct from the NF group (only Cheryl is a member of both). Both are not only closed but also 'secret' groups, meaning they cannot be found via Facebook searches, and all members must be invited to join. Cheryl shared everything she posted to these two groups between May 2018 and May 2019. Her posts include a range of media: some were exclusively text-based, and some included hyperlinks to media such as articles from relevant websites or surveys. Occasionally, Cheryl shared others' Facebook posts, including several memes. When we were creating her network diagram, Cheryl suggested that she posted to these groups for a range of reasons, for example to vent, share information, share funny memes and to generally get support from other adopters. The full range of functions I identified across these posts is listed in Table 10. Sometimes, Cheryl posted the same content to more than one group. For example, two of the 'venting' posts, one of the 'humour' posts and one of the 'celebrating achievements' posts, were shared, in identical form, in both the PAA and NF groups.

In the sections that follow, I analyse a selection of Cheryl's posts to the PAA and NF Facebook groups, which are representative of her two most common post types: venting and info-relational sharing. These post types also have

Table 10 Types of Post in the Parenting Adult Adoptees and New Families Groups

Type	Number (PAA)	Number (NF)	Description	Example
Venting	10	2	Disclosing negative feelings or experiences	Feels like I'm fighting the world at the minute. Just been in a complaints meeting with K's support provider as they are not even trying to meet his needs . . . (PAA group)
Info-relational	2	8	Sharing information, often from an expert or professional source, in a way that builds in-group solidarity or points to common experiences	[hyperlinked article from teenagewhisperer.co.uk] 'Because that always goes so well 😀' (NF group)
Humour	1	3	Sharing light-hearted or witty comments, observations, images or memes, often deploying irony, mockery or self-deprecation	[shared 'teenager for sale' image–text combination from 'WTF Stuff' page] (PAA and NF groups)
Direct information sharing	1	2	Sharing information, often from an expert or professional source	[shared post from parenting page] "This infographic is a condensed version of the book *The Whole-Brain Child* by Daniel Siegel. If you haven't read it . . . read it! . .' (NF group)
Celebrating achievements	2	1	Sharing a positive experience, milestone or achievement	'I've done it!! I've got him to 21 without any major (ish) incidents' (PAA and NF groups)
Asking for support	1	0	Sharing a (usually negative) experience or feeling and asking for support or advice	'What would you do? K has just phoned, he's in Leeds and taking the girlfriend home on the bus to York so he won't make it back some of the way. Not the first time he's done it' (PAA group)
Introductory post	1	0	Sharing an introduction for the benefit of new people, including details of family circumstances, experiences and needs	'So I've got K whose now 20 adopted at 6, he has learning difficulties but no specific diagnosis. We were doing ok up to 17 . . . but he hit 18 like a ton of bricks . . .' (PAA group)
Holiday wishes	1	0	Sharing seasonal good wishes, e.g. Christmas, Easter and other holidays or celebrations	'Wishing all of us a peaceful and stress free Christmas . . . Or enough booze to get through it 😀' (PAA group)
Total Posts	19	16		

particular relevance for this chapter, since they can support the construction and maintenance of collective connection through allusion to shared experience and practice.

Venting and info-relational sharing are comparable with key functions identified in other researchers' investigations of supportive posts and interactions on Facebook. For example the first type, described by Cheryl herself as 'venting', is similar to Buehler et al.'s (2019) category 'disclosing directly'. In their typology of support-seeking strategies on Facebook, Buehler et al. (2019) suggest that direct disclosures of negative experiences or feelings are a way of seeking support by articulating a source of distress. The source of distress or dissatisfaction in Cheryl's 'venting' posts is usually her son's actions or behaviour, or the failure of services and professionals to take appropriate actions that would support him. Cheryl's discussion of these posts in our second interview suggests that 'venting' posts tend to elicit supportive interactions that are based not on advice and information-giving but on expressions of understanding and empathy. As she explains, when sharing negative experiences in these groups 'you have a moan and other people go oh god I know how you feel and then someone's listened to you'.

Cheryl's second most frequent post type usually includes hyperlinks to articles about parenting and teenage development from relevant websites. The posts also tend to include a brief comment from Cheryl that alludes to connections between the content of the article and the group's own family practices and experiences. Following Fage-Butler and Jensen (2013), I categorize these as 'info-relational' posts. In their exploration of posts to an online forum for thyroid patients, Fage-Butler and Jensen (2013) found that 'insider' information about the biomedical system was often filtered through patients' narratives about their personal experience with this system. For example, these authors found that participants shared specific details around what clothes to wear post-surgery, and how to ice their post-surgery bodies, when writing about their experiences of surgery. Similar practices of 'info-relational sharing', whereby biomedical information is filtered through personal experience, have been found in studies of a Facebook support group for people with type 2 diabetes (Pounds et al., 2018) and in studies of parents' interactions through digital media such as Mumsnet (Jaworska, 2018) and WhatsApp (Lyons, 2020). However, Cheryl's info-relational posts are a little different from those explored in these studies, since the primary content comes from professional and/or institutional domains, and her comments do not reference her personal experience directly or in detail. This difference is further discussed in the analysis that follows.

Solidarity through info-relational sharing

This section focuses on Cheryl's info-relational posts to the New Families Facebook group, a closed, secret group with eighty-four members who are predominantly LGBT adopters of older children. As explained in the previous sections, Cheryl perceives this group as a 'safe space' where she can share her experiences and feelings openly and honestly, without feeling judged or being given unwanted advice. In our second interview, as Cheryl was showing me her posts to this group, I noted that she had shared quite a lot of content from a website called *teenagewhisperer.co.uk*. Figure 13 presents a screenshot of this website's homepage. The founder of the teenage whisperer is Sam Ross, a teen behavioural consultant working in the UK. As well as the advice on the website, Ross consults one-to-one with teens and parents, and has written the book *What I Need from You: The Essential Guide to Reaching Troubled Teens*. The description on the site's homepage describes it as a place for parents, carers and professionals to come for advice 'that will help you to successfully live or work with troubled teens'. Scrolling down the homepage, the site's goal is expressed thus: 'to help you all become teenage whisperers: people who can relate to, understand and help teenagers break out of negative behaviour cycles so that they can truly flourish.' Cheryl explained in our second interview that although the teenage whisperer is not exclusively concerned with the needs of adopted children, it explored issues that were very relevant to members of the New Families group.

Figures 14, 15 and 16 show three of Cheryl's posts to the New Families Facebook group from April 2019.[2] In each of these posts, she recontextualizes content from the teenage whisperer website by inserting a hyperlink into her post, accompanied by her own comment. In each post, as the figures show, the hyperlinked text appears on screen with the name of the website, the title of the article and an image from the article. From this information, given their experience as adoptive parents, group members will likely have a good sense of each article's key messages. In these hyperlink-with-comment posts, all three dimensions of connected parenting are intertwined. For example, they constitute and consolidate epistemic connections between members, with Cheryl contributing to the group's shared knowledge around parenting troubled children and teens. Further, the collective and affective connections between group members come to the fore when Cheryl foregrounds her affective reaction to the content and suggests that her own perspective will be shared by other members of the group. Whilst all three dimensions overlap in these posts, the analysis that follows will focus on the significance of *collective*

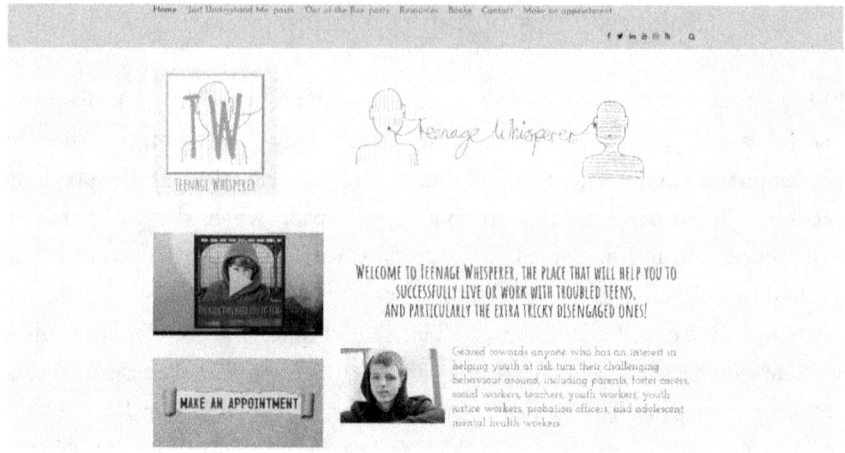

Figure 13 The Teenage Whisperer homepage by Sam Ross © Sam Ross 2022. Retrieved 04.03.2022. Reproduced with the permission of Sam Ross, teenagewhisperer.co.uk.

connection at these moments of discursive action. More specifically, it will show how Cheryl recontextualizes the actions and practices that are entextualized in the teenage whisperer articles as *shared practices and experiences* within the New Families group.

The content shared in Figure 14 is an article titled 'Instead: Tell Me What You Actually Want Me To Do'. This content takes the form of a poem, in which Sam Ross adopts the voice of both a 'troubled teen' and their carer. The poem begins in the voice of the carer, who tells the young person what they *shouldn't* be doing through a series of negated imperatives – 'Don't do this, don't do that, don't be such a stupid prat'. The poem then switches to the perspective of the young person, who asks, 'what do you want me to do instead'? As the poem unfolds, the roles of the adult and young person are reversed, and the negated imperatives become positive imperatives. For example, the imagined teen directs the adult to better support them by telling them what they *should* do, rather than telling them what they *shouldn't* do, namely 'show me how to take calm simple actions' and 'show me alternate places to make new friends'. The actions and practices that are entextualized in this poem have two components: first, the adult is encouraged to take the caring action of *showing* rather than *directing*. Further, they are encouraged to support their teen in establishing positive practices such as 'tak[ing] calm simple actions' and 'mak[ing] new friends'. These actions are then *re*contextualized by Cheryl in the form of the hyperlinked text and accompanying comment 'because that always goes so well'. In Cheryl's comment, the referent for the demonstrative pronoun 'that' seems to be the set of caring

Figure 14 'Because that always goes so well' (04.04.2019). 'Tell me what you actually want me to do', title and image by Sam Ross © Sam Ross 2022. Reproduced with the permission of Sam Ross, teenagewhisperer.co.uk.

practices outlined by Ross, which emphasize positive reactions over negative reactions, encourage care over control and promote specific guidance rather than reprimands.

Cheryl's comment in Figure 14 begins with the connective 'because', as if answering an unstated question. This creates the impression that Cheryl is entering an ongoing dialogue with her fellow group members, mid-conversation. The rest of her comment consolidates her collective connection with the group, through the presumption that they will share her perspective on the hyperlinked text and understand this in the context of ongoing dialogue between members. For example, through the simple, unmitigated declarative 'because that always goes so well', Cheryl presumes that others have experienced the caring practices entextualized in this article. Further, the 'eyeroll' emoji that punctuates the comment makes it very clear that Cheryl assumes other members of the group will read her statement as ironic. Through this comment, then, Cheryl suggests not only that the caring practices advocated by Ross are universally well known, tried and tested amongst members of the group, but also that they aren't so easy to carry out as the poem's simple imperative constructions imply; they don't always go 'so well'. In other words, Cheryl's comment largely dismisses the caring practices that are set out by Ross as unrealistic in the context of adoptive parents' lived experiences. By challenging the advice that is encoded in the poem, Cheryl offers reassurance to group members who may be finding it difficult to enact positive caring practices in their own family lives and consolidates a sense of in-group solidarity by implying that they *all* have trouble successfully implementing these practices. Cheryl achieves this multi-layered recontextualization of specific caring practices by signalling that this post feeds into ongoing conversations within the group and relying on shared understanding, experience and familiarity with those conversations.

The teenage whisperer content that is hyperlinked in Figures 15 and 16 has also been written in the voice of a troubled teen, this time in prose form. Both texts have a similar structure, beginning in a stream-of-consciousness style. For example, the first one narrates the imagined teen's actions whilst 'on high alert' in real time, deploying the first person and present progressive: 'I'm buzzin', I'm buzzin'. Looking from left to right, right to left, over my shoulder, off in the distance'. The narrative begins in a school setting, before moving to the home, where the teen ignores their foster parents' questions about their day and vents

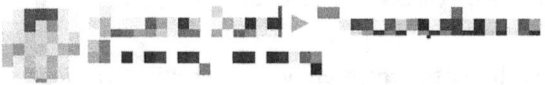

25 Apr · · Exactly this isn't it

TEENAGEWHISPERER.CO.UK

On High Alert: Hyperarousal + 'losing it' over nothing

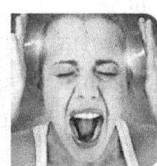

Figure 15 'Exactly this isn't it' (25.04.2019). 'On high alert', title and image by Sam Ross © Sam Ross 2022. Reproduced with the permission of Sam Ross, teenagewhisperer.co.uk..

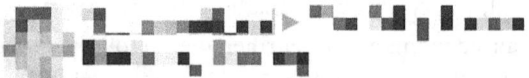

30 Apr · · Another one that feels like our life

TEENAGEWHISPERER.CO.UK

It's safer if I do nothing: overcoming fear and apathy

Figure 16 'Another one that feels like our life' (30.04.2019). 'It's safer if I do nothing', title and image by Sam Ross © Sam Ross 2022. Reproduced with the permission of Sam Ross, teenagewhisperer.co.uk.

their frustrations by putting their fist through a wall. 'The more you talk at me', the teen voice explains, 'the more I will try and survive. Which means I'll lash out more.' The second text focuses on the way fear and apathy can be manifested in negativity and inaction, with the teen voice narrating the words 'I sit on my backside. I don't want to go to school. I don't want to work. I don't want to talk to anyone. The world can just f*** off.' Again, as the narrative develops, the imagined teen's behaviour escalates with potentially dangerous consequences, with the teen saying that 'as far as "doing" goes I might immerse myself in drinking or taking drugs or getting a buzz from nicking cars ... I'll do anything that helps me to stop feeling'. The first part of these texts thus entextualizes (and dramatizes) the troubled teens' actions and thought processes when they are in an immediate state of distress. This includes actions and behaviours such as ignoring adults, drinking and drug taking, refusing to engage in any kind of activity and putting their fist through a wall. The second part of these texts again speaks directly to parents, with the first article asking 'what can you do when I go into my survival mode?' and the second imploring readers 'please don't give up on me'. The advice again revolves around supporting teens who are struggling to self-regulate through acts of care and warmth, such as 'skin-to-skin contact', 'a hug' or even just simple interactions such as 'hello, how are you?' or 'a hand on my shoulder'.

In the comments that accompany these hyperlinked texts, Cheryl again suggests that the actions and practices entextualized in them are *shared* and *recognizable* by all group members. Figure 16, which includes the comment 'another one that feels like our life ☺' begins, like Figure 14, in medias res, with the words 'another one' positioning this post as part of a shared, ongoing dialogue. Further, Cheryl's use of the plural pronoun 'our [life]' consolidates her assumption of shared experience. The comment in Figure 15, 'exactly this isn't it ☺', suggests that Cheryl recognizes her own child's behaviour in the teenage whisperer text. The rhetorical tag question 'isn't it', further, points again to a presupposition that other group members will share Cheryl's practices and experiences, and thus echo her recognition. Both comments, like Figure 14, take the form of unmitigated declaratives and are punctuated with an emoji that confirms the affective tone of the post – in this case, one of frustration and exhaustion. The emojis' position alongside collectivizing strategies implies that these affective responses will be shared by others: that as a group, they are all exasperated to the point of tears. As with the post displayed in Figure 14, the entextualized actions and practices at the heart of these teenage whisperer texts are distilled in Cheryl's comments through deictic pronouns ('this', 'isn't it' and 'another one that . . .'). These words capture a complex set of actions, experiences and meanings in a highly condensed form, simultaneously referring to the practices that are addressed in each article and to group members' own experiences of these practices. As such, they might be described, as with Lynne's reference to images and use of deixis (see Chapter 3), as micro-entextualizations, which rely on shared knowledge, understanding or experience in order to decode the actions and practices to which they refer.

To sum up, in these posts we see Cheryl working to consolidate and mobilize collective connection between members of the New Families Facebook group. She does so through the persistent implication that they have an extensive bank of shared experiences: more specifically, that their children have exhibited similar actions and behaviours to those described in Ross' articles, and that the parenting and family practices advocated by Ross are very well known, tried and tested amongst members of the group. Cheryl's recourse to these shared repertoires of action and practice is the foundation for her connection with the group. Through Cheryl's recontextualizations of the teenage whisperer texts, she is able to position group members as caring, competent parents who have researched and practised a range of strategies to support their children. Further, by sharing content from an external source, Cheryl can reference specific shared actions, practices and experiences, without herself appearing to give advice or singling out any particular group member. As explained in the previous section, this particular kind of info-relational sharing is comparable to that identified in Fage-Butler and Jensen's (2013) explorations of health-related Facebook groups and similar contexts where institutional or biomedical information is filtered through narratives of personal experience. However, there is a key difference here: rather than narratives of personal experience being imbued with 'expert' information, in these posts 'expert' texts are imbued with personal experience. Through this combination, Cheryl is able to both collectivize *and depersonalize* the group's experiences. By filtering the group's shared practices through a genericized and fictionalized article, she sends the message that the parents in the group are not alone, suggesting that both they and their children are experiencing problems that countless families have experienced before them and will continue to experience long after. She also takes the spotlight away from individual parents' practices and experiences, thereby mitigating the potential for personal blame or responsibility. This is a creative strategy for building collective connection amongst individuals who haven't all met in person or interacted one-to-one.

Collective venting

The second Facebook group, Parenting Adult Adoptees, is a closed, secret group with twenty members who all have older adopted children and mostly know one another quite well. As a result of the small, close-knit nature of the group, and members' similar family circumstances and experiences, Cheryl feels she can be completely open in this context, without fear of negative judgement (see discussion in previous sections). It is perhaps not surprising, then, that 'venting' posts, where Cheryl shares negative actions, events, experiences and feelings, are the most common type of post she shares with this group. Extracts 5, 6 and 7 show three of these venting posts, which were written between December 2018 and May 2019, and have a similar theme and structure. Cheryl also shared the third of these posts, reproduced in Extract 7, with the New Families group.

Extract 5. 'Where do they get their ideas from?' (17.12.2018)

1. Where do they get their ideas from?
2. K in supported living, doesn't work
3. and his ESA is gone as soon as he gets
4. it (he has a boomerang £20 he can borrow
5. but has to pay it back before he can
6. borrow it again) has decided he's having
7. driving lessons 🙄 😔
8. I'm leaving him to it

Extract 6. 'Here we go again!' (08.04.2019)

1. Here we go again! Keir was doing ok
2. and settling into his new flat, working
3. with support who is a young lad but
4. getting Keir to do as 'he looks like my
5. mate not support' now somethings gone
6. on, not related to Keir and so they've
7. changed his support, cue refusing to
8. engage, trauma response, them not
9. listening and now a report to the tenancy
10. manager and safeguarding. I wish they'd
11. listen!

Extract 7. 'It's never enough, is it?' (06.05.2019)

1. We're in London celebrating the boys 21ˢᵗ,
2. this was instead of a big present. He's
3. seemed at his happiest feeding the
4. squirrels and parakeets in the parks and
5. apart from that he's just wanted to explore.

6. Blip last night as I wouldn't sit in Piccadilly
7. Circus or wander round til the small hours,
8. it stunk of cannabis and was being openly
9. smoked.
10. It's never enough is it? 😔

The actions and experiences that Cheryl entextualizes in these posts largely relate to her son Keir's *in*action and struggles to regulate his behaviour independently. In this respect, they are strikingly similar to those of the teenage whisperer articles explored in the previous section. For example, in Extract 5 Cheryl juxtaposes Keir's inaction with his spontaneous, unregulated behaviour, noting that he 'doesn't work' and doesn't save his money: 'his ESA is gone as soon as he get it', yet has 'decided he's having driving lessons'. In Extract 6, Cheryl recounts a situation with Keir's support worker that upset him, with the result that he 'refus[ed] to engage' and exhibited a 'trauma response'. Finally, in Extract 7 Cheryl entextualizes a trip to London with her son with an emphasis on his extreme behaviour, noting that he wanted to 'wander round til the small hours' and implying that he was attracted to cannabis, which 'was being openly smoked'. Cheryl's use of negations and negative evaluations throughout these posts all point to conflict between her own, her son's and support services' actions, expectations and feelings. Further, the 'pensive face' emoji that punctuates Extract 7 consolidates Cheryl's disappointed and regretful perspective on these past events, whilst the hyperbolic laughter emojis towards the end of Extract 5 imply, in the context of this post, exasperation and despair. The key difference between these posts to the PAA group and the teenage whisperer articles that she shares with the NF group is that Cheryl does not centre her own actions as a parent nor any caring practices that might ameliorate her son's distress or troubling behaviours. Instead, through an entirely self-authored post that is shared with a closed, homophilous community, Cheryl is able to just 'vent': to focus on the distressing nature of other's actions and practices (including her son), without turning attention to her own parenting practice or any counteractive course of action.

Each of Cheryl's disclosures is framed by a statement that addresses the group as a whole and implies that other members will have had similar experiences with their children and possibly with support services: 'Where do they get their ideas from?' (Extract 5), 'Here we go again!' (Extract 6) and 'It's never enough is it?' (Extract 7). These statements are similar in form and function to those of her info-relational posts, and they work, similarly, to position her words as part of an ongoing dialogue between group members. For example, in Extract 6, her exclamation 'here we go again!' signals that bad experiences with professionals are familiar to the group; that this is just one of many examples that will come as no surprise to members. The plural pronoun 'we' in this instance can be read both as a reference to Cheryl and her son, and to the wider group. In Extract 7, the closing tag question 'is it?', like the tag question of her second info-relational post, indicates a presumption of understanding and alignment with her assessment that 'it's never enough'. Further, the deictic references to 'their ideas' and 'it' in Extracts 5 and 7 can again be seen as micro-entextualizations that capture an unspoken set of actions and practices in condensed form. As with the other examples of micro-entextualization across Cheryl and Lynne's digital data, these usages presuppose shared understanding: in this instance, of what 'ideas' their children have and the parenting practices that will 'never [be] enough' to satisfy their needs. Finally, all of these statements again take the form of simple, unmitigated declaratives: Cheryl does not ask if others have experienced similar problems or mitigate her assumption that they have. Cheryl thus signals that the actions and experiences detailed in her posts are representative of group members' ongoing experiences and that her posts are reliant on a shared history and shared set of references.

As explained in Chapter 2, comments on posts to closed Facebook groups were not included in the data collection process for this study. However, Cheryl's interview talk around her interaction and engagement within the PAA group does shed some light on the kind of replies she (and others) tended to receive when they posted 'venting' messages such as those shown in Extracts 5, 6 and 7. For example, in our second interview, I asked Cheryl what kind of replies she got when she wrote about 'having a bad time' in the PAA group. Her subsequent response, which is reproduced in Extract 8, provides an impression of the typical comments she received in this context.

Extract 8. Excerpt from interview 2
(interviewer interjections in square brackets)

1. from here you'd get oh I understand that we've been through that [yeah] erm a lot of
2. empathy but you wouldn't get oh you need to do this or you need to do that [you wouldn't

3. get advice] you wouldn't get advice no this [no] this board isn't for advice this is just for so
4. you can vent and someone can go yeah I understand that [yeah]
   [3 minutes discussion of specific group members omitted]
5. so yeah there's a lot of us just moaning on this one [yeah] really if I'm honest [laughs] yeah
6. but it do but it does its job you have a moan [yeah] and then you go back and you get on
7. with it don't you [yeah yep yep] you have a moan other people go oh god I know how you
8. feel [mmm] and then you c you can someone's listened to you and you can go back and get
9. on with it
   [30 seconds talk about 'funny memes' omitted]
10. there's lots of moaning and does has anybody else gone through this [yeah] or like Sophie's
11. saying you know we're having the same here so you've got a bit of solidarity there as well
12. haven't you [mmm] you know you can go oh god it's awful and someone else'll go oh yeah
13. it's awful here as well [mmm] and you don't have to explain yourself [mmm] cos everybody
14. knows what you're going through

At this point in our second interview, Cheryl suggests that people commenting on her 'venting' posts often express 'solidarity' (line 11) by using language that echoes and mirrors the content of others' posts. For example, between lines 10 and 11 she recounts a common question – 'has anybody else gone through this' – and a typical response that confirms shared experience: 'we're having the same here'. Between lines 12 and 13, Cheryl gives the (hypothetical) example of posting 'oh god it's awful' and a responder echoing these words in their reply: 'oh yeah it's awful here as well'. Both illustrative replies deploy expressions of sameness: 'the same here' and 'here as well'. This re-voicing of one another's experiences is comparable with the deictic and mirroring devices used in Lynne's Messenger chat, as well as that identified in studies of the UK-based Mumsnet Talk forum (Jaworska, 2018; Pedersen & Lupton, 2018; see Chapter 3). Further, these examples again employ micro-entextualizations, where complex actions and experiences are encapsulated through deictic reference to 'it' and 'this'. By using undefined deictic expressions in her description of these interactions, Cheryl points to a shared understanding of common occurrences within members' families. This assumption of shared understanding nullifies any need to specify the details of what is actually happening in their lives. Cheryl also repeats the words 'understand' (lines 1 and 4) and 'know' (lines 7 and 14) throughout this excerpt to explain how others respond to her posts. She suggests that responses such as 'I understand' (line 4) or 'I know how you feel' (line 7) are very powerful; that being understood whilst not having 'to explain yourself' (line 13) is extremely valuable to her within the context of the PAA group. She also suggests it is the expression of shared experience and understanding, rather than specific detail about what those experiences entail, that is useful to her. These examples illustrate Cheryl's claim that the PAA group provides a space where she can 'have a moan', other people listen and offer solidarity, and she is then able to carry on with her life – to 'go back and get on with it' (lines 8–9).

Chapter summary

This chapter has elaborated the concept of collective connection through a second case study, which examines Cheryl's use of Facebook groups to sustain and mobilize shared actions, practices and experiences amongst her fellow adoptive parents. The analysis of Cheryl's posts to a group for LGBT adopters, *New Families*, shows how she filters members' shared family practices and experiences through recontextualized content from an advisory website, using the hyperlink-with-comment format. I suggest that this form of info-relational sharing is a creative strategy that allows Cheryl to both collectivize and depersonalize group members' experiences. The second analysis focuses on Cheryl's 'venting' posts to a Facebook group for parents of adopted adults (PAA), in which she relays her son's struggles to regulate his behaviour independently and the failure of support services to meet his needs. In both cases, Cheryl's posts operate on the presumption that others' children exhibit the same behaviours, that they will have experienced similar problems with support services and that parents will have attempted the same caring and supportive practices to counter these issues. I argue that the circulation of these actions, practices and experiences is not the *result* of these groups' collective connection; rather, it is taken as the starting point for this connection. Cheryl's posts (and others' responses) work to further consolidate and mobilize this collective connection through oblique reference to shared actions and experiences, for example through the simulation of ongoing dialogue, unmitigated declaratives, frequent micro-entextualizations and through echoing and mirroring devices. As we saw in the previous chapter, these strategies often function as communicative 'shortcuts' that signal shared, unspoken experiences and reference points. The implications of these connective practices are twofold. First, as shown in other explorations of online support groups, Cheryl is able to construct a reassuring sense of togetherness, understanding and solidarity which is extremely valuable in her life, offering a sense of validation and security. Further, as suggested in Chapter 3, these collective connections also relate directly to her own and others' parenting and family actions, which are constructed not as individual but as *collective* practices.

Together, the explorations presented in Chapters 3 and 4 suggest that practices of collective connection may be particularly significant for those who encounter multiple, intersecting challenges in their everyday family practice – in this case, single adoptive parents. Whilst these parents' practices and experiences may not always align with wider social presumptions around family lives, through collective connection they are able to construct a sense of reassuring solidarity and togetherness. These connections are often based on very specific axes of similarity, with participants' networks being restricted to those who are perceived to share a precise set of experiences. Such measures seem to be a form of self-preservation that protects these adoptive parents from being challenged or misunderstood by 'outsiders'. These chapters have also moved beyond the themes of support, solidarity and validation that dominate existing research with online parenting collectives, to show how collective connection has the potential to reshape contemporary family life in flexible and dynamic ways. Indeed, Cheryl and Lynne's construction of parenting and family actions and practices as *collectively* undertaken can be seen to stretch the boundaries of 'family' beyond the parent–child unit, to include a more expansive network of parents, friends and other supporters.

5

Introducing Epistemic Connection

The previous chapters have suggested that *collective connection* forms the foundations for a connected parenting practice that has the potential to reshape contemporary family life. Building on this discussion, I now introduce the second dimension of connected parenting, *epistemic connection*, which concerns the formation of ties through the construction and exchange of knowledge and information. Whilst this chapter will explore epistemic connection as a significant dimension of connected parenting in its own right, it will also show that the domains of epistemic and collective connection are intimately intertwined, with epistemic connection relying on and mobilizing a collective epistemic background that is rooted in shared practice and experience. The relational perspective I adopt in this chapter promotes a circular exploration of how knowledge is constructed *through* connection with others, how that knowledge is evaluated and valued, and how co-constructed ways of knowing, in turn, shape the quality of connections between people.

In the first part of the chapter, I elaborate this relational perspective through an exploration of interdisciplinary research that concerns information-sharing and knowledge-construction practices in online groups, networks and communities. This discussion introduces key theories and concepts that are particularly relevant for the case studies that follow, including connected knowing and connective action, which attend to the co-production and mobilization of knowledge resources through online networks. It also explores some of the ways in which expert and experiential advice and information are negotiated in supportive group contexts.

The chapter then introduces the first case study on epistemic connection. This study focuses on Jenny, who adopted her two children as a single woman. After outlining Jenny's use of the microblogging platform Twitter, I home in on her use of quotes as a resource for recontextualizing and reinterpreting knowledge and information resources within a network of adoptive parents. Through analysis of Jenny's retweets, I examine the ways in which actions, moments, events and practices are made 'tangible' and thus 'knowable' through the transformative processes of decontextualization, entextualization and recontextualization. Further, I consider how Jenny's connections with individuals and groups are constructed, sustained and mobilized through these transformative processes. This analysis provides a basis for exploring how parents can mobilize collective connections between their peers to construct and consolidate forms of knowledge about children, parenting, families and education that challenge (and sometimes sustain) dominant and institutional points of view, and enact positive social change for children and families. These themes will be elaborated in Chapter 6, which focuses on Rachael, a single woman who conceived her infant daughter with the help of donor insemination and in vitro fertilization (IVF).

Connected knowing, action and expertise

In this chapter's exploration of epistemic connection, I take the position that the construction and exchange of 'knowledge' are not solely a matter of moving information from one place to another or accruing facts as a 'store' of information. Rather, I suggest that when people share, evaluate or elaborate information, they also take a particular stance in relation to that information; they assign value to it, and in turn, they create bonds with people who share that stance and distinguish themselves from those who don't. The concept of *epistemic connection*, consequently, is based on the premise that the construction of 'knowledge' is deeply interconnected with the positioning of self in relation to others and in relation to the wider social world. This relational perspective is consistent with Miller and Fox's (2001) claim that 'knowledge' does not exist in isolation; that we cannot conceive of knowledge as a tangible but disconnected store of facts, information or data that can be selected and discarded at will. Rather, knowledge will always be responsive to the culture in which it's embedded and will always be constructed *through* interpersonal connections between individuals and groups who are working towards a common endeavour.

A significant body of research across the social sciences has examined information-sharing and knowledge-construction practices in online discussion groups, forums and communities from such a relational perspective. Much of this research has focused on health-related and parenting groups, as contexts in which knowledge construction frequently intersects with the formation of social connection and solidarity. For example, Landqvist (2016) has pointed to the interrelation between epistemic and interpersonal goals, such as support-seeking, rapport-building and community, in the context of the Swedish social networking site *Familjeliv* ('family life'). Within the discussion forum of this site, he suggests, information is shared in a way that establishes rapport between contributors through an emphasis on personal experience and compassion. Others have shown how online groups like these have mobilized their shared experiential knowledge to effect social and institutional change. For example, in Akrich's (2010) ethnographic exploration of a French list server group called CIANE (Collectif Interassociatif Autour de la NaissancE: *Interassociative Birth Collective*), she shows how this group worked to reframe problems around episiotomy practices. As she explains, members of the group came together as an informal collective and consulted with professional groups to combine their medical and technical knowledge with experiential knowledge drawn from the online list server group's testimonials. The CIANE network's practices may be described as *connective action*, a form of collective action that operates through the co-production and co-distribution of personalized content across media networks (Bennett & Segerberg, 2012). Their positive results illustrate the power of connective action for reworking dominant forms of knowledge and their associated practices.

The rise of online forums in which people seek advice and information about matters relating to health and parenting coincides with a broader neoliberal trend towards the production of informed citizens who take personal responsibility for every aspect of their life. For example, in the context of health care, Kivits (2004, p. 526, 2009) has explored the evolution of the 'informed patient' as a responsible citizen who 'take[s] responsibility for, and ... constantly improve[s], their health'. Kivits (2004) suggests that active information seeking, through online or other resources, is a central practice for the informed patient, which indicates their awareness and acceptance of these responsibilities. In terms of parenting expertise and responsibility, the expectation that parents, specifically mothers, should be well-informed 'experts' when it comes to matters of parenting and childhood has been well documented (e.g. Wall, 2010, 2013). Further, it has been suggested that the constant availability of information via digital and mobile media has increased the demands of 'knowledge-intensive' parenting practices that place responsibility on mothers to make the most appropriate, well-considered decisions for their children (Lehto, 2021; Schofield Clark, 2012). As a result, the negotiation of medical and parent-related knowledge in digital contexts is often intertwined with parents' self-positioning as informed, legitimate, competent and generally 'good' parents (see Hine, 2014, and Jensen, 2013, on the construction of 'informed', 'responsible' mothers on Mumsnet).

In taking up the role of informed, responsible and consequently 'good' mothers, users of online parenting groups and forums have been shown to navigate a careful balance between personal and professional/institutional expertise and experience (see Holland, 2018; Papen, 2013; Zaslow, 2012). Some authors (e.g. Song, West, Lundy, & Smith Dahmen, 2012) have suggested that when weighing this balance, most women still turn to online resources that affirm and supplement, rather than contradict, mainstream medical authority. Others, however (e.g. Hine, 2014; Zaslow, 2012), have suggested that women's subjective experience tends to be given equal weight, if not precedence, in online networks of mothers. In her ethnographic exploration of an online listserv community for mothers to children with special needs, for instance, Zaslow (2012) shows how participants privilege 'connected knowing' (Belenky, Clinchy, Goldberger, & Tarule, 1986) as a form of collaborative, subjective and experiential knowledge production. For example, in her response to a mother who was having problems with her son's play therapy, one participant, 'Julia', both shared details of her own son's aggressive behaviour and offered up the experiences of other list members as a 'knowledge base' that had value beyond institutionally valorized treatments. In this way, Zaslow (2012, p. 1366) suggests, participants used the collaborative nature of the community 'to re-position traditionally feminine ways of connected knowing as valuable and legitimate'. Similarly, in Hine's (2014) analysis of Mumsnet 'Talk' discussions, she points to the way traditional forms of expertise are reconfigured in peer-to-peer interactions about head lice treatment, as part of a process of *apomediation* in which 'official' advice and information is filtered through personal perspectives and experiences. This is comparable with the 'info-relational sharing' identified in Fage-Butler and Jensen's (2013) examination of an online forum for thyroid patients (see Chapter 4). As they share advice and information, Hine (2014, p. 588) suggests, contributors construct a 'collective' in which, as in the listserv communities explored by Akrich (2010) and Zaslow (2012), 'personal experience was evaluated on a par with . . . formal scientific knowledge'. These studies suggest that in online networks and communities of mothers, being an 'informed', and therefore 'good', parent is often a shared endeavour, with relevant information being evaluated, valued and subsequently valorized on a collective level.

A number of discourse analysts have conducted close investigations of *how* mothers negotiate the complex positions of the 'informed' and 'good' parent at the micro-level of digital interaction (see Mackenzie & Zhao, 2021, for an overview). For example, Lyons' (2020) analysis of messages within a WhatsApp chat group focuses on new mothers' negotiation of the 'expertise paradox', which positions mothers as needing expert help, but also bearing full responsibility for their children. Lyons draws on positioning theory (Harré & van Langenhove, 1999) to consider how participants use a range of discursive moves to locate themselves and others in relation to different forms of knowledge. This approach allows her to show that the position of expert shifts between different group members, in combination with external expert sources, depending on the topic and individual members' experiences. She is therefore able to elaborate the micro-level strategies through which institutionally validated forms of expertise intersect in complex and subtle ways with mothers' experiential knowledge. Jaworska's (2018) narrative analysis of threads about postnatal depression in Mumsnet Talk, similarly, points to the way institutional knowledge can be filtered through personal experience in this context, specifically through the narrative form of the *exemplum*. Further, she shows how the exemplum benefits users by allowing them to speak from the position of 'knower', which lends authenticity to institutional forms of knowledge. Jaworska (2018, p. 31) suggests that these negotiations constitute 'an experiential knowledge resource' that can support readers in understanding and validating their own lives and experiences. Finally, Hanell and Salö's (2017) exploration of the Swedish parenting site Familjeliv ('family life') elucidates some of the processes by which sharing experience online can actually *produce* knowledge and enable future actions (see further discussion in Chapter 1). These examples again show that sharing personal experience online can be an extremely powerful act, which contributes to the construction of new, collective forms of knowledge and practice.

As the discussion in this section has shown, the construction and mobilization of epistemic connections between parents have become increasingly important in a social context that demands high levels of medical and parenting expertise, especially from mothers. Given their marginalized and often stigmatised positions as single women who have used donor conception or adoption to bring children into their lives, parents like Jenny and Rachael will likely experience even more pressure to be knowledgeable and well informed about their children's specific needs. Further, being well connected within networks of their peers is likely to have particular value for Jenny and Rachael as they raise their children independently and navigate the range of challenges that come with their particular family circumstances. In the following section, I briefly consider these participants' positions in their respective networks, before introducing the subject of the first case study, Jenny, in more detail.

Introducing Jenny

All nine of the parents who took part in the Marginalised Families Online study engage in practices of online information sharing and knowledge construction to an extent. However, in this chapter and the one that follows, I focus on two single parents for whom epistemic connection is a particularly significant dimension of their connected parenting practice: Jenny and Rachael. As these chapters will show, both Jenny and Rachael are deeply embedded in very active communities of adopters (Jenny) and solo mums (Rachael). Indeed, they are important figures within these communities: Jenny works for an adoption charity and has written a book about attachment and trauma in educational settings, whilst Rachael has a business, *Going Solo*, which supports solo mums and is involved in consultancy work with fertility clinics. Both participants are very well-connected individuals, who are engaged with a number of intersecting personal, institutional and professional networks. Further, both Jenny and Rachael have worked to mobilize their connections within these networks to drive forward new ways of understanding and thinking about conception, parenting, family life and educational practice. For example, Jenny has drawn on some of the experiences shared by adoptive parents on Twitter for her book. Similarly, Rachael has used some of the anecdotes solo mums have shared to her Facebook group to inform her consultancy work. As such, these women both seek and share information related to their family and parenting circumstances not only for themselves but for the groups, networks and communities in which they are embedded and which they serve as part of their professional roles.

This chapter's case study focuses on Jenny, a 45-year-old heterosexual adoptive parent who works part-time for the charity Adopter Network, alongside caring for her two children and home-schooling her son. She has a master's degree in education and extensive experience of working with children, in both the UK (as a secondary school teacher) and abroad (as a carer at an orphanage). At the age of thirty-six, Jenny began to seriously consider the possibility of becoming a foster carer. At this point in her life, Jenny explained, she felt she was 'getting on a bit' and probably wasn't going to meet anyone she could have children with. At the same time, she didn't feel it was particularly important to have biological children with a partner. Jenny subsequently adopted her son Jack in 2013 and her daughter Charlotte in 2015. Although Jenny adopted both of her children as a single woman, she is no longer single, having married and begun co-habiting with her husband halfway through the fieldwork for the Marginalised Families Online study, in 2019. As noted earlier, Jenny is well known within the adoption community, due to her professional role as an educational advisor with Adopter Network and her expertise in the area of public and home-schooling for adoptive children.

Jenny is an intensive user of social media. When she first started fostering in 2009, she set up a blog, using the pseudonym 'The Instant Parent', as a way of keeping her friends and family up to date with her life. She later set up a Twitter account and Facebook page using the same name, and now uses these platforms to communicate with other adopters, as well as professional organizations and institutions. Talking about the height of her social media usage, Jenny told me in our second interview that she used to sit on the sofa 'for four hours at night' because the conversations she had online were the only adult conversations she would have for several days. Although Jenny no longer feels so reliant on her digitally mediated interactions, checking social media on her phone is still the first thing she does when she wakes up each morning. It is perhaps not surprising, then, that the network diagram she produced in our final interview contained a significant proportion (4/9) of exclusively digital contacts. These connections are illustrated in Figure 5, which shows the nine alters in Jenny's network and the means by which their communication is mediated (see Chapter 2 for a detailed explanation of network diagrams).

As with the other single adopters in the Marginalised Families Online study, forming collective connections with other adopters was very important to Jenny. Like Cheryl and Lynne, she felt that homophilous friendships and communities were particularly valuable because her family had many adverse experiences

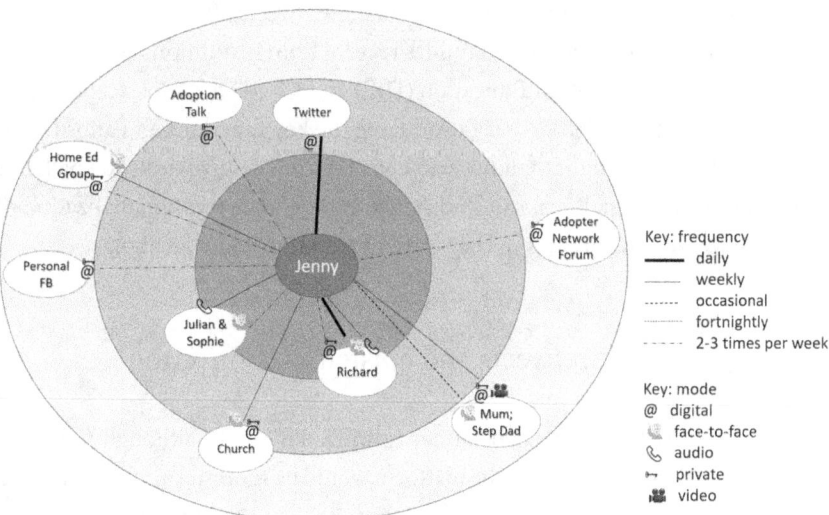

Figure 5 reproduction of Figure 5, Jenny's modes of contact diagram.

that would be unfamiliar, and perhaps shocking, to other parents (see Chapter 4). To give a specific example, Jenny felt that no one could really understand what the child-to-parent violence she had experienced was like unless they had experienced it themselves. As she quite vividly explains, 'you can't really get across to somebody how awful it is when your child pulls you to the ground and kicks you in the face'. Further elaborating on the importance of being able to openly and honestly express negative feelings without judgement, Jenny explained in our second interview that 'when you're parenting [in] sometimes quite extreme situations . . . you need to be able to go somewhere and say my life is shit actually and not have four thousand people coming after you going . . . this is the life you chose'. Jenny tended to use more private and closed-network digital media, such as Facebook groups and mobile messaging apps, to mediate collective connections with other adopters and 'vent to people who understand'. In this respect, Jenny's connected parenting practice has much in common with Cheryl's (see Chapter 4).

The collective and epistemic dimensions of connected parenting practice frequently intersect in Jenny's digitally mediated communication, which often centres on the sharing of knowledge, information and advice about parenting and education with fellow adoptive parents. Further, through her professional role, print publications and public-facing digital media content, Jenny works to negotiate, challenge and reconstruct dominant forms of knowledge around adoption, trauma, childhood behaviour and education. For example, she often uses the microblogging platform Twitter to engage with institutions, media groups and individuals who have the power to effect positive change for adopted and/or home-educated children. In particular, her tweets often draw attention to the inadequate support adoptive families receive from institutions such as social services, the Department for Education (DfE) and Child and Adolescent Mental Health Services (CAMHS). After introducing the key functions and affordances of Twitter, the analysis that follows will consider how Jenny works to challenge expert and institutional forms of knowledge through her recontextualization of tweets by well-known figures in the world of adoption and education.

Twitter, retweets and epistemic connection

Twitter is widely known as a social networking site (SNS), although there is a historical tension over whether the platform would be more accurately described as an 'information network' (Burgess & Baym, 2020, p. 12). This tension between social and information networking, Burgess and Baym (2020, p. 15) suggest, contributes to Twitter's 'unique culture, where friendly chatter, food updates, and pet portraits mingl[e] with election campaigns and world news events'. Over the years, however, they argue that the balance has tipped in favour of Twitter as a 'world-centered, public, and newsy' platform, strongly influenced by the company's concern with engagement and metrics (Burgess & Baym, 2020, p. 13). In line with Twitter's growing status as a key source for global information and news as it happens, it is the norm on Twitter to have a 'public' profile (i.e. open and accessible to anyone with an internet connection), making it possible for information to circulate quickly and freely. However, it is possible to lock individual accounts, which makes them less accessible, or to use a range of privacy settings that limit visibility, interaction and engagement.

Twitter users build their network by 'following' others, and unlike Facebook's 'friend' relationship (see Chapter 4), following need not be reciprocated. The platform's participatory structure revolves around the tweet, a short post that is shared with an individual's followers. These tweets can be no longer than 280 characters, a limitation that contributes to Twitter's distinctive character as a fast-paced information network. Individuals will see the tweets of people they are following in their timeline and sometimes tweets created by followers-of-followers or tweets that are 'recommended' through the site's engagement algorithms. Users can interact with a tweet by liking it, replying to it or retweeting it, and these metrics are displayed below a tweet, so others can see how much engagement it has garnered. These and other evolving functions, such as retweets and mentions, have become important metrics for a platform that depends on 'measurable user interaction' to 'generate data that makes user engagement visible' (Puschmann, 2015, p. 29).

According to Burgess and Baym (2020), three key technological features have shaped Twitter's distinctive architecture and culture: mentions, hashtags and retweets. Although all three functions can be found, in various forms, across other social media platforms such as Tumblr, Instagram and Facebook, they were established and popularized on Twitter and remain central to Twitter's character. Hashtags, described by Burgess and Baym (2020, p. 60) as 'the hash symbol (#) immediately followed by a string of alphanumeric characters', have an organizational function, thematizing tweets and thus making them more 'searchable' for users. They can also serve social and interpersonal functions, as a resource for building 'ambient affiliation', which Zappavigna (2011, p. 801) describes as 'affiliat[ion] with a copresent . . . community by bonding around evolving topics of interest'. The mention and the retweet allow for more direct and targeted interaction and affiliation. For example, Twitter users can draw a specific person's attention to a tweet by including their username, prefixed with the @ symbol (e.g. @JaiMackenzie). The targeted user will then receive a notification telling them that they have been mentioned. Mentions can serve a number of social functions, including the initiation of a dialogue (e.g. what do you think @JaiMackenzie?), the flagging of a useful resource (e.g. @JaiMackenzie have you read this?), marking an account as a useful resource for others (e.g. @JaiMackenzie might know the answer to your question) or mutual promotion (e.g. @JaiMackenzie's new book is a fantastic read).

The third feature, the retweet, is a particularly salient resource for recontextualizing and reinterpreting knowledge and information resources on Twitter, and will thus be the focus for this chapter's exploration of epistemic connection. Retweeting, along with email quoting and other digital practices such as the Facebook 'share' function that is mentioned in Chapter 4, has often been examined within the historical context of reported speech as technology-facilitated iterations of this spoken practice (Draucker & Collister, 2015; Gruber, 2017; Puschmann, 2015). It has been described by Burgess and Baym (2020, p. 35) as 'a way to share other users' contributions accurately and with attribution'. After a few years of user-led tweet-sharing practices, Twitter introduced the retweet function in 2009, which allowed users to directly reproduce someone else's tweets on their timeline at the touch of a button. Two types of retweet are built into Twitter's participatory structure: the direct 'preserving' retweet and the 'retweet with comment' (RwC) (Draucker & Collister, 2015). This chapter focuses on *retweets with comment*, a distinctive form of recontextualization that makes the link between the quoter and the quotee highly visible, with both the retweeter's comment and the original tweet appearing as one unit in the audience's rolling timeline.

As explained in Chapter 4, retweets and other digital recontextualization practices allow users to both share information or material and take an evaluative stance in relation to that recontextualized material (Draucker & Collister, 2015; Du Bois, 2007; Gruber, 2017; van Leeuwen, 2008). Retweets are therefore not just acts of sharing information; they also serve an important function in terms of the retweeter's public self-positioning and alignment with others. For example, Gruber (2017, pp. 4–5) suggests that retweets establish 'staged "micro-dialogues" between the retweeter and the retweeted text (and/or its authors) in front of the retweeter's followers'. Page (2018, p. 139), similarly, discusses the 'staging' of dialogue through retweets as a way of 'display[ing] connection with others' and suggests that such displays 'can be co-opted for various socio-political purposes, such as activism . . . or to manage a fan base as a form of celebrity practice'.

boyd et al.'s (2010, p. 6) 'non-exhaustive list of motivations' for retweeting outlines a wide range of stances and participation roles that can be taken by a retweeting user. Most of these motivations can apply to both preserving retweets and RwCs, although some (such as 'commenting on someone's tweet by retweeting and adding new content'; boyd et al. 2010, p. 6) apply specifically to RwCs. Although boyd et al. (2010) mention agreement, validation, amplification and loyalty as possible motivations for retweeting, they do not explore the potential for *negative* alignment through retweets. Nevertheless, just as retweeting practices create opportunities for positive alignment, in-group formation and rapport-enhancing interactions, they also create opportunities for negative alignment, out-group formation and rapport-threatening interactions (Gruber, 2017; Page, 2018). The analysis of this chapter covers both forms of evaluative alignment, exploring three types of RwC in Jenny's Twitter data: rejections, takedown threads and endorsements. These types are introduced and contextualized in relation to Jenny's full Twitter data set in the section that follows.

Jenny's use of Twitter

As noted earlier in this chapter, Jenny is keen to engage with powerful institutions, media groups and individuals on issues that affect adoptive and home-educating families. It is clear from both her interview and digital media data that Jenny sees Twitter as a highly effective medium for this kind of advocacy, activism and influence. Further, Jenny uses Twitter to engage with other parents who have shared circumstances and experiences, most notably the community she calls 'adoption Twitter', as well as a sub-community of adopters who educate their children at home. Jenny emphasized, throughout our interviews, how much she had learned from adoption Twitter and how the connections she had made through this network had significantly impacted her life. For example, in our third interview she explained that, if it wasn't for the connections she made on Twitter, she would have missed a lot of learning about the issues currently facing adopters and adoptees, she wouldn't be in her current job and she wouldn't have published her recent book. Jenny has also expressed her gratitude for Twitter's adoption community on the site itself, writing in one tweet from November 2018 that 'without everyone here I would still be clueless'. She is therefore very aware of Twitter's potential as an 'information network' that supports information sharing, learning, campaigning and activism. Jenny also uses Twitter in much more informal ways, for everyday social interactions and updates about her life.

For example, as well as her public-facing and information-focused tweets, she often shares humorous, informal anecdotes about her life with her children, participates in frivolous quizzes and shares trivial facts.

As of 1 April 2019, the end point of my data collection, Jenny had 2,626 followers and had posted 28,200 tweets in total.[1] Jenny's Twitter account has remained public throughout her time using the platform, but she has rigorously protected her privacy and anonymity by using a pseudonymous username and not displaying images of her face. Jenny explained in our final interview, however, that she was gradually adjusting these practices, given that so many of her followers know who she is through her professional role, where it is necessary to use her real name. She had also written a book using her real name, which she was keen to promote through her Twitter account. However, Jenny continues to deploy a range of strategies to keep her children anonymous, such as mentioning them infrequently, using initials or pseudonyms for their names, disguising their faces in photographs (e.g. with emojis) and taking photos from behind. Such practices are increasingly common for social media users who are concerned about their children's privacy (see Autenrieth, 2018; Locatelli, 2017). A heightened concern with children's privacy and anonymity is especially prevalent within the adoption community, where some children may be put in danger if they can be identified by birth parents and other relatives.

I collected tweets posted by Jenny between 1 October 2018 and 1 April 2019. Whilst I read and reviewed all of Jenny's tweets, retweets and replies from this period, I only collected and stored the 125 tweets, RwCs and tweet threads[2] that she posted during this time. Of these, 77 were sole-authored tweets and 48 were RwCs. In order to respect the privacy and autonomy of others in her network, I only collected RwCs of well-known or institutional accounts with large numbers of followers (see detail on the data collection process in Chapter 2). For this chapter's investigation of epistemic connection, I focus on Jenny's use of RwCs as a strategy for recontextualizing and reinterpreting knowledge and information resources on Twitter. From these forty-eight RwCs, I identified four main types, covering four interpersonal functions: rejection (including a 'takedown' sub-category), endorsement, response and addition. These are detailed in Table 11, which includes definitions, examples and sub-categories for each type.

These four types of RwC can be subsumed within the broader categories of evaluative RwCs (rejection, takedown and endorsement) versus non-evaluative RwCs (response and addition). For the purposes of this chapter, I am particularly interested in Jenny's use of evaluative RwCs to express a stance (positive or negative) in relation to the quoted material or author and thus to

Table 11 Types of RwC in Jenny's Twitter Data

Type	Sub-type	Number	Description	Example
Rejection		11	Taking an evaluative, oppositional stance in relation to the retweeted content/author (or part of it)	[RwC Sally Bundock] 'It's nobody's job to get a child "school ready". Schools exist for children, not the other way around.'
	Takedown thread	2	A rejection tweet that goes on to offer in-depth critique in a thread of (three or more) tweets	[RwC Sue Crocombe] 'I can't get past the first few paragraphs of this Telegraph article, which cites a historical case of abuse by a foster carer on a home ed foster child. Thread'
Endorsement		12	Taking an evaluative, positively aligned stance in relation to the retweeted content/author (or part of it)	[RwC Sally Donovan] 'HOORAY!!!!'
Response		2	Providing a response to a question, game or prompt that is set out in the original retweet	[RwC Al Coates] 'During my adoption prep we were given old profiles of real children and asked if we'd consider adopting them.'
Addition		21	Adding further detail, information or elaboration to a tweet (including her own and other people's tweets)	[RwC one of Jenny's own tweets] 'Today we achieved Stage 2: Try on the Clothes'

recontextualize and/or reinterpret the knowledge and information presented in the original tweet. In the sections that follow, I take a typical example of each evaluative RwC in turn. In each case, I first consider the content Jenny is retweeting, in terms of both who has produced the content and how knowledge and information are represented. I then look more closely at Jenny's comments, considering the evaluative stance she takes in relation to the retweeted content, the way she positions herself in relation to her audience of Twitter users and how this contributes to the construction of *epistemic connections* with that audience.

Rejecting the 'naughty child' trope

The first retweet, posted by Jenny in December 2018, is an example of a *rejection* RwC (see Figure 17). Here, Jenny retweets Tes, an organization that began as a print magazine, the *Times Educational Supplement*, and now brands itself as 'one of the largest professional digital communities, connecting and supporting more than 13 million educators globally' (Tes Global Ltd, 2022). Tes' tweet reads 'Challenging behaviour is never an easy feat, but if the parents don't believe their child is naughty, then it can be even trickier – here are four things that should help'. This text is followed by a hyperlink to an article, which is available on their website. The first part of this article, including the title, subtitle, attribution and primary image, is shown in Figure 18.

In terms of the retweeted content and author, Tes is well known as a leading authority on educational practice in the UK. It covers and responds to a range of education-related policy, research and experience through articles, analysis and teaching resources. By retweeting Tes, Jenny signals to her followers that she follows the work they do. By commenting on the content of the article in her tweet, she also shows that she reads their content in full. Jenny's retweet-with-comment therefore positions her as someone who keeps up to date with current

Aagh!! There are a couple of reasonable points in this article (tho no mention of behaviour as communication, natch), but the title!! Wonder if this is the wording the author chose?

> **tes Tes** ✓ @tes · Dec 7, 2018
>
> Challenging behaviour is never an easy feat, but if the parents don't believe their child is naughty, then it can be even trickier – here are four things that should help
>
> bit.ly/2QAd2GX

5:20 PM · Dec 7, 2018 · Twitter for Android

Figure 17 'The wording the author chose' (07.12.2018), title details and tweet by Tes © Tes 2018. Reproduced with the permission of Tes.

What to do when parents refuse to believe their child is naughty

Tackling challenging behaviour depends on parental input, but that is not always a given, says Lisa Jarmin

7th December 2018, 12:02pm

Figure 18 Excerpt from a Tes article (07.12.2018). 'What to do when parents refuse to believe their child is naughty', title details and image by Tes © Tes 2018. Reproduced with the permission of Tes.

developments in education, debates about education and educational practice. By using her comment to dispute the author's choice of words, Jenny also signals that she has the expertise and conviction to oppose and challenge a prestigious institution such as this.

The Tes article itself begins with an invented scenario that entextualizes a set of actions relating to a teacher and their student. This exposition is reproduced in Extract 9. The opening statement 'there's this child in your class' relies on the presupposition that the reader is a teacher, and the statements that follow, many of which continue to address the reader directly through second-person pronouns, indicate a presupposition that they will be very familiar with the presented scenario. The exposition ends with direct address to the reader, in the form of the rhetorical question 'so what do you do?'. The article goes on to offer several 'solutions' to this 'problem' scenario, under four headings: 'find out about behaviour at home'; 'understanding is key'; 'have they had the full picture?'; and 'is the child giving a different version of events?'. In these subsections, the author (Lisa Jarmin) frequently entextualizes pupils' dispreferred actions and practices (such as conducting a reign of terror, swearing, shouting and administering dead legs) as the 'naughty' behaviour of a specific schoolchild (Lewis), which needs to be rectified. The Tes article's use of the problem–solution format, together with the construction of an imagined scenario between an adult and a young person, makes it similar in some respects to the teenage whisperer articles seen in Chapter 4. However, this article is written from the perspective of an adult, rather than a young person.

Extract 9. Exposition of the Tes article

> There's this child in your class; we'll call him Lewis.
> Lewis has been conducting a reign of terror that he inflicts on the school. He swears and shouts, he's disobedient and he makes his friends' lives a misery.
>
> You know full well that Lewis calls you a knobhead and regularly administers dead legs in the playground, but any attempt to bring up his challenging behaviour with his parents leads to stone-cold denial and a refusal to cooperate with you to improve the situation. They insist he would never act in such a way.
>
> So what do you do?

Jenny begins her commentary on this article with the exclamation 'Aagh!!', taking an affective stance of frustration and exasperation from the start. The intensity of her frustration (marked by the double exclamation marks) suggests that the problem she is about to point out is one she has seen many times before. In the remainder of the comment, Jenny evaluates the article in more detail, suggesting that it has some merit, but this is limited to a small number ('a couple') of points, which are met with the lukewarm evaluation 'reasonable'. However, she questions 'the wording' of the title, which reads 'what to do when parents refuse to believe their child is naughty'. The double exclamation marks again indicate her frustration and exasperation with the way children's behaviour is presented here ('the title!!').

Jenny mentions 'behaviour as communication' as a key omission in the article. This indicates her alignment with a school of thought that takes a non-evaluative perspective, understanding children's behaviour as a way of expressing needs or communicating feelings. To give a specific example of this approach, the teenage whisperer articles discussed in Chapter 4 adopt such a 'behaviour as communication' perspective. Given Jenny's alignment with this approach, it is reasonable to assume that her objection to 'the wording' of the title centres on its use of the word 'naughty', which negatively evaluates the child, rather than considering what they are trying to communicate. By drawing attention to an alternative perspective through which children's actions and behaviours can be interpreted, Jenny's tweet challenges the epistemological lens through which the article interprets actions such as shouting, swearing and fighting as 'naughtiness' or 'misbehaviour'. In turn, Jenny implies that these actions could be entextualized differently, for example not as a hyperbolic 'reign of terror' that is 'inflict[ed]' on others but as a way of communicating distress or anger, perhaps as a cry for help. In this way, Jenny's tweet works to challenge and reconstruct the epistemological perspectives through which children's actions and behaviours are defined and understood, both within the article and beyond it, in the wider audiences that it might reach. The harmful behaviours that are described in the Tes article (i.e. swearing, shouting and kicking) have in this instance become a tool for connection, through shared (re)interpretation of those actions. The retweet-with-comment function allows Jenny to position two opposing interpretations of those actions alongside one another and to foreground the epistemological perspective that she and her follows are presumed to share.

Jenny's recontextualization of the Tes tweet relies on a number of presuppositions. For example, she doesn't explain exactly what has caused her frustration, presupposing that her audience (a) understand the problem without her having to spell it out and (b) will also share her exasperation with certain approaches to understanding behaviour. The most explicit expression of Jenny's objection comes through the words 'the title!!', but she doesn't explain what is wrong with the title, leaving her readers to deduce this for themselves. The presumption that Jenny's audience will share her interpretation and evaluation of the article is particularly apparent in the words 'no mention of behaviour as communication, natch', where the adverb 'natch' (naturally) suggests it was entirely predictable and obvious that Jarmin would *not* take a behaviour-as-communication perspective. The underlying message of the tweet is therefore a sort of collective groan, as if to say 'look everyone, they're at it again!' This message both relies on and consolidates a combination of epistemic and collective connection between Jenny and her audience, a strong sense of togetherness and solidarity that is forged through collective knowledge, experiences and perspectives.

Endorsing superparents

The second tweet I will analyse in this chapter, also posted in December 2018, is an example of an *endorsement* RwC (see Figure 19). Here, Jenny retweets Sally Donovan, an author who has written several popular books about adoption and is an adopter herself.[3] Donovan's tweet reads 'A few thoughts about Channel 4s Superkids and why Superparenting should be super-valued #C4 #superkids', and links to a post on her own blog, called 'Superkids need Superparents'. The header image, title and first few lines of this blog post are displayed in Figure 20. The post itself is Sally's response to the Channel 4 documentary 'Superkids: Breaking Away from Care', which follows the poet and care leaver Lemn Sissay as he supports seven care-experienced teenagers in telling their stories. Donovan's response transposes the 'super-' prefix from 'superkids', who are the focus of the documentary, to 'superparents', who are the focus of her blog. Her post reflects on the lack of state support given to the very people who are best placed to improve the life chances of children going through the care system – their adoptive parents and foster carers. She suggests that this lack of support leaves families so 'broken and dispirited' that many do not even feel able to watch the programme.

Jenny's retweet-with-comment, like the Tes retweet analysed in the previous section, relies on a series of entextualizations that can be traced back to the actions of children. The 'Superkids' documentary itself focuses on young people's entextualizations of their experiences: the documentary charts the process of them coming together, being tutored by Sissay, writing poetry about their lives in care and ultimately performing these poems in front of an audience that includes influential and powerful figures from the government and social services. Through these actions, the young people are able to entextualize their

Cried a bit at this, but glad I read it anyway.

Just like #ChildrenInNeed, our collective response to #Superkids needs to be more than a fleeting emotional spasm. If we really want to do right by these kids, then its going to take a lot more.
twitter.com/sallydwrites/s...

This Tweet was deleted by the Tweet author. Learn more

5:03 PM · Dec 3, 2018 · Twitter Web Client

Figure 19 'Cried a bit at this' (03.12.2018). Sally Donovan's tweet has now been deleted, but the content of the original tweet and blog post is reproduced with her permission.

Sally Donovan
writer, editor

Superkids need Superparents

2 Replies

Many of my Superparent friends; foster carers, adopters, kinships carers, guardians chose not to watch Superkids on Channel 4 last week. They said being Superparents had left them too broken, exhausted and sad and all they could face was a bit of I'm a Celebrity and an early night. The programme could have carried an irony warning.

Although everyone says they bloody love those who care for the state's children, words can come up empty when the shit hits the fan. I took a deep breath of sweet-smelling air, thought of the poetry and Lemn Sissay and switched over. I'm glad I did – the kids, the poetry, the human spirit....

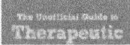

Figure 20 Excerpt from Sally Donovan's blog post (03.12.2018). Sally Donovan website header and 'Superkids Need Superparents' post and images by Sally Donovan © Sally Donovan 2022. Reproduced with the permission of Sally Donovan.

experiences as culturally valuable, and valued, information. Their actions and experiences are then further entextualized in the form of a documentary. In this video documentary form, the young people's actions travel into people's homes, including the living rooms of adoptive parents, where they can be recontextualized in relation to individual viewers' lives and experiences. One of these living rooms belonged to Sally Donovan, a valued member of the adoption community, who entextualizes *her* experience of watching the documentary in the form of a blog post. This blog post, in turn, is shared by Jenny in a RwC in which she comments on *her* experience of, and reaction to, reading Donovan's blog post. Thus, we can see how actions and moments from the lives of care-experienced young people, many of which are quite distressing (such as Stacey being made to swallow soap and Liam breaking his wrist by punching a wall), travel through multiple cycles of decontextualization, entextualization and recontextualization, being defined and assigned value in different ways as they go. The following analysis of Jenny's RwC will focus on her recontextualization of *Sally Donovan's response* to the programme.

The content and author being retweeted in this example can be distinguished from those featured in Jenny's Tes retweet (Figure 17) in two important ways. First, Donovan is an independent author publishing to her own blog, without institutional support. Second, Donovan is an adopter herself and is situated firmly within the 'adoption Twitter' community, where her work is regularly shared, and she is regularly mentioned by other adopters. By posting a retweet that endorses Sally Donovan's blog content, Jenny therefore signals her alignment with, and support of, a respected and influential member of the adoption community to her audience of followers. Further, Jenny and Sally know one another personally and are on friendly terms; they often interact on Twitter and have met in person. Indeed, following on from this retweet, the two of them exchange a series of twelve replies (six tweets each) where they further discuss their experiences of being 'superparents' and their feelings about the 'Superkids' documentary. Given the relationship between these two women, and their extended interaction, Jenny is therefore signalling her alignment with Donovan not just to her audience of followers but also to Donovan herself, in a way that constructs and sustains a more individual connection between the two women. This connection relies not only on their shared experience as adoptive parents but also on their shared epistemological backgrounds as two experts and published authors who have a similar outlook and body of expertise on adoption and education-related issues.

Jenny begins her comment by taking an affective stance in relation to what she has read, through the words 'cried a bit at this'. Jenny's reference to crying is not a negative reaction to Donovan's post, but rather an echoing of both Donovan's and other carers' affective reactions to the 'Superkids' documentary. As Donovan explains in the second sentence of her blog post, many adopters, foster carers, kinship carers and guardians told her that 'being Superparents had left them . . . broken, exhausted and sad'. In the second clause of Jenny's opening line, 'but glad I read it anyway', Jenny expresses her affective response to Donovan's post itself, which contrasts with her unhappiness around the situation for 'superparents' and their children. As with the Tes retweet, Jenny's retweet of Sally Donovan can therefore be said to take affective connection as a starting point, foregrounding shared affective evaluations of adoptive (and foster) families' experiences.

The second part of Jenny's tweet, separated by a line of white space, moves from commentary on Donovan's post to an extension of it, acknowledging 'our collective response' but also calling for extended action that goes beyond this 'fleeting emotional spasm'. As in Jenny's Tes retweet, this call to action presupposes that her audience has a shared perspective on the issues raised by Donovan's post. Through her use of plural pronouns ('our', line 2; 'we', line 3), Jenny not only alludes to shared perspectives but also works to mobilize them, positioning herself as a spokesperson for her community. Her statements '#Superkids needs to be more than a fleeting emotional spasm' and 'if we really want to do right by these kids, then its going to take a lot more' function as a call to action for the adoption Twitter community. The call is driven by an appeal to morality, through Jenny's use of the deontic modals 'needs' and 'wants' and the binary ideal of doing the 'right' thing. Jenny also presupposes shared experience when she positions the proposed response to Superkids in relation to past responses, for example to Children in Need.[4] Thus, Jenny draws on a shared history of collective viewing, interpretation and response to public appeals, mobilizing her audience to channel their emotional energy into action.

In sum, Jenny's 'superkids' tweet takes the actions and affective responses of parents and carers such as herself, Sally Donovan and the wider adoption and fostering community, and mobilizes them as a tool for both connecting with others and appealing for collective action. In this way, the 'relentless parenting' and 'care' that Sally mentions in her blog post, as well as the tears and emotional response referenced by Jenny, become a tool for change. The retweet format, as in the previous example of Jenny's Tes retweet, allows Jenny to reference complex chains of entextualized actions in a condensed format. These actions include the distressing experiences of the young people featured in the documentary, their empowered entextualizations of these experiences, adoptive parents and foster carers' reactions to the documentary, and the parallels drawn between what they see on screen and their own families' actions and practices.

Taking down Anne Longfield

The final retweet is an example of a distinctive kind of 'rejection' retweet that I call the 'takedown thread' (see earlier explanation of retweet types). In this series of sixteen tweets, posted on 6 February 2019, Jenny begins by retweeting @C4Dispatches. This initial retweet-with-comment is displayed in Figure 21, whilst the original tweet by @C4Dispatches is shown in Figure 22.

@C4Dispatches is the Twitter account of a long-running UK investigative current affairs programme, which often involves undercover investigation and has sometimes unearthed ground-breaking findings of corruption, malpractice or illegal operations, especially by large organizations, institutions or groups who are of interest to the general public. C4 Dispatches' tweet (Figure 22) relates to the Dispatches episode aired on 4 February, called 'Skipping School – Britain's Invisible Kids', which offers an investigative report on home education in the UK. The tweet begins with a quote from the programme's interview with Anne Longfield, who was Children's Commissioner for England at the time, and ends with the claim that '@AnneLongfield is calling for a "complete overhaul" of the system'. The tweet also includes the video clip from the programme in which

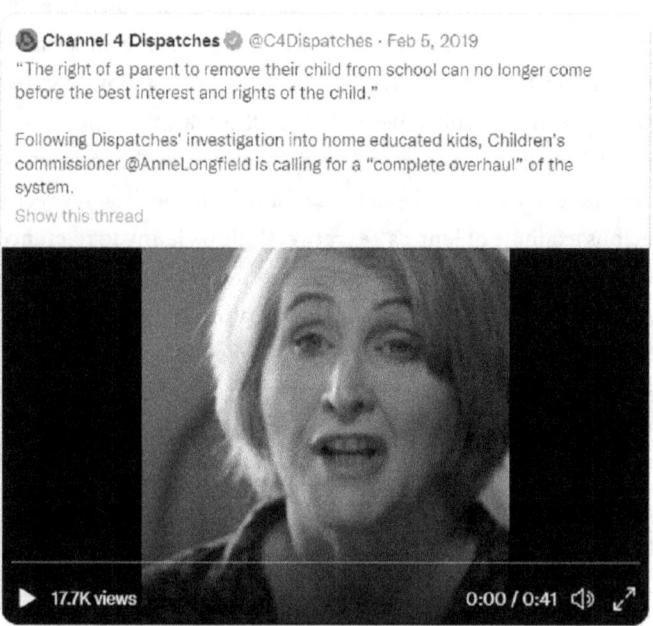

Figure 21 Jenny's initial retweet-with-comment (06.02.2019). Original tweet by @C4Dispatches (05.02.2019), @C4Dispatches tweet and image by Channel 4 © Channel 4 2019. Reproduced with the permission of Channel 4.

Longfield makes these statements. The argument being reproduced here is that in order to properly monitor and protect vulnerable young people, there has to be a better register of who is being educated at home. This issue is particularly relevant to adoptive parents, who often feel that state schools are unable to meet their children's complex needs (see Introduction and Chapter 3 for discussion of adoptive families' experiences), and it is particularly relevant to Jenny because she home-educates her son. Jenny also has a good deal of expertise in UK education, especially for adoptees and children in care, as a former teacher, an educational advisor for Adopter Network and the author of a book about supporting care-experienced children in the classroom. Given her expertise and

Introducing Epistemic Connection

Channel 4 Dispatches
@C4Dispatches

"The right of a parent to remove their child from school can no longer come before the best interest and rights of the child."

Following Dispatches' investigation into home educated kids, Children's commissioner @AnneLongfield is calling for a "complete overhaul" of the system.

Figure 22 Original tweet by @C4Dispatches (05.02.2019), @C4Dispatches tweet and image by Channel 4 © Channel 4 2019. Reproduced with the permission of Channel 4.

experience, Jenny is well placed to respond to this programme generally and Anne Longfield's words specifically. Jenny's full thread of sixteen tweets critiquing Longfield's statement has been transcribed and presented in Extract 10.

Extract 10. Full text of Jenny's takedown thread (06.02.2019)

Tweet 1

There is a lot to be concerned about in this comment by @annelongfield on @C4Dispatches. Let's take it line by line…

Tweet 2

"The current system needs completely over-hauling"

Yes, yet it does, when disadvantaged and SEND children are disproportionately excluded, off-rolling used to massage league table standings, 12% of adoptive parents told to remove child or face PEx, ECHPs not complied with etc.

Tweet 3
"Ultimately there has to be a register"
Oh wait, she's not talking about schools, she's talking about home ed! Well, that's a shocker – attempting to deal with massive failings towards some children by schools through a home ed register.
Really, who'd a thunk it?!

Tweet 4
"With the powers for local authorities to be able to visit, to see children, assess their education…"
LAs already have stat duty to identify children not receiving an education and to issue SAOs to force them back into school. What more is needed exactly?

Tweet 5
"… but also check their well-being"
And there we have it – inevitable spurious connection between home ed and safeguarding. Never mind that SCRs where home ed implicated almost universally cite child known to authorities but multiple failures to intervene. #NotInvisible

Tweet 6
"A lack of proper education is a real blight on a young life and there's a huge cost to society too"
As those whose children have been excluded, off-rolled, or forced out will no doubt confirm. Loss of earnings (and tax), mental health concerns and unmet SEND included.

Tweet 7
"So we need a real shift in thinking, where…"
Here it comes…

Tweet 8
"the right of a parent to be able to remove their child from school, and educate them as they see fit, no longer comes before the best interest and rights of the child"
Sounds so reasonable talking about the best interests and rights of children.

Tweet 9
But… "remove their child from school"? My children are electively home educated but many are not. For many, parents didn't choose to remove their

child, they felt forced to, or their child was put out of school. Many would love to find a suitable school for their child

Tweet 10

but there isn't one, or there are no spaces, or the LA won't pay for it. These children we're already not receiving a proper education, and families are sacrificing to try to provide one at their own cost while still contributing taxes towards the state education of their child

Tweet 11

should have been entitled to.
And what are the "best interests" of a child anyway? Who decides? We have generally assumed that parents decide what is in their children's best interests unless their is egregious failure when social services step in. Is this to change?

Tweet 12

Sorry *there!

Tweet 13

Let's be clear: Las can ALREADY step in if a child is not receiving a suitable education and issue a School Attendance Order. So, again, what extra power are needed here?
Children have a right to an education and current UK law places the responsibility on parents to secure

Tweet 14

That, whether by attendance at school or otherwise.
Do we propose to change that law?
Home educated children are #notinvisible.
Children are registered at birth. If they are removed from school, that is registered. They are registered with GPs, Dentists, etc.

Tweet 15

And if some unscrupulous parent manages to avoid all that registration, it is likely they'd be able to avoid your home ed register too.
State education needs to get its own house in order. If the DfE can do that, then thousands of children will re-appear on school rolls.

Tweet 16

Let's start solving our education problem please, rather than using failings as a smokescreen to denigrate families who are providing what the state, apparently, cannot, often at great personal cost. /end

As with the Tes RwC, Jenny's extended comment thread recontextualizes the post of an institution that is both widely known and respected, Channel 4, and more specifically, the Channel 4 programme Dispatches. Further, since the tweet mentions and contains the words of the (then) Children's Commissioner for England, Anne Longfield, Jenny can also be said to retweet Longfield herself, a powerful individual, with a powerful institution behind her. Through this RwC thread, Jenny therefore signals to her audience that she follows serious, political current affairs related to education and adoption, and stays up to date with current developments in educational policy and practice. Further, Jenny again shows that she has carefully engaged with the content shared in the original tweet (in this case, a video clip) by quoting and responding to excerpts throughout the thread. By using the 'reply' function to create a chain of connected tweets, Jenny is able to offer multiple comments that engage with the @C4Dispatches tweet in full. This takedown thread is also a neat display of her skill and confidence in using the affordances of Twitter to persuade and engage.

As well as retweeting C4 Dispatches, Jenny mentions both @C4Dispatches and @annelongfield in her own comment, further signalling who she is responding to and notifying both accounts of her commentary. This use of mentions lends a dialogic quality to her thread. However, given the unlikeliness that either account will respond (they both represent large institutions and do not have a known relationship with Jenny), the mentions may function more as a signal to Jenny's followers that she is addressing these powerful figures head-on, as more of a 'staged' dialogue (Gruber, 2017) than a genuine attempt to engage in conversation with them. Jenny sustains this staged dialogic quality throughout the thread, with nine of her sixteen tweets including a quote from the interview clip, followed by her own response. Often these responses seem to address Longfield directly, as if the two of them are engaged in a face-to-face conversation. For example, in the second tweet, Jenny follows a quote from Anne Longfield with the response 'Yes, yes it does . . .', signalling agreement with her statement that 'the current system needs completely overhauling'.

Jenny's opening statement, 'there is a lot to be concerned about in this comment' (tweet 1), makes her oppositional position clear from the start. Nevertheless, her statement represents a more controlled, professional and detached expression of negative affect than we see in the Tes and Sally Donovan retweets. Following this statement with 'Let's take it line by line' further signals that this thread will not be an emotive or knee-jerk response but a measured, critical engagement with the specifics of Longfield's claims. Jenny continues to adopt this relatively detached, focused and professional stance throughout the thread, for example through her use of statistics ('12% of adoptive parents . . .') and specialist terminology, including acronyms ('SEND children are disproportionately excluded, off-rolling used to massage league table standings') in her second tweet. In this way, Jenny constructs her tweets as a series of measured counter-claims, meeting expert commentary with expert commentary. Indeed, paired with Longfield's statements, Jenny's rebuttals arguably come across as *more* authoritative and expert, given that Longfield, in the quoted statements, does not evidence her claims in the way Jenny does. Through the construction of an extended comment thread, Jenny is therefore able to address and reframe several key assumptions around the relationship between home education and mainstream education that are presented in the C4 Dispatches programme. This reframing takes an epistemological perspective that is markedly different from Longfield's, placing the onus on educational institutions and authorities to include and provide adequate provision for adopted children, rather than to scrutinize home-educators.

The detailed, specific and expert rebuttal that Jenny presents in her thread prepares the ground for her final appeal to Longfield, and the broader systems of which she is a part (specifically the Department for Education), in tweets 15 and 16. As with her call to action in the Donovan retweet, Jenny uses imperatives and deontic modality to position her call as a moral imperative, in the statements 'state education needs to get its own house in order' and 'let's start solving our education problem please'. Here, as before, Jenny positions herself as a spokesperson for her community, and her tweet can be read as a form of activism that mobilizes adoptive parents' experiences and expertise to effect real change in the systems their children move through and rely upon. However, in this instance she is calling for *institutions* to effect change, rather than adoptive parents themselves.

Jenny signals from the start of this thread that she is bringing her wider audience of followers with her, almost as co-collaborators in the construction of this takedown thread, through the inclusive pronoun 'let's' in 'let's take it line by line' (tweet 1). Throughout the thread, Jenny then moves between calculated, formal, evidence-based statements that are directed at Longfield and more informal, 'knowing' gestures of collective action and understanding, which are directed at her audience of followers. For example, Jenny's third tweet begins with Longfield's quoted statement 'ultimately there has to be a register', followed by a comment which refers to Longfield in the third person: 'Oh wait, she's not talking about schools, she's talking about home ed!' This comment has a distinctly less formal style than other parts of Jenny's commentary, with the conversational interjection 'oh wait' and the closing exclamation mark giving the impression that she is now addressing those 'in the know' – her intended audience of adoptive and home-schooling parents. Jenny uses a similar conversational style throughout her third tweet, for example in the phrases 'well, that's a shocker' and 'who'd a thunk it?!'. As phrases that index sarcasm through hyperbolic surprise in British English, these words have the effect of mocking Longfield and implying that the creation of a home education register is a foolishly simplistic way of trying to solve significant, deep-rooted problems with the education system. The expressions also point to the obviousness of Longfield's words, implying (as she does in the Tes retweet) that her long-suffering audience will emit a collective groan at this disappointingly predictable stance. Jenny's iterative style-switching further sustains the impression that this takedown thread is a 'staged' dialogue that has been written, at least in part, for the benefit of her followers.

The presumption of shared experience in these community-facing comments echoes the tone of Jenny's Tes retweet, in which she also pointed to adoptive parents' wearied lack of surprise at having their children overlooked by common educational practices and perspectives. This underlying message of solidarity is perhaps most apparent in the seventh tweet to the thread, in which Jenny implies that Longfield's gambit is entirely predictable by quoting the first part of her statement, 'So we need a real shift in thinking, where . . .', followed by the interjection 'Here it comes . . .', before completing Longfield's statement in tweet 8. Through this anticipatory interjection, Jenny brings her audience of followers with her in this line-by-line critique, implying that their experiences and perspectives will be so closely aligned with her own that they, like her, will anticipate Longfield's words before they have been uttered. This RwC therefore provides a further example in which Jenny constructs and mobilizes the intersecting collective and epistemic dimensions of connected parenting, this time in a way that adds weight to her critical recontextualization of Anne Longfield's policies and perspectives. The thread format offers a particularly effective tool for recontextualizing Longfield's statements through an alternative epistemological lens and gives Jenny the space to bring her audience of adopters with her in an apparently collective challenge to this perspective.

Chapter summary

This chapter has introduced epistemic connection as the second dimension of connected parenting. It began by showing how a relational perspective has been deployed in previous studies of information-sharing and knowledge-construction practices in online health and parenting groups. It also introduced key concepts from this body of work that feed into the concept of epistemic connection, most notably *connected knowing* and *connective action*.

The case study of this chapter focuses on Jenny's use of Twitter to recontextualize, and sometimes challenge and reinterpret, expert and institutional knowledge and information within a network of adoptive and home-educating parents. The in-depth analysis of three evaluative retweets-with-comments has revealed several key insights. The first two analyses show how Jenny uses the retweet function to pit different epistemological perspectives against one another and to unite her audience in shared opposition to an institutional stance. The final analysis shows how the retweet format allows Jenny to entextualize, and subsequently mobilize, complex chains of intersecting actions and practices in an appeal for collective action and systematic change that will benefit care-experienced young people and their families. Together, these analyses show how Jenny is able to mobilize connection, knowledge and action to engage in social advocacy and activism that has the potential to benefit the communities to which she belongs.

Across the tweets analysed in this chapter, Jenny deploys strategies of collectivization, argumentation and 'staged' dialogue to challenge institutional perspectives and practices, and to valorize the epistemological perspectives that she and her followers are presumed to share. This strategy relies upon and consolidates a combination of epistemic and collective connection between Jenny and her audience, a strong sense of togetherness and solidarity that is forged through collective knowledge, experiences and perspectives. The analyses of this chapter have also begun to show how the epistemic and affective dimensions of connected parenting are intertwined. For example, Jenny's opposition to institutional practices and viewpoints are underpinned by collective expressions of rage, frustration and sadness at the inequalities and disadvantages that arise for adoptive and home-educating families. This affective dimension of connected parenting will be further elaborated in Chapters 7 and 8.

6

Elaborating Epistemic Connection

In the previous chapter, I introduced *epistemic connection*, which is centred on information sharing and knowledge construction, as the second dimension of connected parenting. This chapter showed that epistemic connection is a particularly significant practice for Jenny and Rachael, two single parents who are very well connected, active and influential members of their networks. The case study in Chapter 5 examined epistemic connection in relation to Jenny's digital media practices, looking at how she maintains a sense of solidarity and togetherness with her audience of followers on Twitter through presuppositions of shared knowledge, experiences and perspectives. This chapter also showed how Jenny mobilizes these epistemic connections to appeal for collective action that has the potential to effect systemic change. In the present chapter, I build on these explorations through a second case study that focuses on Rachael, a single woman who used donor conception and in vitro fertilization (IVF) to conceive her infant daughter. After introducing Rachael, I provide an overview of the photo-sharing app that will be the focus for this chapter's analyses: *Instagram*. I then consider how Rachael selects moments from her own life and recontextualizes them in the form of shareable knowledge, information and advice in her Instagram posts. Through this analysis, I show how Rachael drives forward new ways of understanding family relations and practices. Further, I continue to foreground the ways in which practices of epistemic connection overlap with the collective and affective domains of connected parenting in Rachael's digital media engagement.

Introducing Rachael

Rachael is a 40-year-old single heterosexual parent who conceived her daughter with the help of donor insemination and IVF. Like many UK-based women who have conceived children in this way, Rachael describes herself as a 'solo mum'. When we first met, Rachael told me about her journey to solo motherhood. She explained that after the sudden end of an engagement in her late twenties, she hoped for many years to meet a man and start a family together. In her mid-thirties, however, Rachael began to fear that if she waited any longer it would be too late and started to think about becoming a mother on her own. She gave birth to her daughter Poppy, now a young infant, when she was thirty-nine. Rachael has worked in business and human resources for most of her adult life, but in 2019, becoming a solo mum inspired her to start a new company, *Going Solo*, which combines her passion for business with her commitment to supporting other solo mums (see further discussion of Rachael's situation in Mackenzie, 2021).

As part of her *Going Solo* venture, Rachael runs a Facebook group for solo mums, as well as a blog, podcast and Instagram account where she regularly posts advice and information. She also offers mentorship and coaching services to single women, and consultancy to organizations such as fertility clinics. The popularity and reach of *Going Solo* mean that Rachael is particularly well connected within a number of intersecting solo mum, infertility and single-parent networks. She largely uses her platform and influence to write about her everyday life as a solo mum, sharing her own story as a way of reaching out to, and inspiring, others. By sharing her experiences online, Rachael explains, she hopes to show prospective solo mums they are not alone and that solo motherhood 'is 100 per cent normal'. Rachael conceptualizes her online sharing and networking as a form of social action and activism, a way of normalizing and correcting the stigma around solo motherhood within a social context that privileges hetero-biological nuclear families. Epistemic connection is therefore a particularly significant dimension of Rachael's digital media engagement, through which she seeks to both challenge and shift common conceptions of solo motherhood and collaboratively construct new ways of understanding parenthood and families.

Rachael considers herself lucky to have a strong support network, and her immediate family (especially her mum) plays a very important role in her life. She primarily uses mobile messaging apps (WhatsApp and Messenger) to stay connected with close friends and family, and social networking sites (Instagram and Facebook) to connect with wider groups, communities and networks of parents, especially solo mums. A key difference between Rachael's network and the networks of other single (adoptive) parents such as Cheryl and Lynne is that Rachael distinguishes more sharply between the role different individuals and groups play in her life. For example, she explained in our second interview that her wider family, brother Dave, friends she met at school ('school friends') and friends she met whilst working in Africa ('Africa friends') primarily offer fun, whilst her mum and dad mainly provide practical help. On the other hand, Rachael usually turns to groups that are directly connected with her business and experiences as a solo mum, such as the National Childbirth Trust (NCT) group, Millburn solo mums, Going Solo (GS) mum tribe and Team Titan (a group of fertility and health professionals and activists based in the North of England), for information and networking. In Cheryl and Lynne's networks, by contrast, adoptive parents play a key role across all of these domains. Figure 23, Rachael's 'forms of support' diagram, offers a visual illustration of these distinctions. However, despite the distinction between subgroups in her network, there is significant overlap between Rachael's professional and personal life. This overlap is very apparent in her use of the *Going Solo* Instagram account to engage simultaneously with her established family and friends alongside the wider solo mum community, as well as some of the institutions and organizations that solo mums and related groups are likely to engage with, such as fertility clinics and maternity services.

Rachael regularly posts to her *Going Solo* blog, Facebook page and Instagram account, but this chapter focuses on her use of Instagram. This is the platform she posts to most frequently, which has the largest number of followers, and the most evidence of engagement with others (measured in terms of likes and

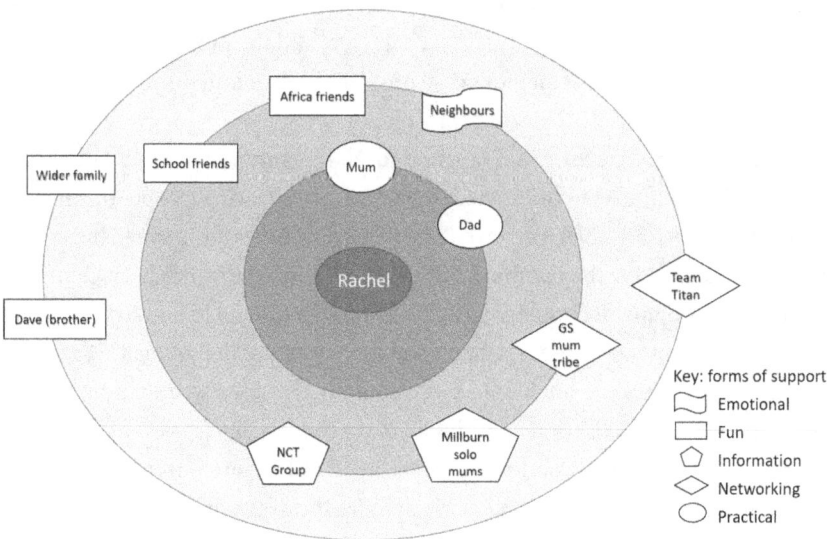

Figure 23 Rachael's forms of support diagram.

comments). At the time of data collection, Rachael's Instagram account had 1,091 followers, whilst her Facebook page had 299. Further, when she shared the same posts to both sites, her Instagram posts consistently garnered more evidence of engagement. For example, an almost identical post about going for a walk with her brother, shared in May 2018, received seventy-eight reactions (likes) on Instagram but only thirty-two reactions (either 'like' or 'love') on Facebook.

Instagram, self-representation and the intensification of parenting experience

Instagram has been described as 'a photo application . . . that allows users to take, edit and share pictures and videos with their social networks or the general public' (Poulsen, 2018, p. 122). At the time of writing (March 2022), this popular and culturally significant photoblogging app, now owned by Meta, had reached over two billion monthly active users (Statista, 2022b). On opening an account, Instagram users create a profile, which can include a picture, name, username and short biography ('bio') explaining who they are and/or what their account is for. To create a standard post, Instagram users take a photo or video within the app or select from the existing photo library stored on their mobile device. Individuals can edit and add filters or effects to the photo or video, add a written caption and hashtag(s), tag people and add a location. Others can interact with the post through 'liking' or 'commenting'. Instagram currently limits photo and video captions to a maximum of 2,200 characters and the number of hashtags to 30. Each photo/video that an individual posts in the standard format is displayed on their timeline, below their user information.

Instagram's architecture has a good deal in common with Twitter (see Chapter 5). First, users curate their newsfeed by following people of interest. Followers' posts are then displayed on the user's rolling timeline. Instagram users can also deploy the mention–hashtag–repost triad that has been central to Twitter's development. Hashtags and reposts, however, tend to be used in slightly different ways on Instagram. Hashtags still serve the function of making content searchable, but they are often used more liberally and consistently in Instagram posts, especially by corporate and influential accounts. Instagram hashtags are usually positioned at the end of a caption, so that they are obscured when the post is seen in a user's feed; some users achieve the same effect by placing them in a separate comment (Leaver, Highfield, & Abidin, 2020, p. 26). Instagram users can also follow hashtags, so that popular posts deploying their chosen hashtags will also be displayed on their timeline. The third function, reposting, is not (at the time of writing) built into Instagram's participatory structure in the same way as retweeting on Twitter. Nevertheless, Instagram users deploy innovative strategies for reposting others' content to their own timelines, as they did in Twitter's early development, for example by using external apps or by sharing screenshots of others' posts.

Despite the features it shares with Twitter, Instagram's formal, aesthetic and social design and functions make it a distinctive social networking platform in a number of respects. Most notably, Instagram has a markedly visual character. Much of the literature exploring this platform's history, technologies and sociocultural status has focused on Instagram's tools for creating and sustaining these aesthetics. For example, Tiidenberg (2018), Wargo (2017) and Zappavigna (2016) have attended to the photographic genres that have been popularized through Instagram, especially selfies. Digital filters, which have been part of Instagram's key affordances from the outset, have been described as the most prominent of Instagram's photo production tools (Poulsen, 2018). This feature not only supports the rapid creation of professional-looking photographs but can also imbue those images with specific meanings (Leaver et al., 2020; Poulsen, 2018). For example, many of Instagram's early filters created a 'retro' look, which has been said to induce feelings of nostalgia (Bartholeyns, 2014) or to 'rende[r] more poignant the present moment' (Zappavigna, 2016, p. 286). These filters are extremely powerful tools for creating visually appealing photographs that are suffused with layers of cultural meaning.

Another distinctive feature of Instagram's character, which is intertwined with its visual aesthetic, is its emphasis on intensive self-representation. For example, the heightened opportunities for digitally manipulating photographs make it possible for photobloggers to engage in processes of continual self-improvement, whereby the self is treated as a project, or resource, to be worked upon, improved and subsequently shared with others as a form of bonding and identity work (van Dijck, 2008). This culture is not unique to Instagram; rather, as van Dijck (2008, p. 62) has argued, it is connected with a wider cultural trend towards the 'individualization and intensification of experience' through digital photography, apps and networks. Jones' (2009) exploration of digital photography as a 'technology of entextualization' is a useful extension of van Dijck's (2008) arguments around the social functions of digital photography from a mediated discourse analytical perspective. Like van Dijck (2008), Jones (2009, p. 293) has pointed to the intensification of everyday, ordinary experience through digital photography, which can make even the most mundane occasions into significant '"events" to be entextualized' (see discussion in Chapter 1).

From Instagram's visual and self-representational character, a culture of self-branding, promotion and commercialization has arisen over time. Leaver et al. (2020, p. 1) suggest this culture has largely been driven by a 'new class of content creators' called *influencers*. An influencer is a type of micro-celebrity who 'court[s] online fame' through 'positive self-branding strategies', 'groom[s] followers to consume their content aspirationally' and 'can parlay their high internet visibility into an income that is lucrative for a full-time career' (Leaver et al., 2020, pp. 4–5; also see Abidin, 2018). Influencers monetize their audiences by cultivating a high 'follower-to-following rati[o]', producing sponsored posts and messages, and engaging with others in a way that is designed for 'maximum visibility and reach' (Leaver et al. 2020, p. 3). Further, groups of influencers often create informal networks, or 'instapods', who share, promote and amplify one another's accounts through mutual engagement with posts, promotion of products and services and participation in 'public thanks and acknowledgements' known as 'shout-outs' (Leaver et al., 2020, p. 14; also see Abidin, 2018). Through these strategies, influencers have made a significant contribution to the commercialization of Instagram (Leaver et al. 2020, p. 3). The platform's rich range of resources for sharing, but comparably limited tools for interacting, further enables this culture, putting control in the hands of the content creator and contributing to an 'asymmetrical relationship between users' (Poulsen, 2018, p. 18).

In the past decade, a number of researchers have examined issues around visual self-representation, the intensification of everyday experience, self-branding and commercialization in the context of parenting and motherhood. This research has shown that photoblogs are more than just a vehicle for conveying parents' experiences; they have become integral to the performance, maintenance and intensification of ideals around pregnancy, parenting and motherhood themselves. Seko and Tiidenberg (2016), for example, show how the online sharing of women's ultrasound images can acquire social currency as symbols of expectant mothers' authenticity, their transitional identities and their status as 'good mothers'. Further, Le Moignan et al. (2017) have suggested that the public sharing of family photography can increase the pressure on women to display good parenting and maternal confidence, and to maintain dominant norms of 'happy' family life. Locatelli's (2017) analysis of breastfeeding images on Instagram, similarly, shows that the representation of breastfeeding on this site often maintains normative ideals of infant feeding. However, along with other studies of parent-related photo sharing on Instagram (e.g. Marcon, Bieber, & Azad,

2019; Zappavigna & Zhao, 2017), Locatelli (2017) has also shown that Instagram representations can contribute to new ways of understanding family practices. For example, some of the breastfeeding images that she examined contribute to the normalization of public breastfeeding, offer new kinds of support for breastfeeding parents and empower mothers through the affirmation of shared experience. This chapter contributes to research in this area by considering how Rachael promotes and legitimizes solo mothering practices on Instagram.

Rachael's use of Instagram

Rachael first posted to her *Going Solo* Instagram account on 7 March 2018. As of 1 April 2019, the end point of my data collection, she had 1,091 followers and had shared 172 posts in total. Her account remains public, which means anyone with internet access can find and follow her account and posts by visiting her page. Rachael's audience of followers includes friends and family, parents and prospective parents in the wider solo mum and (in)fertility communities, and other organizations that provide services and support to these groups, including fertility clinics.

As explained previously, one of Rachael's key motivations for using social media in relation to her *Going Solo* business is to share her personal experiences in an effort to support other single women, normalize solo motherhood as a valued and legitimate family form and address sociocultural stigma and misunderstanding around solo motherhood. Further, because Rachael is shaping and promoting her business *through* her first-hand experience as a solo mum, its success is highly dependent on encouraging others to get to know her on a personal level. Rachael thus very explicitly ties her Instagram account to her personal life and image, working to *show* others what solo motherhood looks like. This focus on self is apparent on first glance at Rachael's Instagram data: fifty-nine of these posts contain an image of Rachael and/or her daughter Poppy, either alone or with other family, friends and colleagues; thirty-five contain 'text posts' (large, stylized text in image form) featuring inspirational words written by Rachael under the *Going Solo* brand; and thirty-one contain links to other written or audio content either authored by Rachael or heavily featuring her words. Instagram's culture of self-representation and promotion is thus likely to be a key factor in Rachael's preference for this platform over others such as Twitter and Facebook.

Rachael's use of Instagram to shape the identity and scope of her business has several parallels with the practices of Instagram 'influencers' that have been discussed in the previous section. For example, Rachael's emphasis on her own identity and experience as a solo mum can be seen as a form of 'positive self-branding' (Leaver et al. 2020, p. 4) that ties her business closely to her personal life. Rachael also works to curate both formal and informal networks of contacts who can support one another's endeavours, for example through promoting one another's products and services, participating in 'shout-outs' (Leaver et al. 2020, p. 14) and collaborating with others to create relevant events, services and content. For example, many of Rachael's posts from March 2019 promote 'TalkFertility', a network of fertility experts in the North of England, including Rachael, with whom she collaboratively organized several events and media publications. However, Rachael's account is not popular enough to be described as significantly influential, and her goals are not entirely consistent with those of an influencer. For example, she does not aim to make money from online activities themselves and as such does not engage with advertising and paid promotion practices. Instead, Rachael uses her Instagram account, alongside her Facebook page, group and blog, to network and build her *Going Solo* business, which in turn generates income through paid coaching, classes and consultancy.

I collected data from Rachael's *Going Solo* Instagram account between the period 1 April 2018 to 1 April 2019, during which time Rachael published 156 posts (including reposts). In these posts, Rachael shares details of her life as a solo mum, both in image–caption combinations and through links to her written and audio content from the *Going Solo* blog, podcast and other websites. She also occasionally reposts material relating to fertility, solo motherhood and parenting from other Instagram users, and signposts her readers to relevant events, networks and products. In her own posts, Rachael tends to favour long-form captions with a large number of hashtags: the average length of captions in her March 2019 posts, for example, was 175 words, and the average number of hashtags was 14. These figures indicate that despite Instagram's visual character, written text is an important component of Rachael's posts, functioning as more than just a label for her photos and videos.

Rachael's Instagram data can be broadly categorized into four types: experiential sharing, cross-platform promotion, inspirational quotes and shout-outs. Definitions and examples of these types are detailed in Table 12. There is significant overlap, however, between the content of these post types. Most notably, nearly all of Rachael's posts include some form of experiential content. For example, her inspirational quotes often include some experiential content in the caption, which positions the quote in relation to Rachael's personal experience. Rachael's cross-platform promotions, too – especially those directing readers to blog posts, articles and podcasts she has authored herself – usually focus on Rachael's experiences.

Table 12 Rachael's Instagram Post Types

Type	Number	Description	Example
Experiential sharing	49	Sharing everyday experiences, actions and moments in Rachael's life	Image: Caption: 'Morning cuddles with my little lady! Nothing makes me happier in the morning! She's even started putting her arm round me!'
Cross-platform promotion	48	Redirecting traffic to a blog, podcast, website or face-to-face events that Rachael has produced or co-produced. Includes promotion of *Going Solo's* classes and services	Image: Caption: 'it took me more than 4 years of consideration to come to the decision to start on the journey of becoming a solo mum. Part of this was struggling with letting go of the idea of finding a partner to share the journey with, but part of it was the feelings of embarrassment and shame when I compared myself to others around me. In this blog post I share how I worked through these feelings to finally make the best decision I have ever made to go for it! Head over to the link in my bio to see this latest blog post'

Table 12 (Continued)

Type	Number	Description	Example
Inspirational quotes	37	Stylized text with inspirational content, distilling a piece of advice under the *Going Solo* brand. Around half of these posts were inspired by a special event, theme or day, e.g. the theme of 'loneliness', Valentine's Day, or International Women's Day	Image: [image of woman holding sparkler with text "EMPOWERED WOMEN MAKE THINGS HAPPEN FOR THEMSELVES. YOU HAVE CHOICES. TAKE CONTROL AND EXPLORE YOUR OPTIONS."] Caption: 'if you are a single lady, and worried about your fertility as you are reaching a certain age. If you'd like to start a family, there are different options available for you. Contact me at Rachael@goingsolo.com to talk through those options. More information available on my website, link in bio.'
Shout-outs	22	Pointing to others' products, services or content	Image: [Fertility Fest 2019 poster] Caption: 'So excited to be part of the #solomum panel. If you're in the Millburn area come along and join us xxxx'

Further, Rachael's 'shout-outs', especially those posted in the first half of the data collection period (April 2018–September 2018), also tend to focus on Rachael's own experience of using others' products and services, such as baby slings, clothes or books. Posts categorized as 'experiential sharing', however, are distinctive in that they focus exclusively on moments, actions and events in Rachael's life, and do not include inspirational quotes, cross-platform promotion or shout-outs.

In the sections that follow, I analyse two posts that are typical of Rachael's 'experiential sharing'. In this type of post, Rachael shares an aspect of her day-to-day experience, usually a specific action, event or series of actions or events, and entextualizes it in a post comprised of a photograph(s) and text-based caption. I focus on this category for two reasons: first, this is the most common type of post in the data set. Indeed, as noted earlier, the majority of Rachael's posts across the four category types include some element of experiential content. Second, looking at posts where Rachael shares her own experiences will facilitate a quite different exploration of epistemic connection than that of the previous chapter, which examined Jenny's retweets of *others'* content. Several themes recur across Rachael's experiential posts, but I focus here on those that exemplify two particularly common themes in this subset of data: 'self-care' and 'male influences'. In the analysis that follows, I consider how Rachael selects actions, moments or events that relate to these themes, and the mediational means she deploys to recontextualize them in the form of shareable knowledge, information and advice.

Entextualizing a Friday night drink

As noted in the previous section, there are several recurring themes in Rachael's 'experiential sharing' Instagram posts. The post I will examine in this section relates to the theme of *self-care*. Rachael's self-care posts make reference to indulgent, pleasurable and/or healthy activities that are associated with well-being, leisure, fun, relaxation and 'good times'. They tend to convey the message that Rachael is able to care for herself and tend to her personal needs whilst simultaneously creating positive experiences for her young daughter (or at least, without detriment to her daughter). For example, one post (dated 19.04.2018) contains a photograph of Rachael in the woods, walking towards the camera and carrying her daughter Poppy in a sling, with the accompanying caption 'it's so good being able to get exercise as well as bond with baby'. Another post (dated 05.02.2019) includes a full-length 'mirror selfie' of Rachael in her home, with a caption explaining that she had her fringe trimmed in her lunch break and offering her 'top tip' to 'utilise

Figure 24 'A little taste of Friday night' (29.03.2019).

lunch breaks for tasks that need to be child free'. In this section, I examine a self-care post which includes a photograph of Rachael at a bar, with a large glass of wine in her hand, and a caption that directly addresses her followers, urging them to 'pick a child friendly [bar] and get involved'. This image–text combination is shown in Figure 24, with the anonymized caption transcribed in full in Extract 11.

Extract 11. 'A little taste of Friday night' caption

1. Top tip for solo mums on a Friday night…
2. The sun is shining, people are filling the bars with after work drinks. Pick a child
3. friendly one and get involved.
4. Poppy and I have come with @LittleJune to have a cheeky vino (me not Poppy) after
5. work before the bedtime routine commences!!
6. It feels like you've had a little taste of a Friday night and caught the last few rays.
   .
   .
   .
   .
7. #solomum #singlemombychoice #singlemumbychoice #singlemotherbychoice
8. #ivfjourney #donorconception #singlewomen #mumlife #coach #lifecoach #smc
9. #fridaynightdrinks

In this post, Rachael takes a specific event – an early evening drink in a local bar, accompanied by her mum June (tagged as @LittleJune) and one-year-old daughter Poppy – and uses it as a tool for connecting with other solo mums on Instagram. Rachael's use of her public Instagram account to share this experience increases the visibility of the post amongst her target audience, so that her actions can be widely seen, shared, approved and possibly repeated. She also uses a series of twelve hashtags to enhance this visibility, as she does with most of her Instagram posts. Rachael's choice of hashtags, nine of which reference motherhood, single motherhood or conception, shapes both her audience and the type of connections she makes with that audience. This connection combines both *collective* and *epistemic* dimensions, since Rachael positions herself as a solo mum who is sharing practical, relatable 'tips' and knowledge resources with other solo mums like her. The post received seventy-five 'likes', each of which may encode a range of meanings but which certainly work to affirm Rachael's connection with other solo mums and to validate and legitimize her entextualization of a very specific version of the 'Friday night drink'.

Rachael's Friday night drink is neatly entextualized in the phrase 'a little taste of a Friday night' (line 6). There is particular emphasis, in both the image and text, on the action of drinking a glass of wine – a 'cheeky vino' (line 4) – which is positioned in the centre of the photograph and held forward, so that it appears larger in the frame. The 'little taste' can be read as both a reference to the taste of the wine and a metonymic reference to the broader action of going out on a Friday night. Through these linguistic and visual means, Rachael's Friday night drink – a single glass of white wine – is imbued with specific meaning. The large size of the glass points to indulgence, wealth and fun, which is further emphasized in the description of the wine as 'cheeky' (and therefore fun and frivolous). At the same time, 'cheeky' and 'little' point to moderation, showing that Rachael's drinking happens within the parameters of 'appropriate' motherhood – she is not getting drunk or spending extended time in a bar. Further, her use of 'vino', a word that is commonly borrowed from Spanish/Italian in British English but tends to be used more informally than 'wine', may further contribute to connotations of fun, frivolity and indulgence whilst at the same time distancing Rachael from the act of drinking alcohol.

Rachael's post recontextualizes her Friday night drink as a set of repeatable actions and advises her audience to repeat these actions. For example, she positions the post as a 'top tip for solo mums' (line 1) from the outset and directly implores her audience to repeat her actions through the imperatives in '*pick* a child friendly [bar] and *get* involved' (lines 2–3). Further, the shift in pronoun referent, from 'I' in line 4 to 'you' in line 6, positions her audience as potential reproducers of this action, marking a shift from *Rachael's* action of having a drink at her local 'child friendly' bar on a Friday night to the *reader's* potential reproduction of the same action in their local setting.

Rachael further encourages her audience to repeat this specific variety of indulgent but moderate activity by drawing on tools that entextualize it in a romanticized and nostalgic way. For example, she appeals to her audience's senses in her references to the light and heat of the bar in lines 2 – 'the sun is shining' – and 6 – 'caught the last few rays'. The metaphors of 'catching' the sun's rays and 'tasting' Friday night encompass touch and taste, as well as suggesting that Rachael has employed singular time management and social skills, in order to participate in this fleeting moment of fun and indulgence. In the photograph, it appears Rachael has used a filter that enhances the vivid blue and cyan in the foreground (Rachael's ring and coat), and the sepia tones in the background (the floor, walls, woodwork and glass of beer in the top right corner). Such vintage aesthetics are well established on Instagram, with retro filters dominating the platform's early collection and remaining at the core of their repository. Zappavigna (2016, p. 286) suggests that this type of filter can have the effect of 'rendering more poignant the banal, everyday present moment' and that certainly seems to be the case here. The setting also has some culturally specific resonance; for example, the large glass of wine is a trope used frequently in British advertising and television to index 'good times' and leisure. Further, the wooden bar, tiled floor and sandwich board are all icons of traditional British pubs, which again represent sites of leisure, socializing and fun. Together, these visual and linguistic means appeal to a sense of nostalgia and pleasure, entextualizing this moment in a way that is typical of a cultural trend towards individualized, intensified expressions of experience through digital photography (see previous discussion; van Dijck, 2008).

There is a potential conflict between the Friday night drink and the culturally idealized role of the 'good' mother, especially the good *single* mother. Drinking on a Friday evening is a culturally specific adult activity in the UK, often taking place (as Rachael notes in line 2) with colleagues immediately after work and sometimes continuing late into the night. It involves a number of actions that may be deemed inappropriate for young children to witness: namely drinking alcohol and all the uninhibited behaviours this may entail. On the other hand, being seen as a 'good' mother, as I have shown in my previous work (Mackenzie, 2017, 2018, 2019), entails a high level of responsibility and a commitment to putting children's needs first. Getting drunk with or in front of children, and/or taking children into 'adult' settings where people are drunk or behaving unpredictably, can therefore be associated with 'bad' motherhood (see Harding, Whittingham, & McGannon, 2021, on the complex relationships between motherhood and alcohol consumption). The image of a *single* mother drinking in a pub or bar is particularly loaded, being tied to negative stereotypes of problematic and irresponsible single motherhood that are associated with young, working-class women in particular (Mackenzie, 2021). It seems that Rachael is very aware of these connotations, and as such, negotiates a careful balance between encouraging other single mothers to enjoy an 'adult' experience, reliving the things they used to do before having children but at the same time fulfilling the normative expectations of 'good' motherhood. In her advice to others, she therefore specifies that the chosen bar should be 'child friendly' and draws attention to the time (early evening) in a number of ways. For example, she mentions that 'the sun is shining', that people are just starting to 'fill' the bars 'after work' (line 2) and that her visit takes place 'before the bedtime routine' (line 5). Rachael's reference to the bedtime routine has the dual effect of both emphasizing the early hour and drawing attention to her careful management of Poppy's life. Further, Rachael draws attention to the *smallness* of the event: by labelling the wine 'cheeky' and a 'little taste', she clarifies that it does not involve extended drinking or time in a bar. She also jokingly specifies that it's not her daughter who was drinking ('me not Poppy', line 4). In all, Rachael makes it clear that she prioritizes her child's well-being, sleep and routine, and that her own self-indulgence does not disrupt this. Rather, by doing the 'Friday night drink' within a specific set of parameters, Rachael is able to have the best of both worlds.

Overall, through her entextualization of a carefully managed Friday night drink for an audience of solo mums, Rachael recontextualizes her actions as a useful knowledge resource for other mums to reproduce in their own lives. Further, she inscribes those actions with specific values: namely, that single mothers *can* 'have it all', but that self-indulgent or 'adult' activities are only acceptable when they take place within specific, child-centred parameters. If Rachael's followers do take her advice, they are potentially not just repeating her actions but taking up all the values around self-care, appropriate single motherhood and 'having it all' that come with it. In the context of Rachael's business, through which she aims to support and encourage other solo mums, her entextualization of the Friday night drink sends out the reassuring message that solo mums need not give up the things they enjoyed doing before they had children or which coupled parents may access more easily. In 'self-care' posts like this, Rachael therefore offers solo mums specific, repeatable actions that may be able to quell worries of loss or deficiency. By doing so, she suggests that solo mums can have a happy and fulfilling family life by adapting their existing practices through careful thought and planning.

Entextualizing a walk in the forest

A second prominent theme in Rachael's experiential sharing posts is *male influences*. Posts focusing on this theme tend to feature at least one male friend or family member engaging in some kind of action or activity with Poppy (and sometimes also Rachael). The captions generally point to the significance of these figures as 'male role models' in Poppy's life and emphasize their regular and physically close contact. For example, one 'male influences' post (shared on 16.09.18) features a close-up photograph of a male friend carrying Poppy in a sling, with their faces close together. They are looking at one another and smiling, and the caption explains that 'Poppy is so lucky to have so many excellent male role models in her life'. A second post (shared on 04.12.2018) includes a series of images, each featuring Poppy with a different male friend or family member, with the caption explaining that 'I am surrounded by awesome male role models for her', so 'I don't worry that she will miss out on male interaction'. In each of these images, the men are either holding Poppy or sitting very close to her, engaging in joint actions such as reading a book, playing with a toy or sitting in a jacuzzi. In two of the images, Poppy is looking directly at the men's faces and reaching out to touch their facial hair.

Before examining her *male influences* posts, it is important to acknowledge that Rachael is writing for an audience of solo mums who have likely faced 'charges of selfishness' for consciously 'depriving' their child of a father (Mendonça, 2018, p. 19; see Introduction). In our first interview, for example, Rachael talked about some of the negative comments that had been directed towards her online, with some suggesting she was 'selfish' for using donor conception as a single woman or that 'every child deserves to be brought into the world knowing who their father is' (see Mackenzie, 2021, for more detailed discussion of this issue). Rachael also suggested that feelings of guilt around 'bringing a child into the world without a father' were a common theme in her coaching sessions with single women. As a counterpoint to these concerns, however, Rachael has suggested, both in our interviews and in her digital content, that solo mums can actually be in a better position than heterosexually

Figure 25 'A walk in this lovely forest' (15.05.2018).

coupled mums to bring male role models into their family lives in 'thoughtful' ways. Rachael's *male influences* posts further exemplify this point, contributing to the message that, although Poppy doesn't have a father, she doesn't miss out because she has plenty of men who contribute to her life in meaningful ways. In this section, I focus on a 'male influences' post that includes a photograph of Rachael, her daughter Poppy and her brother Dave. Rachael is carrying Poppy in a sling, with one arm around Dave, against the backdrop of a forest scene. This image–text combination is shown in Figure 25, with the caption transcribed and anonymized in Extract 12.

Extract 12. 'A walk in this lovely forest' caption

1. I'm really conscious to ensure that Poppy is surrounded by lots of positive male role
2. models and is used to being around men. It could be very easy for her to be mainly
3. around women as she spends most time with my mum and I and other mum
4. friends. That's why I find it important to ensure she grows up very close to her uncle
5. @iamdave Dave and Grandad Julian.
6. We got the train to Lynwick for a visit and a walk in this lovely forest.

7. #siblings #uncle #lynwick #lynwickwoods #babywearing #solomum
8. #singlemombychoice #singlemumbychoice #singlemotherbychoice #ivfjourney
9. #miraclebaby #donorconception #solomum #singlewomen #goingsolo #instamum
10. #newmum #mummyblogger #mumlife #mommyblogger #newmom #coach
11. #lifecoach #smc #ninjamum #mumtribe #supportnetwork

In this Instagram post, Rachael again entextualizes a set of actions as an aspirational event. More specifically, she suggests that a walk in the forest with her brother, Dave, and daughter, Poppy, contributes to a set of family practices that provide her daughter with meaningful 'male role models'. As with her 'little taste of Friday night' post, Rachael uses hashtags to target an audience of solo mums and increase the post's visibility amongst this target audience. Indeed, here she has increased the number of hashtags, from twelve to twenty-seven, with nineteen of these hashtags relating to motherhood, single motherhood or conception. The inclusion of additional hashtags such as #instamum, #mummyblogger and #mommyblogger suggests that Rachael is working to align herself with other mothers who regularly use social media to share their parenting experience and is keen to connect with a broader audience who follow this kind of content. Some of the more specific hashtags she includes here, such as #siblings, #uncle and #ninjamum, will be considered in more detail as this section progresses. The post received seventy-six 'likes' in total, which indicates that a significant number of Instagram users validated and legitimized this entextualization of a moment in her life and the values it inscribes.

Unlike the 'little taste of Friday night' post, and many of Rachael's other experiential sharing posts on the theme of 'self-care', this post is not positioned explicitly as a piece of advice or useful knowledge. Nevertheless, by tying her opening statement 'I'm really conscious to ensure that Poppy is surrounded by lots of positive male role models' to an event – going for a walk with her brother – she provides her audience with a specific, repeatable way of ensuring their children have meaningful relationships with men. Further, Rachael positions this walk in the forest as part of a deliberate, careful cultivation of her relationship with her brother. For example, she takes an agentive position in the opening statement 'I'm really conscious to ensure', underlining her very deliberate role in making sure her daughter is 'surrounded by' male role models through the intensifier 'really' and emphatic process 'conscious to ensure' (she also uses 'important to ensure' in line 4). The implication is that, through careful attention to their actions and dedicated cultivation of relationships, solo mums can access the same family roles and relationships (most notably the 'father figure') that are available to heterosexually coupled parent families. Rachael's inclusion of the hashtag #ninjamum at the end of her post encapsulates this aspirational image of a woman who has a mastery of motherhood and is able to fulfil multiple, complex familial obligations through careful thought, planning and selection of specific events, activities and companions.

Rachael deploys a number of visual and digital tools to foreground her brother's important role in her family practice. First, she chooses an image in which her brother Dave takes a prominent position, leaning slightly forward, whilst Rachael is standing slightly back, with her arm around his shoulders, positioning him as the central figure. The scenery in the background is slightly out-of-focus, and Rachael also backgrounds the scene in her caption: the first five lines focus on the importance of being 'surrounded by lots of positive male role models', whilst reference to the event and its location is left until the last line (line 6; 'we got the train to Lynwick for a visit and a walk in this lovely forest'). Further, the list of twenty-seven hashtags at the end of the post begins with her brother's familial roles – #siblings and #uncle. In the caption, Rachael's description emphasizes the closeness of Poppy's relationship with male figures in particular, through the intensifier '*very* close' (line 4) and the preposition 'surrounded' (line 1), which implies an abundance of male figures (as does the quantifier 'lots'). This language contrasts with the less intensive 'spends most time with' in relation to the women in Poppy's life. In this way, Rachael suggests both that Poppy has a balance of differently gendered people in her life and that the male figures are even more significant than the female ones. Further, Rachael implicitly responds to known critique around the children of solo mums being 'deprived' of masculine figures, in the form of fathers.

In sum, this post captures a quite complex set of assumptions around how families operate and what children need, in a single, highly repeatable entextualized action – going for a walk in the forest with a male family member. Rachael uses this action to promote alternative ways of enacting solo motherhood in connection with a network of 'male role models'. Whilst this post challenges the assumption that children need a *father*, it reproduces the assumption that children do need some kind of male role model and thus that 'men' and 'women' take up dichotomous and fundamentally different roles in family lives and relationships. Further, there is an underlying assumption that single mothers should address any 'gaps' in their children's lives through dedication and careful planning. In this way, Rachael's post implicitly values the idea of single mothers 'having it all' through the promotion of specific, tangible and manageable actions and practices. This family practice is easily repeatable by her audience of followers, who in turn may reproduce the values that Rachael encodes in it.

Chapter summary

This chapter has built on the introduction to epistemic connection in Chapter 5 through a second case study that focuses on Rachael's use of Instagram. The analyses of this chapter have shown how Rachael uses Instagram to position herself alongside other solo mums and share practical, relatable knowledge resources with them. In each analysis, I have shown how Rachael entextualizes a set of everyday actions (going for a drink/a walk in the forest) as aspirational events, encouraging others to reproduce her actions in their own family practice. The value of 'having it all' underpins Rachael's entextualization of these actions. The implication is that through close attention to their actions and careful cultivation of relationships, solo mums can overcome broader sociocultural stigma around single-parent families being somehow deficient. The analyses thus show how Rachael is working to circulate and promote new ways of understanding, reinterpreting and 'doing' family roles and parenting practice as a form of social action and advocacy. Despite this positive goal, however, I have suggested that Rachael's posts also reproduce restrictive ideals around the significance of gendered roles in family life, as well as suggesting that women, in this case *single* women, should be able to 'have it all'. These values feed into a neoliberal and individualized perspective on parenting and families, and may place significant pressure on solo mothers to take personal responsibility for emulating, or assimilating with, 'mainstream' families.

There are many parallels to be drawn between the case studies of Chapters 5 and 6. Most notably, both Jenny and Rachael are keen to advocate for their communities, to influence others and to effect systemic and social change that will benefit other families like theirs. From their central networked positions, both Jenny and Rachael drive forward new ways of understanding institutions, such as motherhood, the family and education, at the same time as navigating personal challenges and supporting the people around them. However, this chapter has shown that Rachael's use of Instagram to achieve these aims is markedly different from Jenny's use of Twitter. Most notably, whilst Jenny's retweets focus on recontextualizing and reinterpreting 'expert' and institutional knowledge from a shared experiential perspective, Rachael's 'experiential sharing' Instagram posts forge connections with other solo mums through the entextualization and circulation of her own family-related actions and practices.

7

Introducing Affective Connection

The following two chapters focus on the final dimension of connected parenting: *affective connection*, defined here as the formation of social ties through the construction and flow of emotions, feelings, moods, dispositions and attitudes. As the previous chapters have begun to illustrate, affect runs through every dimension of connected parenting. However, in these chapters I isolate the affective dimension in order to closely examine how the digitally mediated construction, movement and circulation of affective states and actions can work to consolidate and mobilize kin-like bonds between friends and community members.

The chapter begins by outlining my approach to analysing affect. This approach follows scholars such as Ahmed (2014), Boler and Davis (2018, p. 81) and Wetherell (2012) in conceiving affects as dynamic and shifting states that are always 'on the move' and are realized through social and relational actions and practices. This emphasis on movement and social action complements a mediated discourse analysis approach that is concerned with the way actions are mediated and (re)produced in and through discourse. The chapter then considers key insights from research relating to parents' and families' affective connection and sharing in digital contexts. The first body of research has tended to explore how the supportive and collaborative dimensions of emotional reciprocity interact with normative constraints around parenting and motherhood in digital 'parenting collectives'. A second body of research focuses on more private digital communication within transnational and migratory family groups, attending to the ways in which affective digital practices can constitute and sustain family relations themselves. I also consider parallels between research that focuses on the affective practices of parents, transnational families, friendships and LGBT communities.

The case study presented in this chapter focuses on Tony, a single gay man who has two sons of secondary school age and co-parents with a lesbian couple.

After introducing Tony, the chapter examines his posts to a Facebook group for the UK Fae Revolutionaries, a queer community that plays a significant role in his life. The second case study, which is the subject of Chapter 8, elaborates this exploration of affective connection through a focus on Peter, a gay man who conceived his infant daughter with the assistance of an egg donor and gestational surrogate. My focus on two fathers in these chapters brings a different dimension to research on affect, parenthood and digital media. Although existing work on affective sharing online has tended to focus on women's and mothers' digital communication, this chapter will show that online emotional sharing and affective connection can also play a significant role in the lives of men and fathers. Another distinguishing feature of these final case studies concerns their theorization of Tony and Peter's practices of affective connection as family practices in themselves. Through these explorations, I draw out links between connection, parenting, community and family in a way that points to the relevance of 'connected parenting' beyond traditional definitions of kinship.

Relational approaches to affect and emotion

The 'affective turn' (Clough, 2008; Clough & Halley, 2007) is now well established across the humanities and social sciences, bringing embodied senses and behaviours to the fore in explorations of identity, community and social action (Clough, 2008; Wetherell, 2012). Whilst there is no scholarly consensus on the meaning of 'affect', and its relation to concepts such as emotion, feeling and attitude, affect usually inhabits one of two broad semantic fields (Wetherell, 2012). The first relates primarily to *emotion*, with affect referring to either physical and behavioural manifestations of emotion (such as blushes or sobs) or the full spectrum of visible and non-visible emotional experience, including inner and subjective feelings such as hate and fear. The second extends beyond emotions and feelings to capture movement, influence and change in a more general sense, as where one thing (including humans, animals or objects) is *affected by* another (Wetherell, 2012). The latter definition of affect can capture a much wider range of social processes relating, as Clough (2008, p. ix) puts it, to both 'our power to affect the world around us and our power to be affected by it'. The former, however, offers a more tangible concept of affect as it works in and through human bodies, practices and discourse. In this section, I briefly consider these two fields of reference, and note how they intersect, before outlining this book's conceptualization of affects as dynamic and shifting states of emotion and intensity that are realized *through* social and relational actions and practices.

Psychological models of affect as emotion have traditionally attended to internalized feelings, which may be externalized through outward expression and potentially passed on to others. Ahmed (2014, p. 9) describes this as the 'inside out' model of emotions. Linguistic and discourse analytical studies of affect have contributed to such 'inside-out' explorations of affect through attention to the comprehension, naming and expression of externalized emotions through a range of semiotic means. For example, Bednarek (2008) and Martin and White (2005) have examined textual representations of affect as linguistic manifestations, construals or references to human emotions and feelings. Bednarek (2008), expanding Martin and White's (2005) framework for analysing the affective dimension of language as part of a broader system of appraisal, focuses squarely on linguistic construals of emotion. Her corpus-based analysis of 'emotion talk' considers how texts 'portray' or 'denote' emotion, primarily through 'emotion labels' such as love, hate, anger or sadness. Other linguistic studies of affective expression have taken in a wider range of subjective states that include emotions alongside other emotionally valenced states such as feelings, moods, dispositions and attitudes (e.g. Ochs & Schieffelin, 1989).

Research focusing on gesture and body language has turned its attention to non-linguistic means for displaying and construing affect. Goodwin, Cekaite and Goodwin (2012, p. 40), for example, have explored interactional displays of affect through intonation, gesture and body posture, conceptualizing affective performances such as high-pitched screams and other sudden changes of pitch, the turning of heads and upper bodies and widespread arms as 'embodied affective stances' (also see Peräkylä & Sorjonen, 2012; Wetherell, 2012). In digital and social media research, pictorial resources such as emojis have been recognized as comparable tools for signalling and intensifying affect, especially positive affect, in digital interaction (Al Rashdi, 2018; Riordan, 2017). Similarly, Lyons (2018) has pointed to the prevalence of kineticons in written digital discourse as a means of representing affective actions and bodily phenomena. Kineticons, Lyons (2018) explains, combine typographic symbols and lexical items, and may represent gestures, facial expressions or bodily responses, such as *blush*, *sigh* and *hug*. Like emojis and emoticons, kineticons can signal or reinforce affective and other attitudinal messages, serving 'to express the sender's attitude to the preceding part of the message by providing a discursive equivalent of embodied action' (Lyons, 2018, p. 24).

Historically, linguists and discourse analysts have given less attention to explorations of affect as a more abstract, fluid domain concerned primarily with movement, influence and intensity of feeling. This is largely because such affective flows are seen to 'ultimately excee[d] discourse', making them difficult to trace *through* discourse (Milani & Richardson, 2021, p. 3). However, the conception of affect as a pre-discursive force defined by fluidity and variation has gained significant traction in media and cultural studies in recent years, driven largely by the work of Massumi (2002). For example, in Papacharissi's (2014, p. 21) influential exploration of 'affective publics' – political movements driven by social media practices – she describes affect as a pre-conscious entity that 'precedes and sustains or possibly annuls feeling and emotion . . . a non-conscious experience of intensity'. She uses the example of human responses to music to describe the unconscious force of affect, as where a piece of music may inspire an intensity that moves us to tap our feet, for example, or bring tears to our eyes. This perspective, whilst compelling in many ways, presents significant challenges for empirical study. As Boler and Davis (2018, pp. 81–2) explain, conceiving affect as a mystified, uncontainable force or energy can leave readers 'wanting a full articulation of the significance (rather than simply the alleged presence) of affect as it circulates in and through digital media'. Nevertheless, an emphasis on the movement and fluidity of affect will be important for the analysis that follows.

This chapter's exploration of affective connection takes a social and relational perspective that does not neatly fit the dichotomies of affect versus emotion that I have touched on so far. Instead, it brings an emphasis on the movement and circulation of affective forces to an understanding of the way connections are forged and maintained between individuals and groups. As noted earlier, the tracing of affective flows presents a challenge for discourse analytical research. However, from a relational perspective, affect and discourse need not be points of tension. As Mortensen and Milani (2021, p. 451) explain, this tension is only relevant if affects are conceived as 'states lodged somewhere in people's minds or bodies'. What Mortensen and Milani (2021) have done instead is to conceive affect as the construction and circulation of emotion *through* discourse and practice. This approach is consistent with Boler and Davis' (2018) view that affect is less about individual subjectivity and personal feeling, and more about the collective and intersubjective manifestation, experience and mobilization of feeling. This perspective is well suited to my focus on affective *connection*, which explicitly attends to the construction and mobilization of interpersonal bonds, affiliations and relationships through the circulation of affective acts (and indeed the construction and circulation of affective acts through interpersonal bonds).

A relational perspective is able to bring personal, intersubjective and structural dimensions to bear in the theorization of affect and emotion beyond individual bodies, as they intersect with and constitute wider sociocultural norms and practices. It is therefore consistent with feminist perspectives on emotion and affect, which have often sought to theorize 'beyond the binaries of body and cognition, and emotion and rationality, showing the ways these mutually shape and form what and how we know' (Boler & Davis, 2018, p. 80). For example, Hochschild's (1979) influential work on 'feeling rules' theorizes emotion in terms of sociocultural norms and practices that are acquired rather than innate, suggesting that unspoken rules regulate the experience, expression and management of emotion across time and context. More recently, Ahmed (2014) has theorized the relationship between emotion, social structures and power through the concept of 'affective economies', which is based on the premise that emotions (such as hate, fear, disgust, shame and love) do not live *within* people or things but circulate *between* them. Through the repetition of affective actions over time, Ahmed suggests, affects, and the objects to which they 'stick', accumulate as a kind of value, forming 'affective economies'. As an example, Ahmed (2014) shows how the repeated description of migrants and asylum seekers as 'floods' or 'swarms' in UK political and media texts results in the accumulation of an affective economy of hate around these figures. This chapter's exploration of *affective connection* is influenced by both Hochschild and Ahmed's work, in its theorization of the personal, intersubjective and structural dimensions of affect and emotion at the intersection between personal feeling, group values and alignments, and wider sociocultural norms and practices.

Affective connection in parenting collectives, families and LGBT communities

Emotional sharing has been identified as a central dimension of parents' (especially mothers') digital practices. For example, both Morrison (2011) and Pedersen and Lupton (2018) suggest that the sharing of intimate, negatively valenced experiences in mothering blogs and discussion forums constitutes an important form of emotional outlet. Further, they suggest that the mutual and collaborative nature of this sharing, described as 'emotional reciprocity'

(Morrison, 2011, p. 41), or 'me too' sharing (Pedersen & Lupton, 2018, p. 61), facilitates the rapid development of maternal communities based on solidarity, empathy and shared understanding. For example, in Pedersen and Lupton's (2018) analysis of 100 Mumsnet Talk posts that begin with the phrase 'I feel', they suggest that contributors seek and receive reassurance through admissions of similar emotional experiences. This finding is echoed in Jaworska's (2018) examination of Mumsnet Talk threads about postnatal depression, where contributors validated and normalized their experiences of postnatal depression by re-voicing one another's feelings (see discussion in Chapter 3). This emphasis on bonding through shared emotion is echoed in studies of networked expressions of feeling in broader, cross-platform contexts. For example, Sundén and Paasonen (2019, p. 2) argue that the #MeToo movement and related accusations against powerful men have been driven by an 'affective homophily' that brings people together 'through expressions of similar feeling'. The implication, ultimately, is that the drive towards affective connection with others is powerful and intense, especially for marginalized and victimized groups.

Much less attention has been given to men's and fathers' emotional sharing online. Indeed, the heightened attention to affective practice and emotional sharing by women may be in danger of reinforcing the normative assumption that women are more emotional than men, and have a more expressive emotional range, in digital as well as face-to-face contexts (e.g. Ahmed, 2014; Beneito-Montagut, 2017; Wolf, 2000). However, Das and Hodkinson's (2019; 2021) work with new fathers suffering mental health difficulties suggests that sharing emotions online can be just as important for fathers but is often complicated by powerful ideals of stoic masculinity. As a result, much of their participants' online 'emotion-work' was more tentative than the overtly emotional expressions seen in research with mothering communities. For example, they show how one participant's struggles were 'hidden behind coded gestures', such as sharing someone else's post on the theme of their struggles 'in the hope that someone would wonder about his reasons for doing so and reach out' (Das & Hodkinson, 2019, p. 7). Das and Hodkinson's (2019; 2021) work shows that online emotional sharing is by no means restricted to feminine domains and that online 'emotion-work' can take a range of forms, including less explicit references to feelings and emotional states.

As noted in the previous section, emotional sharing practices can have significant implications beyond the expression of individual feeling and construction of community bonds. For example, Pedersen and Lupton's (2018) exploration of Mumsnet Talk has shown how the naming of negative emotions such as anger and material ambivalence can contribute to the redefinition of dominant 'feeling rules' (Hochschild, 1979) of motherhood in this context, repositioning these emotional taboos as a normal part of 'good motherhood'. Discourse analytical explorations of Mumsnet Talk have further elaborated this point, showing how other negative affects that flout the feeling rules of 'good motherhood' such as depression, suicidal thoughts and regret (Jaworska, 2018; Matley, 2020) can be reworked in this context, disrupting these affective taboos. Given the significance of affective expression and negotiation in the specific context of Mumsnet Talk interactions, Pedersen and Lupton (2018) suggest that this online forum might be conceptualized as a 'community of feeling' (Ferreday, 2003; Kuntsman, 2009), a local site where norms of emotional expression and experience are (de)constructed through collective expressions of feeling. Lehto (2021, 2022) has argued that the affective social media landscape for some mothers can be even more complex. On Instagram, she suggests, whilst affective states such as anxiety and depression may still conflict with the feeling rules of 'good motherhood', they have also become a form of social capital amongst influencers, who may use negative affective experiences to garner visibility, engagement and interest for their accounts. Established feeling rules, then, may come into conflict with the emerging rules of social media cultures, as well as with individual and group experiences and practices.

The aforementioned studies of online parenting communities and collectives have focused primarily on the supportive and collaborative dimensions of emotional reciprocity alongside the normative constraints of 'feeling rules'. In a different vein, research with transnational and migratory family groups has attended to the ways in which affective digital practices can constitute and sustain family relations themselves. For example, Wilding et al. (2020, p. 641) draw on Ahmed's (2014) concept of 'affective economies' to explain how the circulation of affect through digital media can 'define and shape' transnational families as collectives comprised of a 'mutuality of being'. These authors also show how the devices that provide access to the 'affective economies' of the family can themselves become deeply personal and precious, and the focus for complex emotions such as love, affection and frustration. For example, one of Wilding et al.'s (2020) older participants, who would spend hours scrolling through images of her family on her mobile device, said that this device helped her feel close to her distant family. As a result, she kept it close to her body, patting it like a close intimate and explaining that she had 'her whole world in her pocket' (Wilding et al. 2020, p. 647). Similarly, Leurs' (2019) work with refugees living in the Netherlands shows how the aural, visual and haptic affordances of mobile phones can facilitate a reassuring co-presence with distant family members that feels grounded and immediate. Building on Madianou's (2016) concept of 'ambient co-presence', Alinejad (2019) has developed the notion of '*careful* co-presence' to reflect the discerning selectivity and emotional care in transnational families' intimacy-facilitating social media practices. This form of co-presence, Alinejad (2019, p. 9) explains, reflects not only *careful* selection of the mode, time and place of digital communication but also *care-full* expressions of emotional care and intimacy through digital media. For example, for many of Alinejad's (2019, p. 5) participants, the choice of one-to-one communication through voice calls, video calls and WhatsApp messages (rather than one-to-many forms of social media) is a deliberate choice 'for maintaining the close relationships that are specifically emotionally intimate'.

The circulation of love, intimacy and care that has been observed in the digital practices of transnational families is by no means limited to kinship groups, or 'families of origin', as Formby (2017) puts it. Sociologists such as Formby (2017), Weeks et al. (2001) and Weston (1991, p. 207), for example, have shown that LGBT friendship groups, communities and 'families of choice' engage in similar practices of love, intimacy and care, for example through emotional support, physical displays of affection and practical help. Further, in Santana's (2019, p. 220) work with transgender women of colour, she argues that everyday acts such as intimate greetings (e.g. 'E ai, mana!' – *Hey Sis!*), coming together to share stories and checking in on the phone are the kinds of caring practices that save lives and 'wi[n] battles'. Digital technologies provide important tools for marginalized groups like these to both find one another and engage in the regular practices of support and care that sustain them. Digitally mediated care and support are shown to be particularly important for individuals who live outside of the liberal, urban localities where geographical LGBT communities often thrive (Adams-Santos, 2020; Tudor, 2018). In these situations, queer media can facilitate the production of global communities that bring geographically distant love, support and care within reach (Tudor, 2018). With these insights in mind, the analysis that follows will examine practices of affective connection as they relate to, but also transcend, families of origin, including a range of intimate and caring practices that can be conceived as broadly 'familial' in nature. Looking at Tony's digital engagement with the UK Fae Revolutionaries, who he describes as his 'queer family', this analysis will examine the ways in which affective connections based on the reciprocal flow of love, care, intimacy and affection can shape connections between members of this community.

Introducing Tony

Tony is a 54-year-old single gay man who co-parents his two sons of secondary school age with a lesbian couple, Suzanne and Emily. He works full-time as a musician and director of a small charity. Tony explained in our first interview that he had seen the potential for queer family formation from a young age. He always assumed he would have children when he was growing up, and as a young man, would talk 'jokingly' with his lesbian friends about 'living in a commune with a whole group of people co-parenting'. Tony generally prefers to connect with his family and close friends on a relatively private and intimate level, either face-to-face, on the telephone or using mobile messaging apps such as WhatsApp and Messenger, where he can interact one-to-one or in small groups. Tony also stays in touch with family and friends, especially those in his wider network, through Facebook, although he guards his family's privacy and personal life quite carefully in one-to-many contexts such as this. When broadcasting to a relatively large audience on Facebook, for example, Tony notes that he is 'quite circumspect about what I post' and only shares images of, or details about, his sons with their express permission. He has a more private website where he shares photographs with his extended family.

Tony's network of family and friends can be grouped into three intersecting spheres, which are visually illustrated in Figure 26. First, he has family and long-standing friends, shown in the lower central portion of the diagram, such as his dad and brother, his two sons, their co-parents Suzanne and Emily, and friends he has known for several decades, such as Soph (who he met at school). Interestingly, Tony was one of only two participants who placed his children within his network; he said that he saw them as a source of fun and emotional support. Tony is also a folk musician, and music is an important part of his life and his social support network, most notably in the form of the 'folk scene', which includes friends and family such as his dad and his friends Gav and Soph (shown in the lower right section of the diagram). Finally, Tony is a member of a queer community called the UK Fae Revolutionaries (henceforth 'UKFRs'). Through this community, Tony has met several close friends and sexual partners such as

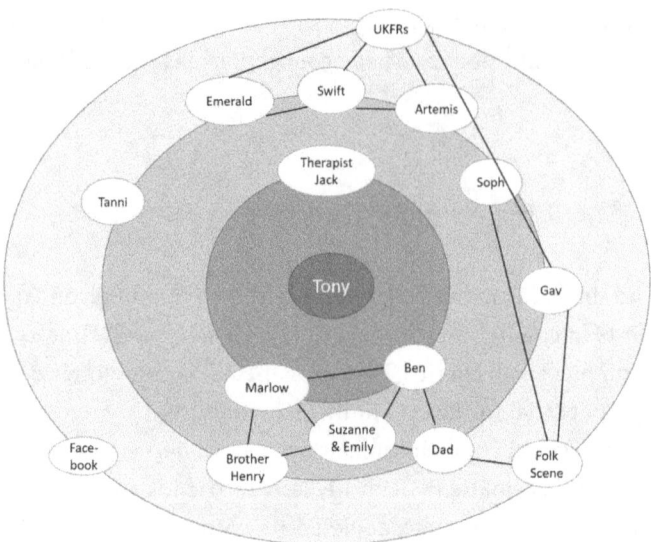

Figure 26 Tony's network connections and density diagram.

Emerald, Swift and Artemis. There is some cross-over between the UKFRs and the folk scene; Gav, for example, is connected with both.

The case study presented in this chapter will focus on Tony's affective connection with the UK Fae Revolutionaries (UKFRs) via a closed Facebook group. In order to understand the nature of Tony's affective connections with the UKFR community, it is helpful to know a little more about the group's history, philosophies and practices. The Fae Revolutionary movement was formed out of necessity at a time when heteronormative society and structures frequently ignored, rejected or threatened LGBTQ people's lives. Tony himself came out as a gay man in the late 1980s, when this was still largely the case in the UK. Tony's description of the Fae Revolutionary movement as a 'rejection of heteronormativity' and a way of 'celebrating our otherness' captures their reclamation and celebration of difference. Whilst the Fae Revolutionaries are a relatively loose, worldwide network, the UK branch that Tony belongs to is more of a community, and they have regular face-to-face meetings (called 'gatherings'). Tony himself describes the UKFRs as a community on several occasions throughout our interviews, in statements such as 'it's a very supportive community'. Members of the UKFRs also maintain regular connections through online groups; for example, Tony uses the UKFR's public Facebook page to stay up to date with local events and national gatherings. The UKFRs Facebook group is both closed and 'secret'; it is only accessible to people who have attended gatherings, who will then be invited to join and the group cannot be found in any other way.

The Fae Revolutionary movement also has connections with paganism, a religion defined by a strong sense of spiritual connection with the earth and compassion for everything that lives within it. As a result, their core values and beliefs have a strongly affective dimension centred on love, acceptance and celebration. The 'about us' summary on the UKFR's website affirms these affective values and emphasizes the importance of creating safe spaces to celebrate members' spirituality, sexuality and personal growth. The community's joint enterprises are also centred around these affective values and goals; for example, they hold regular ritual-based events including 'heart circles'. This traditional ritual practice involves gathering in a circle to 'speak from the heart' and supporting one another's revelations 'with unconditional love'.[1] A second key practice is the 'drum circle', which again involves coming together in a circle formation and finding emotional expression and release through rhythm, drumming, movement and dance. The descriptions of both rituals on the UKFR website focus on building a community through honest emotional expression, trust, healing and unconditional love. The UKFRs also have a shared linguistic repertoire. One distinctive language practice within this community, for example, involves choosing a unique name, which usually has a connection to nature and/ or spirituality. Tony's Fae Revolutionary name is Flower, and he has several friends who he only refers to using their fae names, such as Artemis, Swift and Qemerald. Further, Fae Revolutionaries often use the collective naming device 'fae' when referring to one another. As Tony explained in our second interview, fae is short for 'faeries' and is often playfully deployed in naming devices such as 'fae', 'anyfae' and 'everyfae'. These naming practices tie in with Fae Revolutionary principles around joyful celebration, identity play and the rejection of established social norms or structures. In our third interview, Tony explained that he saw the Fae Revolutionaries as his 'queer family', suggesting that the concept of family remains relevant, useful and comforting in relation to LGBTQ+ friendships and communities such as the UKFRs (see discussion in the previous section). The analysis in this chapter will further explore how Tony's affective connections with the UKFR Facebook group relate to family practices as they extend beyond traditional concepts of family and parent–child relationships.

Facebook, Facebook groups and affective connection

A good deal of academic literature has explored norms of affective sharing and interaction within Facebook networks and communities. For example,

McLaughlin and Vitak (2011, p. 307) suggest that intimate and emotional disclosures in posts to the Facebook timeline are seen by some users as norm violations – as too 'overly emotional' for this relatively public sphere and better suited to a more private forum. Lambert's (2016) ethnographic study of friendship and intimacy amongst six Australian Facebook users revealed similar findings. However, as I have shown in Chapter 3, Facebook groups are distinct from the Facebook timeline in a number of ways and are likely to have quite different norms of sharing, engagement and interaction. In Facebook groups, for example, intensely emotional and intimate disclosures may be welcomed, even expected, by members, as is the case with many of Cheryl's Facebook groups for adoptive parents (see Chapter 4). In this section, I build on the introduction to Facebook groups in Chapter 4, with a specific focus on the ways in which these groups can shape and enable affective connections.

Studies of Facebook group interactions, in common with much research exploring online parenting collectives (see discussion earlier in this chapter), have shown that these groups can be key sites for the circulation of emotional reciprocity, or 'affective homophily' (Sundén & Paasonen, 2019). This work has also suggested that the 'rules' of emotional sharing in any given context may be strongly influenced by both global normative structures of feeling and local group norms. For example, Pounds et al.'s (2018) study of a closed Facebook-based diabetes support group, which was introduced in Chapter 3, reveals that sharing negative experiences and seeking support from others are very common practices in this context. They found that the most common response type in group members' comments was 'core and peripheral empathy giving', which is realized through a range of responses including 'sharing similar feelings and experiences' and 'acknowledging feelings' (Pounds et al., 2018, p. 39). Giaxoglou's (2021, p. 140) case study of a memorial Facebook group, created as a tribute to a young, US-based adult, shows how the affective practices circulating in this group are shaped by norms related to online mourning in general, as well as specific norms evolving within this group. For example, Giaxoglou (2021, p. 140) suggests that posts are shaped by norms of the '"good" mourner', who 'views death as a transition to a better life and who commits themselves to the "duty" of remembering the dead'. She explains that members (re)construct these norms through group practices such as engaging in 'group memorial activities' or sharing 'personal, everyday acts of remembrance' (Giaxoglou, 2021, p. 140). As a final example, Hutchings' (2017) exploration of posts focused on death and grief within the Church of Sweden's Facebook page suggests that the page was used to construct and maintain an 'emotional brand' centred on 'empathy with sorrow'. However, whilst Hutchings (2017) suggests that affirming sadness and sorrow is given 'priority' in page admins' responses to community comments, he also notes that they work hard to value all emotional experiences, shifting between emotions in response to the affective timbre of members' comments. In the sections that follow, I build on existing studies of emotional sharing and affective connection in Facebook groups. The analysis will consider, specifically, how Tony's relationship with the UK Fae Revolutionary Facebook group is shaped through the circulation of affective actions, states and intensities.

Tony's use of the UKFR Facebook group

On his main Facebook page, Tony has quite a large number of 'friends' who can see and interact with his posts. Tony explained in our first interview that he tends to use this page as 'a way to keep in touch with [people] and to keep up with photos and things', and that he mostly posts about political campaigns, environmental issues and folk music on his main timeline. However, Tony uses the UK Fae Revolutionaries (UKFR) Facebook group quite differently. He suggested in our second interview, for example, that he wouldn't be likely to share an emotional or vulnerable side on his main Facebook page, because he wouldn't want 'to seem too needy'. However, he said he was much more likely to show vulnerability or ask for help within the UKFR Facebook group, because 'it's a very supportive community'.

At the time of data collection, the UKFR's closed Facebook group had 378 members. Tony explained that he didn't post to the group very often, because he generally preferred to communicate with other Fae Revolutionaries one-to-one or in small groups, via messaging apps such as WhatsApp and Messenger. Tony therefore posted to the group just seven times between May 2018 and May 2019. He was happy to share all of these posts with me, but for reasons of ethics and privacy (see Chapter 2), I did not collect others' replies to these posts. However, a good deal of insight around the wider UKFR Facebook community, and the way others responded to Tony's posts, can be gleaned from his interview data, particularly interview 2, where Tony talked me through his 'digital life' (see details in Chapter 2). In the section that follows, I therefore draw on excerpts from this interview in order to contextualize his posts and shed light on the way others responded to them.

Tony's posts to the UKFR Facebook group can be loosely organized into three categories: queer observations, music promotion and asking for support (see Table 13). All of Tony's queer observation posts include an image–text combination, in which he shares a photograph or screenshot that references an aspect of queer culture, community or dating/sexual activity, and relies on the shared understanding of members to interpret meaning. For example, the 'fruit stoners' post, which includes a photograph of a tool for removing the stones from fruit, is a play on words, with 'fruit' and 'stoner' being slang terms for a gay man and someone who regularly smokes cannabis, respectively. Both of the queer observation posts include a sexual and/or flirtatious element, indicating a playful dimension in Tony's posts. In his music promotion posts, which are often connected with his own folk music, Tony encourages others to engage with music events or media. In these posts, Tony often shares hyperlinks that will take the reader directly to another website. These posts

Table 13 Types of Post in Tony's UKFR Facebook Group Data

Type	Number	Description	Example
Asking for support	3	Sharing a (usually negative) state of mind and asking for support or advice	Text: My kin … I'm asking for help, as I'm having a hard time at the moment. Messages of support, phone calls, virtual hugs, physical hugs and cuddles, good vibes, healing energy, mentions in ritual, you know the sort of thing. Thank you. Love, Flower x
Queer observations	2	Making reference to an aspect of queer culture, community or dating/sexual activity that relies on in-group understanding or experience	Text: I've met a few Fruit Stoners … Image:
Music promotion	2	Encouraging others to engage with music events or media, often connected with Tony's own folk music	Text: Hey Fae! There are still spaces bookable for the Fae Revolutionaries Music Gatherette at the end of June, please do get your booking in if you plan to come as places are limited xxx [Link to the Fae Revolutionary website booking page]

illustrate the intersection between the UK Fae Revolutionary community and the folk music community. Finally, the asking for support category includes text-based posts in which Tony shares his (usually negative) state of mind and asks for support.

The analysis that follows will focus on the first and most frequent of Tony's post types, 'asking for support'. These posts are examples of an intimate sharing practice that Tony tends to reserve for relatively private, one-to-one or small-group interactions with close contacts through face-to-face meetings, phone calls or messaging. However, as noted previously, Tony feels able to engage in a more intimate way with the relatively large UKFR Facebook group because of its supportive nature. Given the relatively intimate and personal nature of these posts, this data is well suited to an exploration of Tony's affective connections with the UKFR Facebook community. Since these posts are quite similar in form and function, I analyse them in tandem.

Affective flows of energy and magic in the UKFR Facebook group

In this section, I analyse Tony's three 'asking for support' posts to the UKFR Facebook group, considering how affective actions and intensities are mediated in this context, how the circulation of those affective actions consolidates and mobilizes kin-like bonds between members of the group and how these affective flows contribute to the familial shape of the group itself. Tony wrote the first post (Extract 13) when he was suffering with a virus, making an appeal to the UKFR community to 'send me healing vibes'. Members of the group left thirteen comments on the post, and seventeen people responded with a reaction. Although it isn't clear from this screenshot how many 'love' versus 'like' reactions the post received, the heart icon is positioned to the left, indicating that it received more 'love' reactions. Tony wrote the second post (Extract 14) when he was having problems at work and his father had become very ill. He again asks for help here, in the form of 'good vibes', 'healing energy' and other affective practices. This post received fourteen 'love' reactions and nine comments. In the final post (Extract 15), also prompted by his father's illness, Tony asks members of the UKFR community to join him in 'working some protection and healing magic' for his dad. This post had twenty-one reactions, again with more 'loves' than 'likes', and five comments.

Extract 13. 'Please send me healing vibes' (21.05.2018)

Please send me healing vibes, I feel utterly shit and I can't sleep. I don't
Often directly ask for help but somehow a virus feel more legitimate than
Depression. That's absurd I know.

[name redacted] [name redacted] and 15 others   13 comments

Extract 14. 'I'm asking for help' (22.03.2019)

My kin… I'm asking for help, as I'm having a hard time at the moment.
Messages of support, phone calls, virtual hugs, physical hugs and cuddles, good
vibes, healing energy, mentions in ritual, you know the sort of thing.
Thank you, Love, Flower x

[name redacted] [name redacted] and 12 others   9 comments

Extract 15. 'Greetings lovely Fae!' (14.05.2019)

Greetings lovely Fae! Today, with his consent, I'll be working some
protection and healing magic for my dad [name], who's having major surgery
right now. Anyfae who feels called to join me, even if just for a moment, is
most welcome ❤ ❤ ❤

[name redacted] [name redacted] and 19 others   5 comments

Extracts 13 and 14 both begin with expressions of negative emotion as personal, inward-focused mental states – first, 'I feel utterly shit and I can't sleep' and second, 'I'm having a hard time at the moment'. These disclosures point to an affective state that might be described as 'misery', and Tony uses language that expresses this misery fairly directly: although both expressions are figurative, they are also quite blunt, direct and unmitigated, especially the intensified expletive 'utterly shit'. These initial statements briefly contextualize Tony's posts in relation to an affective impetus – a feeling of misery and personal turmoil – that has driven him to ask for help and support. Such open expression of negative feeling amongst like-minded others is comparable with the emotional sharing that has been identified across a range of parenting collectives and Facebook groups, as a form of emotional outlet that facilitates the rapid development of communities based on solidarity and shared understanding (see discussion earlier in this chapter).

However, these posts are not exclusively focused on the expression of negative feeling: all three of the previous examples also reference affective states and acts of love, care, intimacy and affection. For example, in Extracts 14 and 14, the opening greetings 'my kin' and 'greetings lovely fae', and the sign-offs 'love, Flower x' and '❤ ❤ ❤', which are positioned at the boundaries of the posts, signal that they have been written, and should be received, in a spirit of love, care, intimacy and affection. The heart emojis, x as an orthographic representation of a kiss and reference to greetings, love and kinship can be said entextualize affective states of care and intimacy, as well as specific affective actions such kissing and greeting, in condensed form. These greetings and sign-offs also include naming practices that are distinctive to the Fae Revolutionary community (see earlier discussion). 'My kin', for example, is a term of address that implies an intimate and loving familial relationship, and is consistent with Tony's feeling that the UKFRs are his 'queer family'. Tony also employs the collective naming device 'fae' and his Revolutionary name, 'Flower'. Each of these address terms not only functions as a signal of Tony's belonging to the UKFR community but also consolidates and mobilizes affective connections based on the reciprocal exchange of love and intimacy.

All three of Tony's 'asking for support' posts also reference the affective act of *healing*, which implies assisted movement from a negative, damaged state to one that is more positive, peaceful or healthy. For example, when Tony specifies what kind of support he's looking for, he asks people to 'please send me healing vibes' (Extract 13) and requests 'healing energy' (Extract 14). In the third extract, Tony writes that he will be 'working some protection and healing magic' for his dad, and welcomes others to join him. In these examples, Tony entextualizes healing forces in the form of vibes, energy and magic, and calls on others to continue the circulation of these affective flows in order to care for one another at a distance. In Extract 14, Tony also references a range of other affective actions as he calls for support from the UKFR community, including 'messages of support', 'phone calls', 'virtual and physical hugs and cuddles', 'good vibes' and 'mentions in ritual'. Each of these examples entextualizes some kind of movement or exchange – of words, energy or physical touch. These entextualized actions can be said to mobilize a sort of spiritual, pseudo-physical connection between UKFR members: the feeling of being hugged or cuddled 'virtually' or of sensing others' positive words and 'vibes' delivered at a distance. Healing, physical touch and other affective energies thus seem to be significant affective practices for Tony and perhaps for the UKFR community more broadly.

As noted previously, 'love' reactions dominate the responses to Tony's 'asking for support' posts. Tony also suggested in our second interview that 'love' is the preferred reaction within the UKFR Facebook community more generally, and that he, too, tended to use this more than the 'like' reaction when responding to others' posts. Tony also explained what he intended to communicate with the 'love' reaction, noting that 'it's not always to mean I love this post but more I'm sending love to you as well'. Given this contextual detail, and the overall affective timbre of Tony's posts, group members' 'love' reactions might be interpreted in a similar way – as 'I'm sending love to you' rather than 'I love this post'. Tony's summary of the comments he received underneath these three posts further supports this interpretation. As he explains in interview 2, 'I was . . . getting quite a lot of responses like hope it goes well sending hearts sending love sending some magic.' In these interview excerpts, the repeated instance of the process 'sending' underlines the point that love, care, intimacy and affection are often expressed as affective actions 'on the move' within this community.

The affective practices of love, care, intimacy and affection that have been identified in this section work to construct and sustain connections that are rooted in compassion, love and acceptance. These practices correlate strongly with the UKFR community's core values, and their in-person connective practices, such as the heart and drum circles described earlier in this chapter. Descriptions of these rituals on the UKFR website focus on the healing value of connections made through physical closeness and touch (e.g. holding hands in a circle), expressions of emotion and vulnerability (e.g. speaking feelings aloud) and movement (e.g. dance). Since all members are required to have attended these events, they will have a co-present reference point for such affective practices, which will likely shape their interpretation and experience of these affective flows. By continuing the circulation of physical caring practices in a digitally mediated context, Tony's posts further consolidate affective connections between members that are rooted in the reciprocal flow of love, care, intimacy and affection, even when they are not physically co-present. Indeed, the groups of respondents that come together around Tony's posts could be theorized as digitally mediated heart circles, since they operate around the same basic premise of one member 'speaking from the heart' and others responding with acts of compassion, love and care. Members are not physically co-present, and they are not able to hold hands in a circle formation, but affective flows of love, care, intimacy and affection, mediated here through linguistic and digital means, are able to transcend these boundaries. The practices of love, support and committed care within this community can be theorized as *family practices* and the

UKFR Facebook group as an important site through which familial intimacy can be performed, consolidated and mobilized.

Chapter summary

This chapter has introduced affective connection as the third and final dimension of connected parenting. This exploration is rooted in a social and relational approach, which brings an emphasis on the movement and circulation of affective forces to an understanding of the way emotions, feelings, moods, dispositions and attitudes can shape connections between groups, networks and communities. The chapter begins to examine affective connection through a fifth case study, which focuses on the way one single gay father, Tony, connects with a queer community called the UK Fae Revolutionaries through their closed Facebook group. The analysis shows how the group's affective connections of love, care, intimacy and affection are maintained and mobilized through repeated caring practices such as the use of affectionate and kin-like naming devices, the entextualization of physical acts of care and intimacy (such as hugs and kisses) and the circulation of affective flows through the language of movement (especially the 'sending' of positive energies from one member to another). The chapter demonstrates that the digital mediation of such physical and intimate acts can sustain supportive connections between members, even when they are physically distant.

The chapter also builds on existing studies that explore the relevance of affect in parenting collectives, family groups and other homophilous networks and communities. Building on research with both transnational families and LGBT communities, my analysis of affective practices within the UKFR Facebook group points to some of the specific practices of love, care, intimacy and affection that can both shape it as a supportive, loving and open community and consolidate its members' sense of connection with one another. Further, the analysis shows how these connections can be mobilized by group members through the circulation of affective flows that bring comfort and hope at times of need. I close by emphasizing the point that there need not be a distinction between the practices of care that constitute traditional, or 'given' families, and those same practices as they operate in other close-knit and supportive groups that are built around care, intimacy and affection, including 'chosen' families and kin-like communities. This argument develops the discussion of Chapters

3 and 4, where I suggest that the construction of parenting and family actions and practices as *collectively* undertaken can stretch the boundaries of the nuclear family unit to include a network of parents, friends and other supporters. The findings of this chapter expand the boundaries of family even further, showing how affective practices of love, care, intimacy and affection can be theorized as family practices in themselves, whether they are connected with parent–child relationships or not.

8

Elaborating Affective Connection

The previous chapter introduced affective connection as the final dimension of connected parenting, together with a case study based on the digital practices of Tony, a single gay father. The chapter showed that affective connection is a particularly significant dimension in Tony's engagement with a queer community called the UK Fae Revolutionaries and considered the means by which affective practices of love, care, intimacy and affection are circulated within this group. I paid particular attention to the entextualization of affective actions such as hugs and kisses, and the digitally mediated movement of 'energies', 'vibes' and 'magic', suggesting that these practices can transcend the boundaries both of physical distance and of family relationships and practices as they are traditionally conceived. In this chapter, I build on these explorations through a second case study that focuses on a very different set of digital data shared by another gay father, Peter. Looking at Peter's dyadic interactions with two of his closest friends via the mobile messaging platform *WhatsApp*, I examine the diversity of affective practices through which these individuals construct and sustain intimate, caring and affectionate connections. I build on the insights of the previous chapter by considering how these practices both extend beyond and intersect with traditional concepts of family and parent–child relationships.

Introducing Peter

Peter, a coupled 29-year-old gay man, conceived his infant daughter Lucy with the assistance of a surrogate and an egg donor. He works part-time as a musician and spends the rest of his time caring for his daughter. Like many of the parents who participated in the Marginalised Families Online study, Peter is very circumspect about his use of digital media for different purposes. For example, he very rarely uses one-to-many social media platforms such as

Facebook, Twitter or Instagram, and when he does, he never posts photographs of his daughter, details about their day-to-day lives or what he calls 'personal stuff'. He explained that this is largely about respecting Lucy's privacy, saying that he wouldn't want to post pictures of her online 'because Lu hasn't said she's happy for us to do that and . . . I believe it's very very difficult to get any media off the internet once it's up'. Like Tony, however, Peter and his partner Malcolm do maintain a password-protected blog, as an alternative way of sharing images and life events with their geographically distant family. Peter also regularly uses WhatsApp to connect (often daily) with his network of friends and family. When communicating in dyads or small groups via WhatsApp, Peter *does* regularly share photographs of his family, and more personal details about his life, which he is unwilling to disclose via more public and one-to-many media.

When we first met, Peter explained that he was well supported by family and friends, and had experienced very little discrimination as a result of either his sexuality or family formation. He suggested that, as a result, he hadn't felt the need to seek out others who shared similar experiences of parenthood and conception, such as gay parents and/or users of donor conception or surrogacy (for further discussion of Peter's experiences, see Mackenzie, in press). In this respect, his social network is quite different from the other participants in this study. These participants have all sought out groups and communities who share specific identities or experiences that are marginalized in a wider social context, such as being queer (Tony), a solo mum (Rachael), a single adopter (Jenny and Cheryl) or a single adopter of disabled children (Lynne). Nevertheless, Peter clearly does seek out and maintain close friendships with people who have other dimensions in common, such as a shared history and interests (e.g. friends from university), as well as being a parent and living locally (such as parents from a local baby group). In our interviews, Peter talked a great deal about these relationships, explaining how they were sustained through very regular communication across multiple modes such as face-to-face meetings, telephone calls, video calls and mobile messaging. This regular and multi-modal communication is another factor that makes Peter's network diagram quite distinct from those of other participants in the Marginalised Families Online study. As shown in Figures 27 and 28, he has daily contact (shown with a bold black line) via at least one mode with his closest, 'inner' circle and at least weekly contact (shown with a standard black line) with those in the secondary circle. Because this network diagram is quite large, it is displayed across two figures for clarity.

Peter's closest and longest-standing friendship group includes Andrea, Al and Dominic, who he met at university (these friends are situated in the bottom

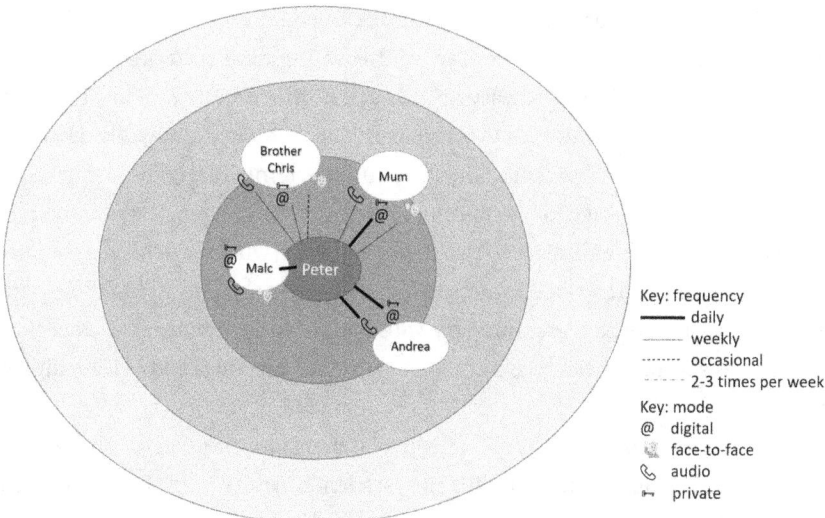

Figure 27 Peter's modes of contact diagram 1.

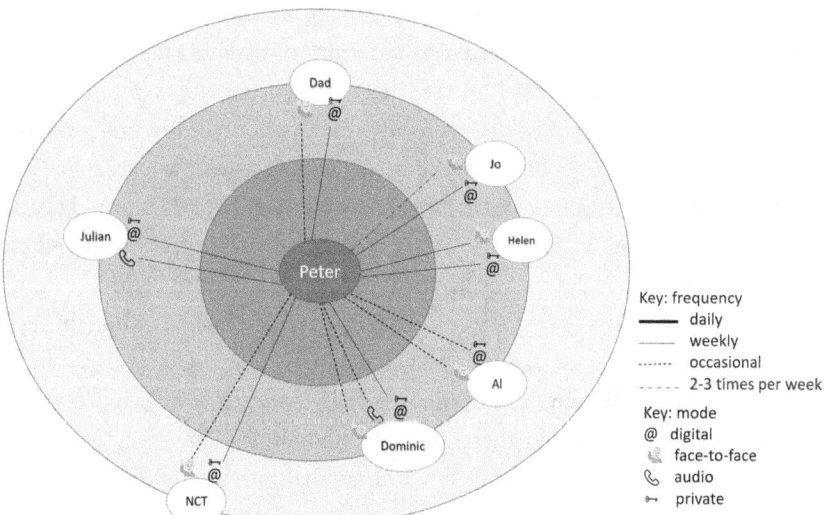

Figure 28 Peter's modes of contact diagram 2.

right portion of Peter's 'modes of contact' diagrams). Peter often described his friendship with this group using the language of kinship, suggesting in our second interview that their frequent and extended physical proximity whilst living together at university fostered strong bonds akin to 'being famil[y]'. Peter has a particularly close, intimate friendship with Andrea; as these diagrams show, he situates Andrea in the innermost circle and communicates with her daily. Further, Peter often referred to Andrea using familial terms, suggesting that their relationship was so easy and effortless, they were 'more like brothers and sisters really'. Since moving to Carville in 2016, Peter had also worked hard to build a network of local parents, largely mums in heterosexual relationships with children of a similar age. Since joining the village baby group, for example, he had become increasingly close to two local mums, Jo (who is also his neighbour) and Helen, who he described in our second interview as 'a really tight little group'. As shown in Figure 28, Peter interacts with both of these friends at least weekly, sometimes several times a week, across face-to-face meetings and private digital media.

This chapter focuses on the affective dimensions of Peter's one-to-one WhatsApp exchanges with two of his closest friends, Andrea and Helen. As noted earlier, Peter has a particularly close, quasi-familial relationship with Andrea, a friend who does not have children of her own. The physical co-presence around which their friendship was initially forged has continued to play an important role in their ongoing friendship, despite their living at almost opposite ends of the country (a four-to-five-hour drive away) and seeing one another face-to-face very infrequently. For example, Peter told me that when Lucy was very young, he and Andrea would often be connected on a video call for hours, without necessarily talking to one another. As he explained in our first interview, 'when Lu had her really difficult period . . . there were times when we'd just sit and Lu would cry on my shoulder and we'd just have the camera on . . . [Andrea] probably muted me but she was there, that was a really invaluable support'. As well as communicating via video call, Peter also regularly connected ('every day') with Andrea through audio calls and mobile messaging. Their interactions frequently traversed these different channels of communication, especially between WhatsApp message and audio call. By keeping these lines of communication open, Peter and Andrea can be said to maintain a sense of familial intimacy and togetherness that is akin to the ongoing 'co-presence' identified in the digital practices of some transnational families and couples (Alinejad, 2019; Ito & Okabe, 2005; Madianou, 2016; see discussion in Introduction). Peter's friendship with Helen is newer but had rapidly intensified during the breakdown of Helen's marriage in early 2019. During this difficult time in her life, both Peter and Jo rallied around Helen to support her. The three of them formed a WhatsApp group, as well as continuing separate one-to-one chats. In our second interview, Peter explained that he regularly exchanged a high volume of WhatsApp messages with Helen, many of which were trivial and humorous (e.g. sharing a meme or commenting on a TV show), and that 'we both have a similar humour'. He also noted that both he and Helen tended to have phones 'in our pockets' at all times and therefore were likely to reply to one another's messages quickly. As a result, many of their messages constitute short, quick-fire exchanges.

WhatsApp and affective connection

WhatsApp is a hugely popular worldwide messaging service, with more than two billion people using it in over 180 countries (WhatsApp Inc., 2021). It is widely used as a mobile-phone messaging application (app), although it can also be accessed online and via computer, using WhatsApp Web. Peter uses both, moving between the app on his phone and WhatsApp web as convenient, so that 'if you're working at a desk ... you don't have to get your phone out'. WhatsApp is very similar in function to Messenger, another messaging app owned by Meta (see discussion in Chapter 3). Both started as simple mobile messaging services that facilitated the sending and receiving of direct messages to specified contacts and have since expanded to support a variety of media including photos, videos, documents, location, audio calls and video calls. Both have the advantage that they are free at the point of use, although they do require access to an internet connection.

The key difference between WhatsApp and Messenger is that, at the time of writing, WhatsApp is independent of the Facebook app, whilst users of Messenger still need to have a Facebook account. Further, WhatsApp enables users to import telephone numbers from their mobile-phone contact list, or add mobile contacts directly to the app, whilst Messenger will only connect the user with people who have a Facebook account or other linked app such as Instagram. WhatsApp also has the strictest privacy policy of all Meta's applications; their use of end-to-end encryption means that messages cannot be intercepted. WhatsApp is therefore extremely well-tailored to intimate, private conversations between close ties. As with all social media platforms, however, the relative privacy afforded to WhatsApp users can shift according to context and use. For example, individuals may be added to WhatsApp groups without their explicit consent and may find it difficult to leave without causing offence. Further, being a member of a group makes certain information (most notably, the user's phone number) available to all members.

As noted in Chapter 3, people tend to use mobile messaging apps to maintain and develop personal relationships between known contacts and intimates

(Asprey & Tagg, 2019; Bazarova, 2012). The possibility of regular, targeted communication within the 'private space' of an individual's phone, further, means that people are more likely to share intimate, personal disclosures through mobile messaging than in more 'open' social networks such as Facebook or Twitter (Lyons & Tagg, 2019; Quan-Haase & Young, 2010; Waterloo et al., 2018). Survey research has suggested that these affordances and perceptions of mobile and instant messaging have a direct effect on users' willingness to express emotions through these media (Quan-Haase & Young, 2010; Waterloo et al., 2018). For example, Quan-Haase and Young's (2010, p. 359) survey of US university students' use of Facebook versus Instant Messaging (IM) suggests that students used IM (but not Facebook) as a way 'to provide and receive social and emotional support from friends'. Further, Waterloo et al.'s (2018) survey of young adult users of WhatsApp, Instagram, Facebook and Twitter revealed that WhatsApp was rated the most appropriate platform for expressing emotion of any kind, largely because the social risks around emotional expression were perceived to be lower in more intimate, dyadic or small-group interactions. These findings are broadly consistent with Peter's, and other participants', claims around their use of relatively 'private' digital media (especially mobile messaging and Facebook groups) for more personal and emotional disclosures. This chapter's exploration of Peter's dyadic WhatsApp exchanges with two close friends will explore the dimensions of such intimate, affective connection in detail.

Peter's use of WhatsApp

This chapter focuses on a selection of Peter's WhatsApp interactions, as his preferred and most-used digital platform for connecting with close friends and family. Peter was the only participant in the Marginalised Families Online study who was keen to share his WhatsApp chats, and he acted as an intermediary to gain consent from relevant friends and family in order to do so (see Chapter 2). In total, Peter shared nine chat logs between the people he contacted most frequently, including messages exchanged between November 2018, when he got a new phone and lost his chat history, and May 2019, when we had our second interview. Rather than taking individual screenshots of messages, Peter offered to export these chats in full, sending them to me in a zipped file that contained the text documents and separate files of any videos, images and documents uploaded to the chat. Six of these chat logs contained dyadic interactions (between Peter and one other), and three were between groups of three to six people. All of the chats were between relatively close friends and family members, with the exception of the 'baby buddies' group, which was also the group Peter engaged with least in this data set. For the purposes of this case study, I focus on dyadic messages between Peter and the two women he identified as particularly close friends – Andrea, who does not have children, and Helen, who has two children, one of whom is similar in age to Lucy. The WhatsApp chat log between Peter and Helen is the largest of the nine he shared with me, consisting of 23,728 words (1,744 individual messages) sent between 27.11.2018 and 15.05.2019. His chat log with Andrea is the fourth largest, containing 7,978 words (738 individual messages) sent between 21.11.2018 and 17.05.2019.

In order to examine Peter's WhatsApp chats with Andrea and Helen, I broke the chat logs down into sequences of messages that were related by time and/or topic. Each of these sequences may contain several utterances (units of meaning), and each participant's utterance may either be contained within a single message or fragmented across several messages (akin to the 'utterance chunks' or 'utterance break pairs' delineated by Baron (2008)). The exact parameters that make a series of messages a 'sequence' are variable, depending on the interactional norms of the dyad. For example, Helen and Peter typically respond to one another's messages within a few minutes. Accordingly, if more than thirty minutes has passed between their messages, and there is a shift of topic in the new message, this is generally considered to be the start of a new sequence. In Peter and Andrea's chats, however, it is usual to have longer time intervals between messages, therefore breaks of several hours may not be commented on or explained. However, if there is a longer time interval *and* a shift of topic in Peter and Andrea's chat log, this is counted as the start of a new message sequence.

I identified eight main communicative functions in Peter's WhatsApp message sequences, each of which may be realized through a range of mediational means – for example through words, emojis, GIFs, images or a combination of these resources (see Table 14). These functions all appear in both chat logs, but some are more frequent in one chat log than another. This chapter focuses on *communicative functions* rather than *message types* because, unlike the majority of digital data collected for the Marginalised Families Online study, Peter's WhatsApp chats represent dynamic interactions rather than single-focus messages, or posts written by one person. The functions identified in this section therefore do not necessarily correspond with discrete messages; indeed, one

Table 14 Communicative Functions in Peter's WhatsApp Message Sequences

Function	Number (Andrea)	Number (Helen)	Description	Example
Greeting	5	8	Sequence-initial welcome, seasonal greeting or term of endearment	'Hello darl'; 'HI FRIEND'; 'Happy Christmas Eve x'
Signing off	21	310	Sequence-final (or message-final) farewell, expression of affect or term of endearment	'Big hugs xx'; 'Xxxxx'
Arranging to meet/call	16	47	Enquiring about the interlocutor's availability to meet in person or call (depending on geographical proximity)	'do you want to catch up tomorrow'; 'When are you home?'; 'Just on the phone. You around for a bit?'
Checking-in	23	55	Enquiring about the interlocutor's well-being, movements or experiences	'How's the weekend been?'; 'How you feeling today?!'
Venting or complaining	7	42	Disclosing negative feelings or experiences	'Mother in law already irritating'; 'Oh god, I'm so ill'
Experiential sharing	57	73	Sharing everyday experiences, actions and moments in the participant's life	'Got out and done stuff and enjoyed the sun'; [photograph of a Normandy tart Andrea made]; [photograph of Andrea's new commute]'; 'She bloody loved soft play toxay [today]'
Reference to external media	14	34	Reference to media both participants are familiar with or have shared interest in (e.g. TV programmes, news/magazine articles, memes or social media posts)	'Have you seen the new QE?' [Queer Eye]'; '[image of the front page of the Guardian Weekend, with Rahul Mandal on the cover] Fuck off Rahul'; 'Unsure if you watch love island 😏'; 'enjoy Derry girls, they're my favourite girls'
Humour	23	85	Light-hearted or witty comments or observations, often deploying irony, mockery or self-deprecation	'Better not turn up to group with hairy pits! Hahaha 😄 x'

message may contain several functions or a single function may span several messages.

The first two functions, *greeting* and *signing off*, are relatively infrequent in Peter's chat log with Andrea. However, signing off a message with an expression of affection or endearment, especially 'kisses' (x, xx), is very common in his chats with Helen. When used, greetings are always positioned at the start of a message sequence. Sign-offs usually signal the end of a sequence, although they may also come at the end of an individual message. Further, several message sequences in both Helen and Andrea's chat logs begin with *arranging to meet or call*. These are often perfunctory exchanges, where a request for information is followed by a response and an arrangement is agreed upon. These kind of short, single-focus exchanges are very common in Andrea's chat log, and they tend not to develop into longer sequences because, if they are both free, the interaction shifts to an audio or video call. In his chats with Helen, however, an 'arranging to meet' sequence often refers to a point in the future, leaving space for further interaction in the present. *Checking-in* and *venting or complaining* sequences, however, do tend to develop into extended message sequences in both Andrea and Helen's chat logs. Checking-in messages, in particular, seem to signal that the participant is available for an extended chat, and these messages usually serve as an invitation to share updates or experiences in-depth. The checking-in function is very common in both chat logs, and Peter checks in with Helen particularly frequently after her separation from her husband. There are also some brief complaint sequences in both chat logs, where a short complaint is followed by an expression of sympathy or empathy.

The sixth function, *experiential sharing*, is particularly common in Peter and Andrea's chat log. This function often takes the form of (or is accompanied by) a photograph, with the subject of Helen's photographs often being food (she is training to be a chef) and the subject of Peter's photographs often being his daughter, Lucy. Some of these exchanges develop into extended message sequences, but many are short, focusing on a single topic. This kind of everyday sharing likely occurs more in Peter and Andrea's chat log because they are geographically distanced from one another and therefore don't spend so much time in the same physical space where they would see, for example, Andrea's cooking, her view of London or Lucy's development, in person. Sharing photographs of their everyday life can therefore be seen as a way of maintaining a regular visual connection, giving Peter and Andrea an ongoing sense of what one another's lives 'look' like and how they experience particular moments and events. Indeed, by regularly sharing snapshots of their lives,

Peter and Andrea can be said to affirm one another's rights to look into, and as such be active participants in, each other's everyday lives (see Jones, 2020b, on digital photography, embodied experience and the 'right to look'). These kind of updates, however, are much less frequent in Helen's chat log. *References to external media*, on the other hand, are very common in Peter's chats with both Helen and Andrea. These may include references to social media posts, news or magazine articles, or memes. References to TV programmes they both watch, including shared evaluations of those programmes, are particularly frequent in both chats. For example, Peter and Helen regularly discuss *Holby City*, *Love Island* and children's cartoons such as the CBeebies programme *Bing*, whilst he and Andrea often discuss *Masterchef* and *Queer Eye*. The final function, *humour*, is very common in both chats, but particularly so in Peter and Helen's chats, which is consistent with Peter's claim in our second interview that he and Helen have 'similar humour'. Humour is not as frequent in Peter's chats with Andrea but is nevertheless present, often in the form of mock-anger. Humour is very rarely an isolated function in these chats; it usually coincides and overlaps with complaints, greetings, references to external media and experiential sharing, as the analyses of the following sections will show.

In order to explore the affective dimensions of Peter's one-to-one WhatsApp chats with Helen and Andrea, I have selected message sequences that are representative of wider patterns in the chat logs and which, between them, span a range of the functions listed previously. The analyses of the sections that follow will consider how affect is mediated in these sequences. In the first instance, I consider short, intense exchanges that are based around a single affective impetus, whilst later examples constitute more complex affective flows, where each interlocutor mobilizes a range of affective practices in a way that is sensitive to participants' history, needs and the emerging communicative context. The analyses will shed light on the mechanisms through which a range of affective practices are mediated in everyday, one-to-one mobile messages and how these practices can sustain intimate, caring and affectionate connections between close friends.

Media references and complaints as moments of shared affect

This section focuses on four short message sequences between Peter and Helen (Extracts 16 and 19) and Peter and Andrea (Extracts 17 and 18), where a single affective impetus serves as a focal point for affective connection between these interlocutors. The first set of examples centres on a reference to external media

Elaborating Affective Connection

with which both participants are familiar, whilst the second set focuses on complaints about family members.

References to external media are very common in Peter's chats with both Helen and Andrea, especially references to TV programmes they both watch. Message sequences that include reference to shared TV programmes tend to include (1) a message checking that the other has watched the programme, followed by (2) a shared affective evaluation of the programme (although participants sometimes go straight to the evaluation). This pattern is exemplified in Extract 16, which begins with Peter asking Andrea whether she has seen the latest episode of 'QE' (*Queer Eye*).

Extract 16. 'Have you seen the new QE?' (27.03.2019)

Message 1: Peter, 11:55
Have u seen the new QE? [Queer Eye]

Message 2: Andrea, 13:03
Yaaaaassssss 🙌

Message 3: Peter, 13:27
The single dad made me cry a lot

Message 4: Peter, 13:27
And how beautiful was Jess

Andrea's response, in message 2, both confirms that she has seen the latest episode of *Queer Eye* and evaluates this episode positively, through the elongated 'Yaaaaaaassssss' and 'raising both hands in celebration' emoji. Peter's subsequent messages build on this enthusiastically positive evaluation through reference to specific moments and characters in the episode. For example, he first evaluates Jess as 'beautiful' and then centres his own affective response to the programme, writing that 'the single dad made me cry a lot'. In this brief exchange, Peter and Andrea's connection around their shared affective response to an episode of *Queer Eye* is comparable with Jenny's connection with other adoptive parents through their emotive responses to the 'Superkids' documentary (see Chapter 5). Peter and Andrea's affective connection, however, is much more implicit. For example, Andrea's response indicates enthusiastic enjoyment of the programme but does not explicitly comment on its content. Further, Peter's positive evaluation 'how beautiful was Jess' relies on the (unconfirmed) presumption that Andrea will share his positive feelings towards Jess. Such presumptions point to a history of shared viewing between these friends.

In the message sequence displayed in Extract 17, Helen sends Peter a photograph of her television, which is showing the CBeebies cartoon *Bing*. In this image Bing, the rabbit star of the show, is standing at the end of a queue for a slide, looking nervous. The photograph is accompanied by Helen's comment 'get it together bing you fucking moron it's a slide'. Presumably, Helen's pre-school child is the one watching the programme, and Helen is co-present with this child.

Extract 17. 'Get it together Bing' (02.01.2019)

Message 1: Helen, 07:29
Get it together bing you fucking moron it's a slide
Message 2: Peter, 08:23
Such a prat

By sharing a moment from *Bing* as it happens, Helen draws Peter into a shared viewing of the cartoon. Indeed, given the frequency with which these friends discuss *Bing* (there are seven separate discussions about the programme and/or character in their chat), Helen may be assuming that Peter *is* watching *Bing* at the same moment, with his daughter Lucy. Helen's accompanying text also draws Peter into a specific affective interpretation of this moment: she labels Bing a 'fucking moron', an emotive but tongue-in-cheek damnation that offers a humorously adult take on a programme designed for pre-schoolers. Peter's response, 'such a prat', echoes Helen's evaluation through a similarly damning insult and thus signals his participation in a shared viewing and affective response to the programme. The brevity of this exchange, like Peter and Andrea's *Queer Eye* sequence, again points to a shared history of viewing between Helen and Peter, which means Helen doesn't have to contextualize her message or explain her response. It also suggests, alongside the expletives and insults 'fucking moron' and 'prat', that they are sharing their genuine reactions as they happen in the moment.

Although *Bing* is a programme Peter and Helen watch with their young children, this exchange represents a distinctly adult moment of affective connection. Helen and Peter can therefore be said to connect not only around their affective response to a cartoon character but around their ability to express apparently unfiltered reactions, even when sharing a physical space with their children. By sharing their affective response to this children's TV programme within the personal space of their mobile phones, Peter and Helen are able to sustain two affective connections simultaneously, being physically present for a shared viewing of the programme with their children whilst at the same time sharing their playful, more adult affective response to the programme via WhatsApp. This capacity for being physically present with a child whilst at the same time communicating with a friend, in silence and without disturbing the child, is an important affordance of mobile messaging that is also discussed by Lynne in the context of communicating with friends whilst a child is in hospital (see discussion in Chapter 3). In Peter and Helen's case, the privacy of the WhatsApp chat is heightened because they have pre-school children who cannot read.

The complaint sequences in Andrea and Helen's chat logs are comparable with these media-related sequences, in that they are often short and centre on the affective evaluation of a single event, object or person who is known to both participants. For example, in Extracts 18 and 19, a short complaint about a family member (or members) is followed by an expression of sympathy, which seems to be the basic utterance-response unit for this kind of sequence.

Extract 18. 'Merry Fuck-Off-mas' (24.12.18)

Message 1: Peter, 12:36
Merry Fuck-Off-mas! Inlaws already irritating me

Message 2: Helen, 13:18

Message 3: Helen, 13:18
Oh god !!!! Why xxx

Extract 19. 'I'm Completely Overrun' (09.02.2019)

Message 1: Andrea, 21:12
SIGH. I'm completely overrun with work and school work and Tom promised me he'd be proactive this weekend and help out. He's been lying horizontal on the bed since 5pm

Message 2: Peter, 21:16

:(

Peter's complaint in Extract 18, like Helen's evaluation of *Bing* in Extract 17, uses an expletive that negatively evaluates his time with his in-laws in playfully abrupt and emotive terms: 'Merry Fuck-Off-mas!'. As with Peter and Helen's shared evaluation of *Bing*, this is not an affective response Peter is likely to share with the family members with whom he is co-present. However, in the private space of his mobile phone, Peter is able to share an alternative, apparently more genuine and unfiltered affective reaction. In Helen's response, she first shares her own affective reaction to Peter's message, in three 'crying with laughter' emojis that sustain the playful nature of this exchange (message 2). In message 3, she echoes Peter's affective reaction, with the words 'Oh god' followed by four exclamation marks and expresses sympathy by asking 'why', followed by three xs (representing kisses). In Extract 19, Andrea offers a similar complaint about a family member – her boyfriend Tom. Her opening affective expression 'SIGH', in capital letters, expresses exasperation, as does the intensified description '*completely* overrun' and the contrast between Tom's 'promise' that he'd be 'proactive' and her description of him 'lying horizontal on the bed'. Peter's response, the sad-face emoticon, echoes and validates the frustration conveyed in Andrea's message.

In each of these short sequences, a media reference or complaint about a family member(s) serves as the affective impetus for the circulation of shared affect. Such circulations, which are a regular feature of these friends' WhatsApp interactions, maintain regular, intimate connections that can operate alongside (and sometimes contradict) in-person connections and interactions with other family members. The kind of alignment through affective evaluation that we see in these exchanges has been widely explored across discourse analytical and social media research. For example, Peter's connections with Helen and Andrea can be theorized using Du Bois' (2007) 'stance triangle', since they align with one another through shared evaluations of a stance 'object'. Alternatively, these 'objects' (family members or television programmes) might be conceptualized as 'bonding icons' (Page, 2018; Zappavigna, 2014) – as symbolic resources around which shared interpersonal meanings can be foregrounded (see discussion in Chapter 3). Further, where we see repeated articulations of shared feeling, as with the example of Peter and Helen's negative evaluation of *Bing*, we might describe this as a more pervasive 'affective homophily' (Sundén & Paasonen, 2019; see discussion in Chapter 7) that articulates the boundaries of these friends' relationship. However, Peter's dyadic exchanges are quite different from the one-off moments of affective 'bonding' or 'homophily' in Page's (2018) exploration of Facebook memorial pages, Sundén and Paasonen's (2019) analysis of the 'me too' movement or Zappavigna's (2014) analysis of tweets about #coffee. Instead, these examples represent recurring moments of affective connection between close friends, which shape and sustain ongoing relationships of familiarity and intimacy. Whilst the sequences tend to be short, then, I would suggest that the connections they sustain are not fleeting. Rather, these affective connections are a mechanism by which Peter, Helen and Andrea draw one another into their lives by sharing in the collective feeling of specific moments, events and interpretations.

Checking-in as an affective practice of care

The previous section has focused on brief exchanges which centre on a single affective impetus. In this section, I analyse a longer message sequence between Peter and Helen (Extract 20) that encompasses both a wider range of interactional functions and a wider range of affects. This sequence moves iteratively between 'greeting', 'checking-in', 'experiential sharing' and 'signing off'. This is a common combination in Peter and Helen's chat log, especially after Helen's relationship breakdown, where an initial 'checking-in' message often serves as an opener to further interaction that shifts through a range of topics and communicative functions. The sequence took place a couple of months after Helen's separation from her husband, soon after she moved into her own house with her children.

Extract 20. 'Felt a little lonely today' (12.05.2019)

Message 1: Peter, 22:55
Hello darl. How's the weekend been? Happy wifi day for tomorrow!! Xx

Message 2: Helen, 22:56
Hellooo. It's been OK! Got out and done stuff and enjoyed the sun. You? Thank goodness for WiFi day xxxx

Message 3: Peter, 22:57
Ahh nice one. Did you enjoy the seaside? Had a nice weekend here thanks, had lots to drink last night which was fun :) xx

Message 4: Helen, 22:58
I did although have felt a little lonely today which I feel guilty about as feel the kids should be enough. Waheyy xxxx

Message 5: Helen, 22:58
I think when you're out seeing other families etc

Message 6: Peter, 23:00
Totally understandable thing to feel, exactly because when you see other families.
Big Hugs xx

Message 7: Helen, 23:00
Xxxxx

Peter opens the sequence with an affectionate greeting, in this case 'Hello darl' (short for 'darling'). Peter and Helen frequently used terms of endearment like this, such as 'friend', 'darl', 'babe' and 'bbz' (an abbreviation of 'babes') in the second half of their chat log, from March onwards, when problems began to arise in Helen's relationship. This may be a sign of their developing closeness and intimacy, accelerated by Helen's need for care and support during this time. As with Tony's greetings to the UKFR Facebook community (e.g. 'my kin', 'lovely fae'), these affectionate terms of address, through repeated use, can be said to build and maintain connections of intimacy, care and affection between Peter and Helen. The checking-in utterance that follows this greeting ('How's the weekend been?') is an affective practice of care that further shapes and affirms this connection, signalling Peter's attentiveness to what is happening in Helen's life, his eagerness to invest in it further and his care for her well-being.

Peter concludes his first message with a second greeting, which takes a form usually reserved for holidays and special occasions, 'Happy [celebration] Day'. By playfully appropriating this formulaic utterance in relation to a relatively mundane moment in Helen's life (the day she gets Wi-Fi in her new home), Peter generates a sort of 'holiday spirit', ending the message in a positive, celebratory affective tone. This tone is consolidated by two xs, as orthographic representations of kisses, at the end of the message. These kisses, as suggested in the analysis of Tony's Facebook posts in Chapter 7, can be interpreted as digital entextualizations of an affective action that physically connects two individuals in a gesture of intimacy and affection. The significance of these 'kisses' is discussed in more detail in the paragraphs that follow. In Helen's reply (message 2), she tentatively echoes Peter's playful and celebratory tone. For example, her responsive greeting 'Hellooo', with the repeated final 'o', signals playfulness and positivity. Although her evaluative update 'It's been OK!' is somewhat vague, the exclamation mark suggests an enthusiastic and light-hearted tone. Helen also takes up Peter's invented celebratory 'WiFi day' in the final utterance of this message – 'thank goodness for WiFi day'. The positivity and celebration in Helen's reply, however, are never enthusiastically realized, and she offers only moderate indications of enjoyment with the vague and neutral references 'ok', 'got out' and 'done stuff'. Further, the initial tone of celebration shifts to something more like relief in the expression 'thank goodness'.

As the exchange between Peter and Helen unfolds, the caring practice of checking-in extends across several messages. In message 2, Helen reciprocates Peter's check-in with the question 'You?', and in message 3, Peter asks for further information ('did you enjoy the seaside?') before responding to Helen's question with his own positive update ('had a nice weekend here'). Peter's second checking-in utterance prompts a slightly different response from Helen in message 4, where she shifts further away from the positive, celebratory affect encoded in their initial messages. This shift, like her initial expressions of positivity and celebration, is tentative, with Helen first agreeing that she did 'enjoy the seaside' but going on to indicate feelings of loneliness and guilt in the elaborated response that follows: 'have felt a little lonely today which I feel guilty about . . .'. This expression of loneliness is mitigated by the qualifier 'little', and Helen ends the message with the positively valenced expression 'Waheyy', which like 'Hellooo', has an elongated final vowel that lends a playful tone. This sign-off could certainly be read as sarcastic, given the content of Helen's message, but it nevertheless indicates some reluctance to close her message on a completely negative note. Further, Helen suggests that her loneliness is not a legitimate emotion when noting that she feels guilty, as 'the kids should be enough'. She also offers a mitigated justification for her loneliness in message 5, which follows directly after message 4, 'I think when you're out seeing other families etc.'

In Peter's response to Helen's negatively valenced emotional sharing (message 6), he definitively takes up Helen's reference to loneliness, legitimizing this feeling in intensified terms that contrast with Helen's tentative expression, as 'totally understandable'. He then echoes Helen's statement 'when you're out seeing other families' almost verbatim, as well as further intensifying and validating her emotional response to this experience with the unmitigated and forceful expression 'exactly'. This message thus signals Peter's affective alignment with Helen, through a flow of emotions that intensifies as it moves between the two friends. This validatory practice is comparable to the 'emotional reciprocity' (Morrison, 2011) or 'me too' sharing (Pedersen & Lupton, 2018) that has been observed in online mothering blogs and discussion forums (see Chapter 7). As in these parenting collectives, the echoing of a negative emotional response connects Peter and Helen through solidarity and shared understanding, as well as acknowledging and validating negative emotions that contradict the dominant 'feeling rules' of good motherhood – in this case, that mothers should always feel happy and fulfilled when spending time with their children. Peter's message ends with the entextualized affective actions of hugs and kisses – 'Big hugs xx' again signalling a flow of embodied physical love, care and affection between these friends. Helen's final message, which simply reads 'Xxxxx', reciprocates this affective action and closes the exchange. This is a fitting sign-off, since the affective act of kissing peppers the sequence, with all but one of the messages ending with between two to five xs. This entextualization of an intimate practice further contributes to an affective connection of intimacy, care and affection that underpins the exchange between these two friends.

The relational construction and shifting of affective states that can be observed in this sequence – from positivity and celebration to negativity and loneliness – points to an affective connection between Helen and Peter that is characterized by emotional shifts and flows. In this sequence, unlike the brief affective exchanges that were explored in the previous section, the flow of emotion is quite tentative at first but can be seen to intensify as it moves between these two friends. I would suggest that, in this instance, the intensely personal focus of the exchange, and underlying difficulty of the experience Helen relates, makes for an affective flow that is 'care-ful' in more ways than one: it is both full of care, and cautiously attentive (see discussion of Alinejad's (2019) work on 'careful' digital practice in Chapter 7). Peter enables this flow through affective practices of love, care and intimacy, in this case affectionate naming, extended checking-in and entextualized affective actions ('hugs' and 'kisses'), as well as the echoing and validation of emotional responses. It is, perhaps, the persistent repetition of these caring practices that allows Helen to draw out a quite complex tapestry of feeling within a caring, supportive and non-judgemental context.

Constructing intimate ease through humour and play

In this final analysis, I explore a light-hearted exchange between Peter and Andrea that combines 'experiential sharing' with 'humour' (Extract 21). This message sequence begins with Peter announcing that he has replaced his phone, an update that also serves to explain why he has had to begin a new chat log with Andrea. He goes on to share a picture of his daughter Lucy, taken on this new phone. Each of the messages in this sequence is very short, and utterances are often fragmented across several messages. This is a common feature of Peter and Andrea's chats, perhaps because they tend to use audio and video calls for longer exchanges and because their familial intimacy and ease make fully formed utterances an unnecessary formality.

Extract 21. 'Changed my phone' (21.11.2018)

Message 1: Peter, 07:26	Changed my phone
Message 2: Peter, 07:26	Don't have an iPhone any more
Message 3: Peter, 07:26	🙃
Message 4: Andrea, 08:11	WHAT?!
Message 5: Andrea, 08:25	How do we FaceTime now?!
Message 6: Peter, 08:43	WhatsApp video instead 😬
Message 7: Andrea, 08:43	No serious
Message 8: Peter, 08:43	Deadly
Message 9: Peter, 09:00	I feel like I should apologise
Message 10: Andrea, 09:02	You should
Message 11: Andrea, 09:02	😟
Message 12: Peter, 09:09	Wellllllllll no?
Message 13: Andrea, 09:23	Lol. Wouldn't expect anything less!
Message 14: Andrea, 09:32	So what have you gone for?!
Message 15: Peter, 09:33	Google pixel 3
Message 16: Peter, 09:33	Loving it
Message 17: Peter, 09:33	[medium shot photograph of Lucy in the bath, smiling and looking to the right of the camera] Camera is so much better
Message 18: Andrea, 09:33	Ahhhhh it's a cheeky baby!
Message 19: Peter, 09:34	Yes especially because she was actually doing a shit whilst I took yhjs
Message 20: Peter, 09:34	This
Message 21: Andrea, 09:34	Oh. Ruined it
Message 22: Peter, 09:34	Yeh
Message 23: Peter, 09:34	Not great

In Peter's first utterance, which is fragmented across messages 1–3, he offers an update about his life, announcing that he no longer has an iPhone. He follows this announcement with an upside-down face emoji, which has a highly variable meaning, but given Andrea's response, seems to indicate that this is a surprising, unexpected announcement and possibly that Peter expects Andrea to disapprove of his decision. Andrea's reply, fragmented across messages 4 and 5, takes an affective tone of mock outrage – a playful mix of anger, incredulity, humour and fun. For example, her first response is a message with a single, unmitigated interjection in all capitals – 'WHAT?!', and the message that follows is a blunt interrogative, 'How do we FaceTime now?!' Both messages are punctuated by interrobangs. Peter plays along with Andrea's mock interrogation by responding, in message 6, as one might to a genuine accusation of wrongdoing: by offering a solution – 'WhatsApp video instead' – followed by a 'cold sweat' emoji that indicates guilt and worry. In message 9, further, Peter points towards an apology – 'I feel like I should apologise.' Andrea's mock outrage continues in messages 10 and 11 with the bald imperative 'You should', followed by a second message that consists solely of an angry red emoji. Following Peter's relatively mundane update, Andrea's transition to outrage appears sudden and blunt, especially when compared with the tentatively shifting affective flows of Peter and Helen's exchange in the previous section. However, in the context of their long-standing familial friendship, this sudden affective shift indicates a level of ease that makes play with extreme affective displays not only possible but a playful validation of their intimate relationship. Such displays are also relatively safe in the context of a comparatively innocuous topic such as brands of mobile phones, compared with the more serious emotional turmoil that flows beneath Peter's message sequence with Helen.

In message 12, Peter redacts his earlier indication of regret and refuses to apologize – 'Wellllllllll no?'. His orthographical play with the final 'l' in 'well', together with the final question mark, indicates fun and playfulness more explicitly than the previous messages. Together with Andrea's reference to laughter ('Lol') in message 13, these messages mark a transition away from mock outrage, through acknowledgement of the playful humour that underpins it. In message 14, Andrea shifts the focus of the exchange, responding to Peter's update in a more conventional way: by asking for more information about the phone – 'So what have you gone for?!' The messages that follow (15 to 18) turn to a fairly well-established pattern of experiential sharing in Peter and Andrea's chat log, where one of them shares a photograph (often unprompted) and the other replies with a positive evaluation (see earlier discussion of Peter's use of WhatsApp). In this sequence, Peter's visual sharing has a dual function, both showing the quality of his new cameraphone and sharing a visual update on life with his daughter. Andrea's response 'Ahhhhh it's a cheeky baby!' responds to the latter, evaluating Lucy as cute and cheeky, and marking a definitive shift away from the playful frame of mock outrage. This kind of admiring and approving response is extremely common in relation to their visual sharing and works to maintain an ongoing affective connection based on mutual care and appreciation.

The sequence ends with a return to humour; in messages 19 and 20, Peter takes up Andrea's evaluation of Lucy as cheeky and cute, and turns this on its head by revealing the less endearing fact that 'she was actually doing a shit whilst I took [this]'. With this humorous juxtaposition, the exchanges fall back into the easy, intimate and light-hearted affective connection that characterizes Peter and Andrea's interactions. Further, by sharing this far less sanitized and photogenic everyday act, Peter lets Andrea into the 'behind-the-scenes' reality of this photo and indeed of his life parenting a young infant. This intimate sharing of a moment that transgresses the picture-perfect family ideal further consolidates the easy connection between Peter and Andrea that can be glimpsed in this message exchange. It may also be compared with the affective evaluations between Peter, Helen and Andrea that were identified in the first analytical section. In each case, the friends let one another into the 'real', unfiltered moments of their lives. The intimacy between Peter and Andrea in Extract 20, however, looks quite different to what we saw in the previous example from Peter and Helen's chat log. Whilst both message sequences undergo a number of affective shifts, in Peter and Andrea's chat these shifts are characterized by blunt transitions and bold assertions rather than careful, tentative movement. The difference in these flows is no doubt influenced by the topic, the use of humour and the nature of the affective connections between each dyad: for Peter and Andrea, this connection seems to be shaped by an undercurrent of intimate, familial ease.

Chapter summary

This chapter has elaborated the concept of affective connection through a second case study that examines Peter's use of WhatsApp to forge affective connections with two close friends, Helen and Andrea. The analysis has shown how Peter, Helen and Andrea deploy affective practices of love, familiarity, intimacy and care to sustain complex and multidimensional tapestries of affective connection. The first analytical section shows how these friends generate moments of shared feeling by centring, and echoing, their unfiltered reactions to an affective impetus that is known to both participants, such as a shared media reference. The longer message sequences examined in the second and third analytical sections undergo a number of affective shifts, showing that these friends' affective connections cannot always be theorized uni-dimensionally. Indeed, as Sundén and Paasonen (2019) have shown in their analysis of responses to the #MeToo movement, Peter's WhatsApp chats demonstrate that the affective flow of emotions, feelings and attitudes between close intimates are rarely static: they shift, merge, combine and can be difficult to isolate. The affective flows of Peter's sympathetic exchange with Helen, for example, are neither exclusively celebratory nor exclusively melancholic, whilst his humorous sequence with

Andrea is neither exclusively angry, ironic, nor admiring. Peter's connections with these friends are therefore best characterized by their range, complexity and nuance, with interlocutors bringing various affective states to bear in their interactions. The affective shifts that ensue can be fleeting and blunt, or they can be tentative, and 'care-ful' in more ways than one, depending on the relationship, the topic and contextual detail around participants' lives.

Together with Chapter 7, this chapter's examination of affective connection makes an important contribution to the book as a whole. The focus of these chapters is quite different from those that came before, since the data explored here does not always relate to directly Tony and Peter's parenting practice. Nevertheless, the chapters develop the discussion of Chapters 3 and 4, showing that parents can expand the boundaries of 'family' not only through the collective construction and maintenance of parenting practices but also through affective connections with significant friends and communities. This line of argument suggests that through the nexus of connected parenting practice, parents can both shape and sustain their parenting actions and practices, and also build and maintain friendship and community relations that are themselves familial in texture.

9

The Theoretical, Methodological and Practical Implications of Connected Parenting

This book set out to examine the relationship between parenting, family practices and digital media for UK parents who brought children into their lives through adoption, donor conception or co-parenting arrangements. Through empirical investigation of six case studies, it has shown how these parents' digitally mediated connections with individuals, groups and communities can be constructed, sustained and mobilized through collective, epistemic and affective actions and practices. Further, we have seen how these mediated actions relate to, and reverberate through, parents' wider family practices, their social lives and personal support networks. The analyses have shown that parents' experience of social marginalization and discrimination is often the driving force in forging connections that can be intimate, supportive and sometimes transformational. Overall, the book has important implications for the way families are theorized and understood, both in a broader social context and in academic research across disciplines. Its emphasis on social action and family practices facilitates a nuanced and flexible exploration of connected parenting that can extend beyond the traditional boundaries of nuclear families and parent–child relationships. Above all, it has shown that family practices are intensely relational. Now more than ever, with the growing potential to form collectives, networks and communities of like-minded others online, family practices are often constructed, realized, maintained and mobilized *through* connection with others. Connected parenting therefore represents a new way of 'doing' family in a digital and networked age.

In this chapter, I review and consolidate the book's key contributions for scholarly and social practice. I begin with a summative discussion of the way collective, epistemic and affective connections can intersect and overlap in the construction of connected parenting practice, before considering the theoretical contributions connected parenting can make to research concerning the relationship between digital discourse, parenthood and family practice. I then outline the book's methodological contributions, emphasizing the value of grounded theory and mediated discourse analysis as a combined approach in qualitative investigations of digital media as it is intertwined with everyday life. As the book draws to a close, I consider its implications for wider social action, policy and practice.

The intersection of collective, epistemic and affective connection

As the start of this book (Introduction and Chapter 1), I introduced connected parenting as a collection of practices – more specifically a 'nexus of practice' (Scollon, 2001) – through which parenting and family practices are constructed, negotiated and maintained between friends, family members, groups and communities. The analytical chapters that followed have examined the three core dimensions of this nexus: collective connection, epistemic connection and affective connection. Separating collective, epistemic and affective connection means that I have been able to explore each dimension in depth and detail, with close attention to the ways in which they are manifested in relation to individuals' family and digital practices. However, this separation may also create the false impression that the three dimensions of connected parenting operate in isolation. This section is therefore dedicated to the re-integration of these dimensions, drawing the findings of the previous chapters together to clarify some of the ways in which collective, epistemic and affective dimensions can overlap and intersect at the nexus of connected parenting practice.

I begin this discussion with a focus on collective connection, defined as the construction, consolidation and mobilization of shared actions, practices and experiences. This is the dimension that is most foundational to connected parenting practice for many of the Marginalised Families Online participants. As Chapters 3 and 4 have shown, connecting with parents who are perceived to have similar family circumstances feels vital for many of these participants because it allows them to forge bonds with others who understand their lives, without having to constantly explain themselves. Groups of peers, further, can offer what one participant describes as a 'safe space' to talk about their experiences without fear of judgement or attack. In Chapters 3 and 4, I looked at some of the ways in which collective connections between parents can be constructed, sustained and mobilized through a focus on the digital media practices of two single adoptive parents, Lynne and Cheryl. I showed how these women work to entextualize and recontextualize their own and others' actions as shared experiences that are already circulating in their network's repertoire of family practices. Parents' recourse to such shared repertoires, I suggest, is the foundation for a collective connection that is forged not just through shared values but through the construction of parenting and family actions and practices as *collectively* undertaken, in a unified and mutually supportive way.

The case studies that are presented in Chapters 5 and 6 suggest that practices of collective connection intersect with, and often form the foundations for, epistemic connection. Practices of epistemic connection, which concern the formation of ties through the construction and exchange of information and knowledge, are explored through a focus on the digital media engagement of another set of single parents: Jenny and Rachael. These chapters show how participants' epistemic connections with their peers often rely upon and mobilize collective experiences, practices and perspectives. In Chapter 5, for example, the analysis of Jenny's recontextualization practices on Twitter shows how she draws on the presumption of shared experience and perspectives with her fellow adopters both to challenge institutional forms of knowledge about care-experienced young people's behaviours and educational backgrounds, and to take social action that will improve their lives. In Jenny's retweet of a post by the educational institution Tes, for example, she connects with her peers by establishing shared familiarity with, and disapproval of, content about how to cope with young people's challenging behaviours in the classroom. This example has a great deal in common with Cheryl's Facebook posts, which are explored in Chapter 4 with an emphasis on collective connection. In both cases, Jenny and Cheryl draw on the shared experience and expertise of their peers to challenge 'expert' perspectives on young people's negative behaviours. Chapter 6 looks at how Rachael uses Instagram to valorize and promote forms of knowledge around parenting, motherhood and family life through the entextualization of her own family practices. The analysis of selected posts in this chapter shows how Rachael's circulation of practical, repeatable knowledge resources about solo mothering relies on collective connections with her audience, who are positioned as a group with similar experiences of family life.

The collective and epistemic dimensions of connected parenting practice also intersect with the final dimension, affective connection, defined as the formation of social ties through the construction and flow of emotions, feelings, moods, dispositions and attitudes. Through Chapters 3 to 6, we began to see that affect can play an integral role in parents' connective practices. In Cheryl's info-relational Facebook posts (Chapter 4), for example, she foregrounds her affective responses to the content she is sharing and presupposes that others will share these reactions. Indeed, the affective tone of frustration and exhaustion that suffuses Cheryl's posts seems to be a core component of the experience that she shares with her peers. A similar affective tone, and a similar presumption of shared affect, can be seen in examples from Jenny's Twitter data (Chapter 5), where she expresses frustration and exhaustion around coming up against the same predictable problems in educational policy and practice, time and again. The analysis of Tony's posts to the Facebook group of a community he describes as his 'queer family' (Chapter 7) and Peter's WhatsApp chats with two close friends, one of whom he sees as a sister (Chapter 8), also point to significant overlap between the affective and collective dimensions of connected parenting. These chapters have shown how the reciprocal circulation of affective responses, expressions and actions can shape relationships characterized by togetherness, solidarity and intimate ease. Just as peers, friends and communities may connect over shared experiences and perspectives, then, they may also connect through shared feeling.

In sum, the analysis that is presented in this book has shown that practices of collective, epistemic and affective connection, although they can each involve distinct actions and effects, are often intimately intertwined. Indeed, there isn't a single piece of digital data from the Marginalised Families Online project that is only relevant to one dimension of connected parenting. The three core dimensions of connected parenting, then, are likely driven by similar forces, namely the desire to reach out to others and forge connections that may be intimate, empathetic, supportive, galvanizing, practically useful or a combination of these values. Together, the nexus of connected parenting practice can be a panacea for the practical difficulties, personal challenges, wider discrimination and lack of social support that many of the Marginalised Families Online participants experienced, alongside the more everyday challenges of parenting and family life. The theoretical implications of connected parenting are discussed in further detail in the section that follows.

Theoretical contributions

This book promotes fresh scrutiny of the relationship between digital discourse, parenthood and family practice in a contemporary context. Through an examination of connected parenting practice in the lives of six UK parents who have non-traditional family structures, it has offered an expansive and inclusive exploration of family practices. Some of the analysis in this book focuses squarely on the digitally mediated entextualization of *parenting* actions and practices, for example through a Messenger exchange about washing nappies (Chapter 3) or an Instagram post about going for a walk in the forest with an infant (Chapter 6). These chapters have illustrated how specific parent-related actions can circulate between families and networks, functioning as tools for connecting with others. However, the book has also shown how mediated family practices can extend beyond parent–child relationships, beyond the household and beyond geographical borders. For example, I have suggested that challenging epistemologies of education, childhood behaviour and family structures through Twitter and Instagram (Chapters 5 and 6) can also feed into connected parenting practice. Further, Chapters 7 and 8 show that connected parenting practice can be realized through the circulation of love, care and affection between intimate friends and communities in Facebook group and WhatsApp exchanges. In all of these cases, I demonstrate that connected parenting practice is not just a supporting act but an integral part of contemporary family life.

Through the explication of three distinct but overlapping dimensions of connected parenting practice, this book also contributes to several strands of interdisciplinary research that concern the relevance of affiliation, knowledge construction and affect in parenting collectives, families, friendship groups and communities. For example, its exploration of collective connection in Chapters 3 and 4 shows that connecting with others who are perceived to have similar experiences can have vital implications for the health and social well-being of marginalized and minority parents and family groups. Echoing research with a range of online parenting collectives (e.g. Bellander & Nikolaidou, 2017; Blum-Ross & Livingstone, 2017; Jaworska, 2018; Pedersen & Smithson, 2018), these chapters suggest that peer-to-peer online connections can help these groups normalize and value their experiences, construct a reassuring sense of togetherness and solidarity, and most of all, feel 'understood'.

The analyses of Chapters 3 and 4 show how, through practices of collective connection, parents like Lynne and Cheryl are able to construct their own and others' parenting and family actions as *collective* practices. These connections can be consolidated and mobilized through simple communicative 'shortcuts' such as hyperlinked texts, micro-entextualizations, metonymies and the simulation of ongoing dialogue, which rely on shared knowledge, experience and understanding for their meanings. The discussion of these chapters moves beyond the themes of support, solidarity and validation that have dominated existing research with online parenting collectives to suggest that collective connections between parents have the potential to expand the boundaries of 'family' beyond the immediate parent–child unit, to include a wider network of parents and families who share in the same family practices. Thus, I suggest that collective connection, especially for parents who may otherwise be isolated or marginalized from mainstream parenting networks, can form an integral part of family life.

Further, the exploration of epistemic connection in Chapters 5 and 6 draws upon scholarly insights around the relationship between connection, action and knowledge. Building on the concepts of 'connected knowing' (Zaslow, 2012) and 'connective action' (Akrich, 2010), these chapters consider how parents privilege the experience-based knowledge resources that are circulating in their networks and mobilize these collective forms of knowledge to promote transformative social action. The chapters show how Jenny and Rachael, two single mothers who are very well connected in their networks, use their influential positions to drive forward new ways of understanding institutions such as motherhood, the family and education. Chapter 5 focuses on Jenny's use of Twitter to recontextualize and reinterpret 'expert' and institutional knowledge from the shared experiential perspective of fellow adopters and home educators. Chapter 6, on the other hand, shows how Rachael foregrounds her personal experiences as a solo mum, entextualizing actions and practices from her own life as practical, relatable knowledge resources to be taken up by other solo mums. These analyses reveal some of the ways in which parents can use social media to subvert established and institutionally valorized practices through new and alternative epistemological lenses. However, the discussion of Chapter 6 also underlines the point that such practices of knowledge-construction and epistemic connection should be subject to critical scrutiny, since they still have the potential to (re)produce restrictive norms and practices.

Finally, building on research with both transnational families and LGBT communities (e.g. Alinejad, 2019; Santana, 2019), my analysis of affective connection shows how practices of familiarity, love, care, intimacy and affection can consolidate intimate bonds between individuals and groups that are familial in texture. In Chapter 7, for example, I point to the way Tony constructs and maintains pseudo-physical affective connections within a queer community's Facebook group through the use of affectionate and kin-like naming devices, the entextualization of physical acts of care and intimacy (such as hugs and kisses) and the language of movement (especially the 'sending' of positive energies). In Chapter 8, we see that similar practices of care and intimacy circulate in Peter's

WhatsApp exchanges with two close friends – for example through frequent checking-in and again through entextualized physical acts such as hugs and kisses. Together, these chapters have shown how the reciprocal circulation of affective responses, expressions and actions can shape the very boundaries of the friendships, groups and communities to which Tony and Peter belong. The focus on Tony's calls for help in Chapter 7 shows how the circulation of affective flows can bring comfort and reassurance at times of need, and work to shape and consolidate the contours of a loving, caring and compassionate community that is characterized by togetherness. Peter's more varied and dynamic WhatsApp data shows how individuals can deploy affective practices of love, familiarity, intimacy and care to sustain multidimensional tapestries of affective connection that are often nuanced, sometimes playful and frequently careful in more ways than one.

The discussion of affective connection in Chapters 7 and 8 plays an important part in the book's argument around connective parenting as a whole. These chapters have shown how Tony and Peter build and mobilize supportive relationships that often feel familial in nature and suggest that affective connections are significant in maintaining these relationships. The chapters underline the important point that there need not be a distinction between the affective practices of intimacy and care that constitute traditional, or 'given' families, and those same practices as they operate in other close-knit and supportive groups, including 'chosen' families. The book's discussion of affective connection therefore points to significant links between familial, friendship and community practices, and shows that 'connected parenting' is a concept that can be extended far beyond the boundaries of nuclear family and parent–child relationships.

So far, this chapter has often foregrounded commonalities between participants in the Marginalised Families Online study. However, it is also clear from the six case studies presented in this book that connected parenting practices can take multiple and varied forms, depending on individuals' histories, identities, circumstances, preferences and the resources at their disposal. Thus, whilst I theorize parents' digital and family practices around the single nexus of 'connected parenting', this book has also shown just how varied that nexus can be. To give an example, Peter, the coupled gay father whose mobile messaging exchanges are explored in Chapter 8, uses digital media in quite different ways from most other participants. He connects almost exclusively with individuals and small groups, via messaging apps, phone calls, video calls and face-to-face meetings. He also has very little contact with other LGBT parents, or parents who have used donor conception and/or surrogacy, preferring to build and maintain connections with local parents, as well as established friends and family.

By contrast with Peter's connected parenting practice, Cheryl, Lynne and Jenny, who have restricted their networks almost exclusively to other single adoptive parents, seem to value very different axes of similarity. For these participants, especially Cheryl, connecting with single adopters seems to be a form of self-preservation in the face of the intersecting difficulties they face. Fear of being attacked, stigmatized, judged or misunderstood leads these participants to closely guard the safe, relatively private spaces in which they can openly share their experiences with single adopters. Looking at a different case again, Rachael, the heterosexual solo mum whose Instagram posts are explored in Chapter 6, is uniquely willing (among these six participants) to share extensive details of her family life in relatively open forums. Indeed, she mobilizes her personal experience as a powerful tool in normalizing solo motherhood and working to bring about positive social change for this group. In sum, each of these participants makes use of different digital tools, technologies and media to realize different levels and combinations of collective, epistemic and affective connection, with dyads and groups of varied sizes, compositions and functions. This diversity illustrates the expansive nature of connected parenting as a flexible constellation of practices that can be adapted for different contexts, cultures and technologies.

Methodological contributions

This book makes a compelling case for the combination of grounded theory and mediated discourse analysis in contemporary applied, sociolinguistic and discourse analytical research that seeks to understand digital media as it is embedded in everyday life and intertwined with a range of social practices. Individually, grounded theory and mediated discourse analyses offer incomplete sets of resources for a qualitative study based on in-depth interviews, digital data collection and micro-level discourse analysis. For example, grounded theory provides strategies for research design and theory development that are rooted in participants' everyday lives, experiences and perspectives, whilst mediated discourse analysis is well suited to in-depth exploration of specific texts, actions and practices. This book presents a complete methodological toolkit that maximizes the benefits of both traditions, taking the analyst from research design to preliminary coding, theory building and in-depth analysis. In the case of the Marginalised Families Online study, it shows how this approach can be used to trace social actions through digital texts whilst situating them in relation to individuals' broader networks, lives and family practices.

In Chapter 1, I explained in detail the rationale for combining these approaches. I showed how grounded theory's emphasis on inductive and person-centred research, socially situated action and the development of explanatory theory is very well suited to the goals of this book. Further, I underlined the synergies between grounded theory and mediated discourse analysis, explaining that although MDA has quite different theoretical origins, it also emphasizes the importance of social action in the mechanisms of everyday life. Indeed, it positions social action as the central unit of analysis, attending to the mediational means through which actions are realized in and through discourse. MDA's dual focus on how discourse can be used to take actions, and how actions can be situated in discourse, means it is well situated to pick up where grounded theory leaves off: to take a grounded theory of how actions are accomplished in everyday life (in this case, the theory of *connected parenting*) and further analyse the specific dimensions of those actions through micro-level discourse analysis. Further, the analyses presented in this book have often paired MDA with entextualization, as a tool for elaborating the specific processes by which actions, when captured and transformed through a range of mediational means, can be used to perform future actions. Through an emphasis on the processes of decontextualization, entextualization and recontextualization, I have been able to scrutinize the ways in which parents' actions and practices are mediated in specific digital texts, in terms of the origins of those actions, the ways in which they are mediated and (re)produced and the future actions they enable.

This book also contributes to the advancement of research ethics in applied, sociolinguistic and discourse analytical projects with a digital component. As in my previous work (Mackenzie, 2017, 2019), I have advocated a case-based and context-sensitive approach to internet research ethics that is guided by the core ethical principle of maximizing benefits and minimizing harm, acknowledges my own positionality as a researcher and treats ethical considerations as an integral and ongoing part of the research process. Applying this approach to the Marginalised Families Online study has had a number of significant implications for the research design. For example, by allowing participants to take control of the digital data selection process, I prioritized their comfort and autonomy, and worked to foster a trusting researcher–participant relationship. Further, in order to preserve participants' anonymity, this book has tended to present digital media data in transcribed and/or pixellated form. Such compromises in the selection and presentation of data, I argue, are necessary for the ethical viability of the research as a whole. The book therefore contributes to an ongoing discussion around researcher priorities when weighing the balance between participant anonymity and autonomy, research design and analytical viability.

Implications for social action

In keeping with the combined methodological impetus of grounded theory and mediated discourse analysis, this book places *social action* at the heart of its investigation. In Chapter 1, I explained that social action is the central unit of analysis for a mediated discourse analytical approach. I also explained that this focus is not limited to the analysis of mediated social action but can include the social action of the researcher and the potential of research itself to both constitute and motivate social action in the world (Scollon & Scollon, 2004). In line with this stance, I bring this book to a close by outlining its implications for social action. This exploration will include consideration of what the book can tell us about the issues and challenges facing single, LGBT and adoptive parents in the UK, the social actions that can be taken to address these challenges and any potential barriers to such transformative action.

I begin by reiterating the significance of *collective connection* as the foundational component of the connected parenting nexus of practice. As explained in Chapter 3, connecting with parents in similar families feels vital for many of the parents who took part in the Marginalised Families Online study. The sense of support, solidarity and togetherness that can arise from peer-to-peer collective connection seems to be particularly important for single adopters, a group who face intersecting prejudices based on the presumption that families should be biologically related and that heterosexually coupled parents provide the most appropriate family settings for children. Further, single adoptive parents often face practical and emotional challenges that stem from being the sole parent to their children, from their children's traumatic early life experiences and from a lack of sufficient support from educational, health and social services. Single adopters like Cheryl and Jenny, for example, made it clear that they had experienced multiple failings in the services of institutions such as social services and CAMHS (Child and Adolescent Mental Health Services) (see Chapters 4 and 5).

Despite some of the Marginalised Families Online participants' negative experiences, in all cases they were able to access and provide help, support and encouragement within dyads, groups and networks of friends, family, peers and communities. The participants were skilled in their mobilization of digital tools and technologies, including a range of digital apps, platforms and technologies, for these ends. Many of them moved with ease between different modes of connection, for example between relatively intimate, personal conversations through mobile messaging apps, telephone calls and face-to-face meetings, to public announcements and appeals through information networks such as Twitter. Through their connected parenting practices, then, it can be said that several Marginalised Families Online participants were empowered to challenge and counter different forms of social inequality and discrimination, to build their own families and support systems, and by doing so, to plug gaps in institutional support. These findings beg the question of whether there are any social issues to be addressed here at all: in many ways these parents are thriving, in terms of their access to social support and their enthusiasm to advance positive social change where it is needed.

However, there are two significant factors that suggest connected parenting practice should not be seen as either a substitute for better state and institutional support or an adequate counterbalance against wider social misunderstanding, stigma and discrimination. First, it must be very clearly acknowledged that the Marginalised Families Online participants are a privileged, well-connected group. Many of these parents are able to operate confidently in a range of social, professional and institutional settings because they have acquired high levels of familiarity, confidence and mastery with digital tools and technologies, and with social and institutional networks, systems and materials, over many years. Of the nine parents who took part in the study, one of them works for an adoption charity; two of them have written books about the experiences of adoptive and solo parent families; two of them are researchers and another runs a business that is influential in the world of fertility, IVF and solo parenthood. Not all parents will have access to the same networks and technologies that enable and support these participants' connected parenting practice.

Bearing this in mind, one form of social action that might benefit diverse and marginalized families would be to improve *all* parents' access to, and proficiency with, digital media and technologies. Some guidance on parents' use of social media already exists, particularly for adoptive parents, through the charity Adoption UK[1] and related organizations such as Childnet International.[2] However, this guidance tends to focus on online safety and anonymity for adoptive parents and children, which is an important issue given that some adoptive children's birth families present a danger to them, and they must therefore withdraw from public view. Nevertheless, the negative focus of this guidance may discourage some parents from using social media entirely. These parents may subsequently lose out on access to the positive relationships and expansive family practices that can be constructed and maintained online. As part of the Marginalised Families Online project, I worked with the charity Adoption UK to produce a guide to social media for new adopters, which attempts to balance caution around the risks of social media with optimism around the meaningful relationships, support and guidance that can be found via digital media. However, the document is only available to adoptive parents who access the services of Adoption UK and their partner organizations, and as such is not likely to reach other diverse and marginalized families who may find it useful and informative.

The second, related counterpoint to any claim that connected parenting is anathema to social discrimination and inadequate institutional support is that digital networking comes with its own problems, and as such, many individuals may not want to bring it into their parenting and family practice. It has already been mentioned earlier, for example, that privacy and anonymity can be vital for many adoptive families. The use of social media may therefore be linked with high levels of anxiety and risk around their children's safety and autonomy. This risk certainly affects the way adoptive parents like Cheryl and Jenny use digital media (see Chapters 4 and 5). Of course, it is not just adoptive parents who feel this way: Peter and Tony, for example, were also extremely careful not to post photographs or information about their children on any social networking sites, restricting this kind of detail exclusively to mobile messages and password-protected photoblogs (see Chapters 7 and 8). Further, several participants suggested that connecting with others via digital and social media came with other stressors. For example, Cheryl explained that she often felt the need to be constantly available to her peers. Lynne, similarly, noted that she sometimes became frustrated and annoyed by other people's online comments and posts on Facebook. Digital media, then, are not for everyone, and their benefits will not always outweigh their drawbacks. That is not to say, however, that connected parenting practice has to involve digitally mediated connections. Whilst digital media certainly can facilitate the process of finding, connecting and sharing information with others at the touch of a button, all of the digitally mediated practices that are explored in this book could quite easily be enacted through different mediational means, such as face-to-face interactions, conferences, rallies, print books and magazines, letters and phone calls. Indeed, the Marginalised Families Online participants' digitally mediated interactions frequently do intersect with these modes of connection.

As I bring this book to its conclusion, I emphasize the point that whilst the benefits of connected parenting should not be underestimated, neither should digitally mediated social support be hailed as a one-size-fits-all solution to the myriad social issues and concerns that disproportionately affect diverse, non-traditional and marginalized families. To do so would be in danger of masking (but not resolving) the problems themselves, which are deeply rooted in discriminatory norms around what makes a family, unequal access to social and medical support, and inadequate funding for struggling children and their carers. Further, working to improve *parents'* access to digitally mediated peer support would put the onus on the very people who are most affected by social stigma and inequality to solve their own problems through peer-to-peer connection, advocacy and kinship. The social actions that are needed to address these issues, however, would likely require better representation, understanding and communication around non-traditional family practices that reach far beyond these parents' networks – for example through popular media, advertising and other public discourse. Further, in political and institutional domains, adjustments must be made to family policy and guidelines that will better support these groups, for example through equal access to health care and fertility, education and improved support from social services. I therefore close this book with a call for further research, social action and advocacy that will advance these social changes, bringing about a more equal, inclusive and accepting environment in which *all* family forms can thrive.

Notes

Introduction

1. Figures published by the Department for Education show that in 2021, one in six adoptions were to same-sex couples: https://explore-education-statistics.service.gov.uk/find-statistics/children-looked-after-in-england-including-adoptions.
2. The subheading of the call read 'Are you a single parent, and/or LGBT parent? Do you use the internet or mobile technology to connect with others or talk about family life?'
3. Demographics by postcode identified via https://www.postcodearea.co.uk/.

Chapter 2

1. I am also indebted to Kelly-Mae Saville (personal communication), who adopted a similar strategy in her work with parents of children with dwarfism.
2. Tamsin Parnell and Marianne Fish, who at the time were part-time research assistants at the University of Nottingham.

Chapter 3

1. Here I refer to participants who entered into parenthood as single adopters and have raised their children largely as single parents. This does not include Anna, who is single, but originally adopted with her ex-wife and continues to co-parent with this woman.
2. These and other demographic details were correct at the mid-point of data collection, 1 May 2019.
3. As explained in Chapter 2, digital data is often transcribed in this book, in order to preserve participants' anonymity.
4. Presumably, 'fuzz' refers to the small particles of material that collect on everything if, for example, you mix in a tissue with the laundry.

Chapter 4

1. These are all real Facebook groups at the time of writing, March 2022, which I found by searching groups from my own Facebook account.
2. As explained in Chapter 3, digital data is often transcribed in this book, in order to preserve participants' anonymity. However, in these figures, screenshots are used because the way the posts appear on screen is relevant to the discussion that follows. Cheryl's name and image, and the name of the group, have been obscured to protect their identities and privacy.

Chapter 5

1. This count is based on the information curated and displayed by Twitter, and shown on Jenny's profile. Twitter's total tweet count includes tweets, retweets and replies.
2. Threads are counted here as a single tweet.
3. Sally Donovan is the pseudonym used by the author herself in her publications and public communication. Because she is quite well known as Sally Donovan and has a public-facing persona, I have not anonymized her further.
4. Children in Need is an annual charity drive in the UK that is organized by the BBC and centres on a televised programme of entertainment and appeals.

Chapter 7

1. Details are taken from the UK Fae Revolutionary website. However, in order to preserve the anonymity of this community, direct quotes are avoided and the url is not specified.

Chapter 9

1. https://www.adoptionuk.org/faqs/social-networking.
2. https://www.childnet.com/resources/foster-carers-and-adoptive-parents/.

References

Abidin, C. (2018). *Internet Celebrity: Understanding Fame Online*. Bingley: Emerald.
Adams-Santos, D. (2020). Sexuality and digital space. *Sociology Compass, 14*(8), 1–15.
Adoption UK. (2021). *Adoption Barometer*. Banbury: Adoption UK.
Ahmed, S. (2014). *The Cultural Politics of Emotion* (Second Edition). Edinburgh: Edinburgh University Press.
Akrich, M. (2010). From communities of practice to epistemic communities: Health mobilizations on the Internet. *Sociological Research Online, 15*(2), 116–32.
Al Rashdi, F. (2018). Functions of emojis in WhatsApp interaction among Omanis. *Discourse, Context & Media, 26,* 117–26.
Alinejad, D. (2019). Careful co-presence: The transnational mediation of emotional intimacy. *Social Media + Society, 5*(2), 1–11.
Androutsopoulos, J. (2008). Potentials and limitations of discourse-centred online ethnography. *Language@Internet, 5,* article 9.
Androutsopoulos, J. (2021). Polymedia in interaction. *Pragmatics and Society, 12*(5), 707–24.
AoIR (Association of Internet Researchers). (2019). *Internet Research: Ethical Guidelines 3.0*. Association of Internet Researchers. Retrieved from https://aoir.org/reports/ethics3.pdf.
Artamonova, O., & Androutsopoulos, J. (2020). Smartphone-based language practices among refugees: Mediational repertoires in two families. *Journal Für Medienlinguistik, 2*(2), 60–89.
Asprey, E., & Tagg, C. (2019). The pragmatic use of vocatives in private one-to-one digital communication. *Internet Pragmatics, 2*(1), 83–111.
Autenrieth, U. (2018). Family photography in a networked age: Anti-sharenting as a reaction to risk assessment and behaviour adaption. In G. Mascheroni, C. Ponte, & A. Jorge (Eds.), *Digital Parenting: The Challenges for Families in the Digital Age* (pp. 219–32). Goteborg: Nordicom.
BAAL (British Association for Applied Linguistics). (2021). *Recommendations on Good Practice in Applied Linguistics*. British Association for Applied Linguistics. Retrieved from https://www.baal.org.uk/wp-content/uploads/2021/03/BAAL-Good-Practice-Guidelines-2021.pdf
Baron, N. S. (2008). *Always On: Language in an Online and Mobile World*. New York: Oxford University Press.
Bartholeyns, G. (2014). The instant past: Nostalgia and digital retro photography. In K. Niemeyer (Ed.), *Media and Nostalgia: Yearning for the Past, Present and Future* (pp. 51–69). New York: Palgrave MacMillan.

Barton, D., & Lee, C. (2013). *Language Online: Investigating Digital Texts and Practices*. London and New York: Routledge.

Bauman, R., & Briggs, C. L. (1990). Poetics and performance as critical perspectives on language and social life. *Annual Review of Anthropology, 19*, 59–88.

Baym, N. K. (2010). *Personal Connections in the Digital Age*. Cambridge and Malden, MA: Polity.

Bazarova, N. N. (2012). Public intimacy: Disclosure interpretation and social judgments on Facebook. *Journal of Communication, 62*(5), 815–32.

Bazeley, P. (2007). *Qualitative Data Analysis with NVivo*. London, Thousand Oaks, New Delhi and Singapore: Sage Publications.

Bednarek, M. (2008). *Emotion Talk Across Corpora*. Hampshire and New York: Palgrave MacMillan.

Belenky, M. F., Clinchy, B. M., Goldberger, N. R., & Tarule, J. M. (1986). *Women's Ways of Knowing: The Development of Self, Voice, and Mind*. New York: Basic Books.

Bellander, T., & Nikolaidou, Z. (2017). Building health knowledge online: Parents' online information searching on congenital heart defects. *Literacy and Numeracy Studies, 25*(1), 4–19.

Ben-Ari, A., & Weinberg-Kurnik, G. (2007). The dialectics between the personal and the interpersonal in the experiences of adoptive single mothers by choice. *Sex Roles, 56*(11–12), 823–33.

Beneito-Montagut, R. (2017). Emotions, everyday life, and the social web: Age, gender, and social web engagement effects on online emotional expression. *Sociological Research Online, 22*(4), 87–104.

Bennett, W. L., & Segerberg, A. (2012). The logic of connective action: Digital media and the personalization of contentious politics. *Information, Communication & Society, 15*(5), 739–68.

Birks, M., & Mills, J. (2015). *Grounded Theory: A Practical Guide* (Second Edition). Los Angeles, London, New Delhi, Singapore and Washington, DC: Sage.

Blommaert, J. (2005). *Discourse: A Critical Introduction*. Cambridge and New York: Cambridge University Press.

Blommaert, J., & Varis, P. (2015). Enoughness, accent and light communities: Essays on contemporary identities. *Tilburg Papers in Cultural Studies*, 139.

Blumer, H. (1969). *Symbolic Interactionism: Perspective and Method*. Englewood Cliffs, NJ: Prentice Hall.

Blum-Ross, A., & Livingstone, S. (2017). 'Sharenting', parent blogging, and the boundaries of the digital self. *Popular Communication, 15*(2), 110–25.

Bolander, B., & Locher, M. A. (2015). 'Peter is a dumb nut': Status updates and reactions to them as 'acts of positioning' in Facebook. *Pragmatics. Quarterly Publication of the International Pragmatics Association (IPrA), 25*(1), 99–122.

Boler, M., & Davis, E. (2018). The affective politics of the 'post-truth' era: Feeling rules and networked subjectivity. *Emotion, Space and Society, 27*, 75–85.

Bourdieu, P. (1972). *Outline of a Theory of Practice*. Cambridge: Cambridge University Press.

Boyd, D., Golder, S., & Lotan, G. (2010). Tweet, tweet, retweet: Conversational aspects of retweeting on twitter. In *Proceedings of the Annual Hawaii International Conference on System Sciences* (pp. 1–10).

Bryan, V., Flaherty, C., & Saunders, C. (2010). Supporting adoptive families: Participant perceptions of a statewide peer mentoring and support program. *Journal of Public Child Welfare*, 4(1), 91–112.

Bucher, T. (2021). *Facebook*. Cambridge and Medford, MA: Polity Press.

Bucholtz, M., & Hall, K. (2005). Identity and interaction: A sociocultural linguistic approach. *Discourse Studies*, 7(4–5), 585–614.

Buehler, E. M., Crowley, J. L., Peterson, A. M., & High, A. C. (2019). Broadcasting for help: A typology of support-seeking strategies on Facebook. *New Media & Society*, 21(11–12), 2566–88.

Burgess, J., & Baym, N. K. (2020). *Twitter: A Biography*. New York: New York University Press.

Chambers, D. (2013). *Social Media and Personal Relationships: Online Intimacies and Networked Friendships*. Hampshire and New York: Palgrave MacMillan.

Charmaz, K. (2008). Grounded theory in the 21st century: Applications for advancing social justice studies. In N. K. Denzin & Y. S. Lincoln (Eds.), *Strategies of Qualitative Inquiry* (Third Edition, pp. 203–42). Los Angeles, London, New Delhi and Singapore: Sage.

Charmaz, K. (2014). *Constructing Grounded Theory* (Second Edition). Los Angeles, London, New Delhi, Singapore and Washington, DC: Sage.

Church, K., & Oliveira, R. de. (2013). What's up with WhatsApp? Comparing mobile instant messaging behaviors with traditional SMS. In *Proceedings of Mobile HCI2013: Collaboration and Communication* (pp. 352–61). New York: ACM Publications.

Clarke, A. E. (2005). *Situational Analysis: Grounded Theory after the Postmodern Turn*. Thousand Oaks, London and New Delhi: Sage.

Clarke, A. E., Friese, C. E., & Washburn, R. S. (2018). *Situational Analysis: Grounded Theory after the Interpretive Turn* (Second Edition). Los Angeles, London, New Delhi, Singapore, Melbourne and Washington, DC: Sage.

Clough, P. T. (2008). The affective turn: Political economy, biomedia and bodies. *Theory, Culture & Society*, 25(1), 1–22.

Clough, P. T., & Halley, J. (2007). *The Affective Turn: Theorizing the Social*. Durham, NC and London: Duke University Press.

Copland, F., & Creese, A. (2015). *Linguistic Ethnography: Collecting, Analysing and Presenting Data*. Los Angeles, London, Washington, DC, New Delhi and Singapore: Sage.

Corbin, J., & Strauss, A. (2008). *Basics of Qualitative Research: Techniques and Procedures for Developing Grounded Theory* (Third Edition). London, New Delhi and Singapore: Sage.

Corbin, J., & Strauss, A. L. (2015). *Basics of Qualitative Research: Techniques and Procedures for Developing Grounded Theory* (Fourth Edition). Los Angeles: Sage.

Correia, H., & Broderick, P. (2009). Access to reproductive technologies by single women and lesbians: Social representations and public debate. *Journal of Community & Applied Psychology, 19*, 241–56.

Cummings, J. A. (2018). Transformational change in parenting practices after child interpersonal trauma: A grounded theory examination of parental response. *Child Abuse & Neglect, 76*, 117–28.

Das, R., & Hodkinson, P. (2019). Tapestries of intimacy: Networked intimacies and new fathers' emotional self-disclosure of mental health struggles. *Social Media + Society, 5*(2), 1–10.

Dewey, J. (1929). *The Quest for Certainty: A Study of the Relation of Knowledge and Action*. New York: Putnam.

Draucker, F., & Collister, L. (2015). Managing participation through modal affordances on Twitter. *Open Library of Humanities, 1*(1), 1–36.

Du Bois, J. W. (2007). The stance triangle. In R. Englebretson (Ed.), *Stancetaking in Discourse: Subjectivity, Evaluation, Interaction* (pp. 139–82). Amsterdam: Benjamins.

Duranti, A. (1997). *Linguistic Anthropology*. Cambridge: Cambridge University Press.

Ellece, S. E. (2012). The 'placenta' of the nation: Motherhood discourses in Tswana marriage ceremonies. *Gender and Language, 6*(1), 79–104.

Ellison, N. B., Steinfield, C., & Lampe, C. (2007). The benefits of Facebook 'friends:' Social capital and college students' use of online social network sites. *Journal of Computer-Mediated Communication, 12*(4), 1143–68.

Enfield, N. J., Kockelman, P., & Sidnell, J. (Eds.). (2014). *The Cambridge Handbook of Linguistic Anthropology*. Cambridge and New York: Cambridge University Press.

ESRC (Economic and Social Research Council). (2021). *Research Ethics: Our Core Principles*. Economic and Social Research Council. Retrieved from https://esrc.ukri.org/funding/guidance-for-applicants/research-ethics/our-core-principles/

Ess, C. (2007). Internet research ethics. In H. Fossheim & H. Ingierd (Eds.), *The Oxford Handbook of Internet Psychology* (pp. 487–502). New York: Oxford University Press.

Fage-Butler, A. M., & Jensen, M. N. (2013). The interpersonal dimension of online patient forums: How patients manage informational and relational aspects in response to posted questions. *HERMES - Journal of Language and Communication in Business, 26*(51), 21–38.

Ferreday, D. (2003). Unspeakable bodies: Erasure, embodiment and the pro-ana community. *International Journal of Cultural Studies, 6*(3), 277–95.

Finch, J. (2007). Displaying families. *Sociology, 41*(1), 65–81.

Fishman, P. M. (1978). Interaction: The work women do. *Social Problems, 25*(4), 397–406.

Formby, E. (2017). *Exploring LGBT Spaces and Communities: Contrasting Identities, Belongings and Wellbeing*. London and New York: Routledge.

Gabb, J. (2011). Troubling displays: The affect of gender, sexuality and class. In E. Dermott & Seymour (Eds.), *Displaying Families: A New Concept for the Sociology of Family Life* (pp. 38–57). Hampshire and New York: Palgrave MacMillan.

Gangneux, J. (2020). Tactical agency? Young people's (dis)engagement with WhatsApp and Facebook Messenger. *Convergence: The International Journal of Research into New Media Technologies, 27*(2), 458–71.

Gee, J. P. (2014). *An Introduction to Discourse Analysis: Theory and Method* (Fourth Edition). London and New York: Routledge.

Georgakopoulou, A. (2017). 'Whose context collapse?': Ethical clashes in the study of language and social media in context. *Applied Linguistics Review, 8*(2–3), 169–89.

Georgalou, M. (2017). *Discourse and Identity on Facebook*. London and New York: Bloomsbury.

Gianino, M. (2008). Adaptation and transformation: The transition to adoptive parenthood for gay male couples. *Journal of GLBT Family Studies, 4*(2), 205–43.

Giaxoglou, K. (2021). *A Narrative Approach to Social Media Mourning: Small Stories and Affective Positioning* (First Edition). London and New York: Routledge.

Gibbs, G. R. (2002). *Qualitative Data Analysis: Explorations with NVivo*. Buckingham, Philadelphia: Open University Press.

Glaser, B. G. (1978). *Theoretical Sensitivity*. Mill Valley, CA: Sociology Press.

Glaser, B. G., & Strauss, A. L. (1967). *The Discovery of Grounded Theory: Strategies for Qualitative Research*. Chicago: Aldine.

Goldberg, A. E. (2012). *Gay Dads: Transitions to Adoptive Fatherhood*. New York and London: New York University Press.

Golombok, S. (2015). *Modern Families: Parents and Children in New Family Forms*. Cambridge: Cambridge University Press.

Goodwin, M. H., Cekaite, A., & Goodwin, C. (2012). Emotion as stance. In A. Peräkylä and M. Sorjonen (Eds.), *Emotion in Interaction* (pp. 16–41). Oxford: Oxford University Press.

Gruber, H. (2017). Quoting and retweeting as communicative practices in computer mediated discourse. *Discourse, Context and Media, 20*, 1–9.

Gumperz, J. J., & Hymes, D. (1972). *Directions in Sociolinguistics: The Ethnography of Communication*. New York: Holt, Rinehart, & Winston.

Hadley, G. (2015). *English for Academic Purposes in Neoliberal Universities: A Critical Grounded Theory*. Cham: Springer International Publishing.

Hadley, G. (2017). *Grounded Theory in Applied Linguistics Research: A Practical Guide*. London and New York: Routledge.

Han, S. (2018). Reproduction and language. In K. Hall & R. Barrett (Eds.), *The Oxford Handbook of Language and Sexuality* (pp. 1–21). Oxford University Press.

Hanell, L., & Salö, L. (2017). Nine months of entextualizations: Discourse and knowledge in an online discussion forum thread for expectant parents. In C. Kerfoot & K. Hyltenstam (Eds.), *Entangled Discourses: South-North Orders of Visibility* (pp. 154–70). New York: Routledge.

Harding, K. D., Whittingham, L., & McGannon, K. R. (2021). #sendwine: An analysis of motherhood, alcohol use and #winemom culture on Instagram. *Substance Abuse: Research and Treatment*, 15.

Harré, R., & van Langenhove, L. (1999). *Positioning Theory: Moral Contexts of International Action*. Oxford: Blackwell.

Heaphy, B. (2011). Critical relational displays. In E. Dermott and J. Seymour (Eds.), *Displaying Families: A New Concept for the Sociology of Family Life* (pp. 19–37). Hampshire and New York: Palgrave MacMillan.

Hertz, R., Jociles, M. I., & Rivas, A. M. (2016). Single mothers by choice in Spain and the United States. In Constance L. Shehan (Ed.), *The Wiley Blackwell Encyclopedia of Family Studies* (pp. 1–5). Wiley Blackwell.

Hine, C. (2000). *Virtual Ethnography*. London, California and New Delhi: Sage.

Hine, C. (2014). Headlice eradication as everyday engagement with science: An analysis of online parenting discussions. *Public Understanding of Science*, 23(5), 574–91.

Hochschild, A. R. (1979). Emotion work, feeling rules, and social structure. *American Journal of Sociology*, 86(3), 551–75.

Hodkinson, P., & Das, R. (2021). *New Fathers, Mental Health and Digital Communication*. Switzerland: Palgrave MacMillan.

Hogan, B., Carrasco, J. A., & Wellman, B. (2007). Visualizing personal networks: Working with participant-aided sociograms. *Field Methods*, 19(2), 116–44.

Holland, S. (2018). Constructing queer mother-knowledge and negotiating medical authority in online lesbian pregnancy journals. *Sociology of Health and Illness*, 41(1), 52–66.

Hutchings, T. (2017). 'We are a united humanity': Death, emotion and digital media in the Church of Sweden. *Journal of Broadcasting & Electronic Media*, 61(1), 90–107.

Hymes, D. (1962). The ethnography of speaking. In T. Gladwin & W. C. Sturtevant, *Anthropology and Human Behavior* (pp. 13–53). Washington, DC: Anthropology Society of Washington.

Hymes, D. (1972). Models of the interaction of language and social life. In *Directions in Sociolinguistics: The Ethnography of Communication* (pp. 35–71). New York: Holt Rinehart and Winston.

Ito, M., & Okabe, D. (2005). Technosocial situations: Emergent structuring of mobile e-mail use. In *Personal, Portable, Pedestrian: Mobile Phones in Japanese Life* (pp. 257–73). Cambridge, MA: MIT Press.

Jamieson, L. (2011). Intimacy as a concept: Explaining social change in the context of globalisation or another form of ethnocentricism? *Sociological Research Online*, 16(4), 151–63.

Jaworska, S. (2018). 'Bad' mums tell the 'untellable': Narrative practices and agency in online stories about postnatal depression on Mumsnet. *Discourse, Context and Media*, 25, 25–33.

Jennings, S., Mellish, L., Tasker, F., Lamb, M., & Golombok, S. (2014). Why adoption? Gay, lesbian, and heterosexual adoptive parents' reproductive experiences and reasons for adoption. *Adoption Quarterly, 17*(3), 205–26.

Jensen, T. (2013). 'Mumsnetiquette': Online affect within parenting culture. In C. Maxwell & P. Aggleton (Eds.), *Privilege, Affect and Agency* (pp. 127–45). London: Palgrave MacMillan.

Johnson, S. A. (2015). 'Intimate mothering publics': Comparing face-to-face support groups and Internet use for women seeking information and advice in the transition to first-time motherhood. *Culture, Health & Sexuality, 17*(2), 237–51.

Jones, L., Chałupnik, M., Mackenzie, J., & Mullany, L. (2022). 'STFU and start listening to how scared we are': Resisting misogyny on Twitter via #NotAllMen. *Discourse, Context & Media, 47*, 1–10.

Jones, L., Mills, S., Paterson, L. L., Turner, G., & Coffey-Glover, L. (2017). Identity and naming practices in British marriage and civil partnerships. *Gender and Language, 11*(3), 309–35.

Jones, R. H. (2009). Dancing, skating and sex: Action and text in the digital age. *Journal of Applied Linguistics, 6*(3), 283–302.

Jones, R. H. (2020a). Mediated discourse analysis. In S. Adolphs & D. Knight (Eds.), *The Routledge Handbook of English Language and Digital Humanities* (pp. 202–19). Oxon and New York: Routledge.

Jones, R. H. (2020b). Towards an embodied visual semiotics: Negotiating the right to look. In C. Thurlow, C. Dürscheid, & F. Diémoz (Eds.), *Visualizing Digital Discourse: Interactional, Institutional and Ideological Perspectives* (pp. 19–41). Berlin and Boston: De Gruyter.

Jones, R. H., & Norris, S. (2005a). Discourse as action/ discourse in action. In S. Norris and R. H. Jones (Eds.), *Discourse in Action: Introducing Mediated Discourse Analysis* (pp. 3–14). London and New York: Routledge.

Jones, R. H., & Norris, S. (2005b). Introducing practice. In S. Norris and R. H. Jones (Eds.), *Discourse in Action: Introducing Mediated Discourse Analysis* (pp. 97–9). London and New York: Routledge.

Kivits, J. (2004). Researching the 'informed patient'. *Information, Communication & Society, 7*(4), 510–30.

Kivits, J. (2009). Everyday health and the internet: A mediated health perspective on health information seeking. *Sociology of Health & Illness, 31*(5), 673–87.

Kuntsman, A. (2009). *Figurations of Violence and Belonging: Queerness, Migranthood and Nationalism in Cyberspace and Beyond*. Oxford, Bern, Berlin, Bruxelles, Frankfurt am Main, New York and Wien: Peter Lang.

Lambert, A. (2013). *Intimacy and Friendship on Facebook*. London and New York: Palgrave MacMillan.

Lambert, A. (2016). Intimacy and social capital on Facebook: Beyond the psychological perspective. *New Media & Society, 18*(11), 2559–75.

Landqvist, M. (2016). Sense and sensibility – Online forums as epistemic arenas. *Discourse, Context & Media*, *13*, 98–105.

Lave, J., & Wenger, E. (1991). *Situated Learning: Legitimate Peripheral Participation*. Cambridge: Cambridge University Press.

Le Moignan, E., Lawson, S., Rowland, D. A., Mahoney, J., & Briggs, P. (2017). Has Instagram fundamentally altered the 'family snapshot'? *Proceedings of the 2017 CHI Conference on Human Factors in Computing Systems*, 4935–47. Colorado: ACM.

Leaver, T., Highfield, T., & Abidin, C. (2020). *Instagram: Visual Social Media Cultures*. Cambridge and Medford, MA: Polity Press.

Lee, J. R., Moore, D. C., Park, E.-A., & Park, S. G. (2012). Who wants to be 'friend-rich'? Social compensatory friending on Facebook and the moderating role of public self-consciousness. *Computers in Human Behavior*, *28*(3), 1036–43.

Lehto, M. (2021). *Affective Power of Social Media: Engagements with Networked Parenting Culture*. Turku: University of Turku.

Lehto, M. (2022). Ambivalent influencers: Feeling rules and the affective practice of anxiety in social media influencer work. *European Journal of Cultural Studies*, *25*(1), 201–16.

Leurs, K. (2019). Transnational connectivity and the affective paradoxes of digital care labour: Exploring how young refugees technologically mediate co-presence. *European Journal of Communication*, *34*(6), 641–9.

Lexander, K. V., & Androutsopoulos, J. (2021). Working with mediagrams: A methodology for collaborative research on mediational repertoires in multilingual families. *Journal of Multilingual and Multicultural Development*, *42*(1), 1–18.

Locatelli, E. (2017). Images of breastfeeding on Instagram: Self-representation, publicness, and privacy management. *Social Media + Society*, *3*(2), 1–14.

Lyons, A. (2018). Multimodal expression in written digital discourse: The case of kineticons. *Journal of Pragmatics*, *131*, 18–29.

Lyons, A. (2020). Negotiating the expertise paradox in new mothers' WhatsApp group interactions. *Discourse, Context and Media*, *37*, 100427.

Lyons, A., & Tagg, C. (2019). The discursive construction of mobile chronotopes in mobile-phone messaging. *Language in Society*, *48*(5), 657–83.

Mackenzie, J. (2017a). 'Can we have a child exchange?' Constructing and subverting the 'good mother' through play in Mumsnet Talk. *Discourse & Society*, *28*(3), 296–312.

Mackenzie, J. (2017b). Identifying informational norms in Mumsnet Talk: A reflexive-linguistic approach to internet research ethics. *Applied Linguistics Review*, *8*(2–3) 293–314.

Mackenzie, J. (2018). 'Good mums don't, apparently, wear make-up': Negotiating discourses of gendered parenthood in Mumsnet Talk. *Gender and Language*, *12*(1), 114–35.

Mackenzie, J. (2019). *Language, Gender and Parenthood Online: Negotiating Motherhood in Mumsnet Talk*. London and New York: Routledge.

Mackenzie, J. (2021). 'I had to work through what people would think of me': Negotiating 'problematic single motherhood' as a solo or single adoptive mum. *Critical Discourse Studies*, online first.

Mackenzie, J. (in press). Negotiating normativities of gender, sexuality and the family in gay parents' small stories. *Journal of Language and Sexuality*.

Mackenzie, J., & Zhao, S. (2021). Motherhood online: Issues and opportunities for discourse analysis. *Discourse, Context and Media*, 40(100472), 1–4.

Madianou, M. (2014). Polymedia communication and mediatized migration: An ethnographic approach. In K. Lundby (Ed.), *Mediatization of Communication* (pp. 323–46). Berlin and Boston: De Gruyter.

Madianou, M. (2016). Ambient co-presence: Transnational family practices in polymedia environments. *Global Networks*, 16(2), 183–201.

Madianou, M., & Miller, D. (2012). *Migration and New Media: Transnational Families and Polymedia*. London and New York: Routledge.

Malmquist, A. (2015). *Pride and Prejudice: Lesbian Families in Contemporary Sweden*. Linköping: Linköping University.

Malmquist, A., Björnstam, T., & Thunholm, A. (2019). Swedish children of single mothers by choice, and children of heterosexual couples, reflect on child conception and other paths to parenthood. *NORA - Nordic Journal of Feminist and Gender Research*, 27(3), 166–80.

Marcon, A. R., Bieber, M., & Azad, M. B. (2019). Protecting, promoting, and supporting breastfeeding on Instagram. *Maternal & Child Nutrition*, 15(1), 1–12.

Markham, A., & Buchanan, E. (2015). Internet research: Ethical concerns. In J. D. Wright (Ed.), *International Encyclopedia of the Social and Behavioral Sciences* (2nd Edition, pp. 603–13, Vol. 12). Amsterdam, Paris, New York, Oxford, Shannon, Singapore and Tokyo: Elsevier.

Martin, J. R., & White, P. R. R. (2005). *The Language of Evaluation: Appraisal in English*. Hampshire and New York: Palgrave MacMillan.

Mason, J. (2018a). *Affinities*. Cambridge and Medford. MA: Polity Press.

Mason, J. (2018b). *Qualitative Researching* (Second Edition). London, Thousand Oaks and New Delhi: Sage Publications.

Massumi, B. (2002). *Parables for the Virtual: Movement, Affect, Sensation*. Durham, NC: Duke University Press.

Matley, D. (2020). 'I miss my old life': Regretting motherhood on Mumsnet. *Discourse, Context and Media*, 37(100417), 1–8.

Mauthner, N., & Doucet, A. (1998). Reflections on a voice-centred relational method: Analysing maternal and domestic voices. In J. Ribbens & R. Edwards (Eds.), *Feminist Dilemmas in Qualitative Research: Public Knowledge and Private Lives* (pp. 119–46). London, Thousand Oaks and New Delhi: Sage.

McDermott, E., & Graham, H. (2005). Resilient young mothering: Social inequalities, late modernity and the 'problem' of 'teenage' motherhood. *Journal of Youth Studies*, 8(1), 59–79.

McLaughlin, C., & Vitak, J. (2011). Norm evolution and violation on Facebook. *New Media & Society*, *14*(2), 299–315.

Mead, G. H. (1934). *Mind, Self and Society*. Chicago: University of Chicago Press.

Mendonça, P. (2018). Situating single mothers through values-based cartooning. *Women: A Cultural Review*, *29*(1), 19–38.

Milani, T. M., & Richardson, J. E. (2021). Discourse and affect. *Social Semiotics*, *31*(5), 671–6.

Miller, H. T., & Fox, C. J. (2001). The epistemic community. *Administration and Society*, *32*(6), 668–85.

Miller, J. J., Cooley, M., Niu, C., Segress, M., Fletcher, J., Bowman, K., & Littrell, L. (2019). Support, information seeking, and homophily in a virtual support group for adoptive parents: Impact on perceived empathy. *Children and Youth Services Review*, *101*, 151–6.

Milroy, L. (1980). *Language and Social Networks*. Oxford: Blackwell.

Morgan, D. H. J. (1996). *Family Connections: An Introduction to Family Studies*. Cambridge: Polity Press.

Morgan, D. H. J. (2011). *Rethinking Family Practices*. London: Palgrave Macmillan UK.

Morrison, A. (2011). 'Suffused by feeling and affect': The intimate public of personal mommy blogging. *Biography*, *34*(1), 37–55.

Mortensen, K. K., & Milani, T. M. (2021). Affect in language, gender and sexuality research: Studying heterosexual desire. In Jo Angouri and Judith Baxter (Eds.), *The Routledge Handbook of Language, Gender and Sexuality* (pp. 450–64). London and New York: Routledge.

Nieborg, D. B., & Helmond, A. (2019). The political economy of Facebook's platformization in the mobile ecosystem: Facebook Messenger as a platform instance. *Media, Culture & Society*, *41*(2), 196–218.

Nissenbaum, H. (2010). *Privacy in Context: Technology, Policy and the Integrity of Social Life*. Stanford, CA: Stanford University Press.

Norris, S. (2004). *Analyzing Multimodal Interaction: A Methodological Framework*. London and New York: Routledge.

Norris, S., & Jones, R. H. (2005). *Discourse in Action: Introducing Mediated Discourse Analysis*. London and New York: Routledge.

Oakley, A. (1981). Interviewing women: A contradiction in terms. In H. Roberts (Ed.), *Doing Feminist Research* (pp. 30–61). London: Routledge.

Ochs, E., & Schieffelin, B. (1989). Language has a heart. *Text*, *9*(1), 7–25.

Ochs, E., & Taylor, C. (1995). The 'father knows best' dynamic in dinnertime narratives. In Kira Hall and Mary Bucholtz (Eds.), *Gender Articulated: Language and the Socially Constructed Self* (pp. 97–120). New York: Routledge.

Page, R. (2010). Re-examining narrativity: Small stories in status updates. *Text & Talk*, *30*(4), 423–44.

Page, R. (2018). *Narratives Online: Shared Stories in Social Media*. Cambridge, New York, Melbourne, New Delhi and Singapore: Cambridge University Press.

Page, R. (2019). Group selfies and Snapchat: From sociality to synthetic collectivisation. *Discourse, Context & Media, 28*, 79–92.

Papacharissi, Z. (2010). *A Networked Self: Identity, Community, and Culture on Social Network Sites.* New York and London: Routledge.

Papacharissi, Z. (2014). *Affective Publics: Sentiment, Technology, and Politics.* New York: Oxford University Press.

Papen, U. (2013). Conceptualising information literacy as social practice: A study of pregnant women's information practices. *Information Research, 18*(2). http://informationr.net/ir/18-2/paper580.html#.YyhX-CVKi3A.

Pedersen, S., & Lupton, D. (2018). 'What are you feeling right now?' communities of maternal feeling on Mumsnet. *Emotion, Space and Society, 26*, 57–63.

Peräkylä, A., & Sorjonen, M.-L. (2012). *Emotion in Interaction.* New York: Oxford University Press.

Poulsen, S. V. (2018). Becoming a semiotic technology – a historical study of Instagram's tools for making and sharing photos and videos. *Internet Histories, 2*(1–2), 121–39.

Pounds, G., Hunt, D., & Koteyko, N. (2018). Expression of empathy in a Facebook-based diabetes support group. *Discourse, Context & Media, 25*, 34–43.

Poveda, D., Jociles, M. I., & Rivas, A. M. (2014). Socialization into single-parent-by-choice family life. *Journal of Sociolinguistics, 18*(3), 319–44.

Price, S. L., Aston, M., Monaghan, J., Sim, M., Tomblin Murphy, G., Etowa, J., . . . Little, V. (2018). Maternal knowing and social networks: Understanding first-time mothers' search for information and support through online and offline social networks. *Qualitative Health Research, 28*(10), 1552–63.

Puschmann, C. (2015). The form and function of quoting in digital media. *Discourse, Context and Media, 7*, 28–36.

Quan-Haase, A., & Young, A. L. (2010). Uses and gratifications of social media: A comparison of Facebook and Instant Messaging. *Bulletin of Science, Technology & Society, 30*(5), 350–61.

Rampton, B., Tusting, K., Maybin, J., Barwell, R., Creese, A., & Lytra, V. (2004). UK linguistic ethnography: A discussion paper. Retrieved from UK Linguistic Ethnography Forum website: https://www.lancaster.ac.uk/fss/organisations/lingethn/documents/discussion_paper_jan_05.pdf

Riordan, M. A. (2017). Emojis as tools for emotion work: Communicating affect in text messages. *Journal of Language and Social Psychology, 36*(5), 549–67.

Rüdiger, S., & Dayter, D. (2017). The ethics of researching unlikeable subjects. *Applied Linguistics Review, 8*(2–3), 251–69.

Salter, E. (2018). A media discourse analysis of lone parents in the UK: Investigating the stereotype. In L. Bernardi & D. Mortelmans (Eds.), *Lone Parenthood in the Life Course* (pp. 55–74). Cham: Springer Open.

Santana, D. S. (2019). Mais Viva! Reassembling transness, blackness, and feminism. *TSQ: Transgender Studies Quarterly, 6*(2), 210–22.

Schofield Clark, L. (2012). *The Parent App: Understanding Families in the Digital Age*. Oxford: Oxford University Press.

Schutt, R. K. (2012). *Investigating the Social World: The Process and Practice of Research* (Seventh Edition). Los Angeles, London, New Delhi, Singapore and Washington, DC: Sage.

Scollon, R. (1998). *Mediated Discourse as Social Interaction*. London: Longman.

Scollon, R. (2001). *Mediated Discourse: The Nexus of Practice*. London and New York: Routledge.

Scollon, R. (2007). Discourse itineraries: Nine processes of resemiotization. In Vijay Bhatia, John Flowerdew and Rodney H. Jones (Eds.), *Advances in Discourse Studies* (pp. 233–44). London and New York: Routledge.

Scollon, R., & Scollon, S. W. (2004). *Nexus Analysis: Discourse and the Emerging Internet*. London and New York: Routledge.

Seko, Y., & Tiidenberg, K. (2016). Birth through the digital womb: Visualizing prenatal life online. In P. G. Nixon, R. Rawal, & A. Funk (Eds.), *Digital Media Usage across the Lifecourse* (pp. 50–66). Surrey: Ashgate Publishing.

Selwyn, J., Wijedasa, D., & Meakings, S. (2014). *Beyond the Adoption Order: Challenges, Interventions and Adoption Disruption*. Department for Education. Retrieved from Department for Education website: https://assets.publishing.service.gov.uk/government/uploads/system/uploads/attachment_data/file/302339/Final_Research_brief_-_3rd_April_2014.pdf

Sharma, D. (2017). Scalar effects of social networks on language variation. *Language Variation and Change*, 29(3), 393–418.

Silverstein, M., & Urban, G. (1996). *Natural Histories of Discourse*. Chicago and London: The University of Chicago Press.

Skeggs, B. (1995). Theorising, ethics and representation in feminist ethnography. In B. Skeggs (Ed.), *Feminist Cultural Theory: Process and Production* (pp. 190–206). Manchester and New York: Manchester University Press.

Song, F. W., West, J. E., Lundy, L., & Smith Dahmen, N. (2012). Women, pregnancy, and health information online: The making of informed patients and ideal mothers. *Gender and Society*, 26(5), 773–98.

Statista. (2022a). Number of monthly active Facebook users worldwide as of 4th quarter 2021. Retrieved 2 March 2022, from Statista website: https://www.statista.com/statistics/264810/number-of-monthly-active-facebook-users-worldwide/

Statista. (2022b). Number of monthly active Instagram users from January 2013 to December 2021. Retrieved 11 March 2022, from Statista website: https://www.statista.com/statistics/253577/number-of-monthly-active-instagram-users/

Strauss, A., & Corbin, J. (1990). *Basics of Qualitative Research: Grounded Theory Procedures and Techniques* (First Edition). Newbury Park, CA: Sage.

Strekalova, Y. A. (2016). Finding motivation: Online information seeking following newborn screening for Cystic Fibrosis. *Qualitative Health Research*, 26(9), 1180–90.

Sundén, J., & Paasonen, S. (2019). Inappropriate laughter: Affective homophily and the unlikely comedy of #MeToo. *Social Media + Society*, 5(4).

Sunderland, J. (2000). Baby entertainer, bumbling assistant and line manager: Discourses of fatherhood in parentcraft texts. *Discourse & Society*, 11(2), 249–74.

Tagg, C., & Lyons, A. (2020). Post-digital linguistic ethnography and the networked individual. *Working Papers in Translanguaging and Translation*. Retrieved from https://wordpress.com/page/tlang.org.uk/12

Tagg, C., & Lyons, A. (2021a). Polymedia repertoires of networked individuals: A day-in-the-life approach. *Pragmatics and Society*, 12(5), 725–55.

Tagg, C., & Lyons, A. (2021b). Repertoires on the move: Exploiting technological affordances and contexts in mobile messaging interactions. *International Journal of Multilingualism*, 18(2), 244–66.

Tagg, C., & Lyons, A. (2022). *Mobile Messaging and Resourcefulness: A Post-digital Ethnography*. London and New York: Routledge.

Tagg, C., Lyons, A., Hu, R., & Rock, F. (2017). The ethics of digital ethnography in a team project. *Applied Linguistics Review*, 8(2–3), 271–92.

Tajfel, H., & Turner, J. (1979). An integrative theory of intergroup conflict. In W. G. Austin & S. Worchel (Eds.), *The Social Psychology of Intergroup Relations* (pp. 33–47). Monterey, CA: Brooks-Cole.

Takahashi, T. (2014). Youth, social media and connectivity in Japan. *The Language of Social Media*, 22, 186–207.

Taylor, Y., Falconer, E., & Snowdon, R. (2014). Queer youth, Facebook and faith: Facebook methodologies and online identities. *New Media & Society*, 16(7), 1138–53.

Tes Global Ltd. (2022). About Us. Retrieved from Tes.com website: https://www.tes.com/about-us

Tiidenberg, K. (2018). *Selfies: Why We Love (and Hate) Them*. Bingley: Emerald.

TLANG. (2021). Translation and translanguaging: Investigating linguistic and cultural transformations in superdiverse wards in four UK cities (TLANG). Retrieved 6 April 2022, from Translation and Translanguaging (TLANG) website: https://tlang.org.uk/

Tong, S. T., Heide, B. V. D., Langwell, L., & Walther, J. B. (2008). Too much of a good thing? The relationship between number of friends and interpersonal impressions on Facebook. *Journal of Computer-Mediated Communication*, 13(3), 531–49.

Tudor, M. (2018). *Desire Lines: Towards a Queer Digital Media Phenomenology* (PhD thesis). Stockholm: Södertörn University.

Tusting, K. (2020). General introduction. In K. Tusting (Ed.), *The Routledge Handbook of Linguistic Ethnography* (pp. 1–9). Oxon and New York: Routledge.

van Dijck, J. (2008). Digital photography: Communication, identity, memory. *Visual Communication*, 7(1), 57–76.

van Dijck, J. (2013). *The Culture of Connectivity: A Critical History*. New York: Oxford University Press.

van Leeuwen, T. (2008). *Discourse and Practice: New Tools for Critical Discourse Analysis*. Oxford: Oxford University Press.

Varis, P. (2015). Digital ethnography. In A. Georgakopoulou & T. Spilioti (Eds.), *The Routledge Handbook of Language and Digital Communication* (pp. 55–68). London and New York: Routledge.

Veazey, L. W. (2019). Glocalised motherhood: Sociality and affect in migrant mothers' online communities. *Feminist Encounters: A Journal of Critical Studies in Culture and Politics*, 3(1–2), 1–15.

Wall, G. (2010). Mothers' experiences with intensive parenting and brain development discourse. *Women's Studies International Forum*, 33(3), 253–63.

Wall, G. (2013). 'Putting family first': Shifting discourses of motherhood and childhood in representations of mothers' employment and child care. *Women's Studies International Forum*, 40, 162–71.

Wargo, J. M. (2017). 'Every selfie tells a story. . .': LGBTQ youth lifestreams and new media narratives as connective identity texts. *New Media & Society*, 19(4), 560–78.

Waterloo, S. F., Baumgartner, S. E., Peter, J., & Valkenburg, P. M. (2018). Norms of online expressions of emotion: Comparing Facebook, Twitter, Instagram, and WhatsApp. *New Media & Society*, 20(5), 1813–31.

Weeks, J., Heaphy, B., & Donovan, C. (2001). *Same Sex Intimacies: Families of Choice and Other Life Experiments*. London and New York: Routledge.

Weistra, S., & Luke, N. (2017). Adoptive parents' experiences of social support and attitudes towards adoption. *Adoption and Fostering*, 41(3), 228–41.

West, L. E. (2013). Facebook sharing: A sociolinguistic analysis of computer-mediated storytelling. *Discourse, Context & Media*, 2(1), 1–13.

Weston, K. (1991). *Families We Choose: Lesbians, Gays, Kinship*. New York: Columbia University Press.

Wetherell, M. (2012). *Affect and Emotion: A New Social Science Understanding*. Los Angeles and London: Sage.

WhatsApp Inc. (2021, July 8). WhatsApp. Retrieved 8 July 2021, from WhatsApp.com website: https://www.whatsapp.com/?lang=en

Wilding, R., Baldassar, L., Gamage, S., Worrell, S., & Mohamud, S. (2020). Digital media and the affective economies of transnational families. *International Journal of Cultural Studies*, 23(5), 639–55.

Wilkinson, S. (1988). The role of reflexivity in feminist psychology. *Women's Studies International Forum*, 11(5), 493–502.

Wolf, A. (2000). Emotional expression online: Gender differences in emoticon use. *CyberPsychology & Behavior*, 3(5), 827–33.

Zappavigna, M. (2011). Ambient affiliation: A linguistic perspective on Twitter. *New Media & Society*, 13(5), 788–806.

Zappavigna, M. (2014). CoffeeTweets: Bonding around the bean on Twitter. In P. Seargeant & C. Tagg (Eds.), *The Language of Social Media* (pp. 139–60). London: Palgrave Macmillan UK.

Zappavigna, M. (2016). Social media photography: Construing subjectivity in Instagram images. *Visual Communication, 15*, 271–92.

Zappavigna, M., & Zhao, S. (2017). Selfies in 'mommyblogging': An emerging visual genre. *Discourse, Context & Media, 20*, 239–47.

Zaslow, E. (2012). Revalorizing feminine ways of knowing: The challenge to biomedical epistemology in an online mothers' health community. *Information Communication and Society, 15*(9), 1352–72.

Zhao, X., & Basnyat, I. (2018). Online social support for 'Danqin Mama': A case study of parenting discussion forum for unwed single mothers in China. *Computers in Human Behavior, 80*, 12–21.

Index

action
  connective 109, 206
  social 1, 4, 24–5, 29–32, 35, 37–9, 46, 62, 138, 156, 159, 203, 206, 209–11, 213
activism 32, 116, 117, 133, 135
adoption
  challenges 7–8, 87–8, 111, 113–14
  community 58, 80–1, 86, 88, 111–14, 117–18, 125–7
  and education 114, 126, 132
  UK charity 41, 211–12
advocacy 117, 135, 156, 213
affect 63, 67, 99, 122, 126, 159–66, 188–92, 203–4
affection 165–7, 174–8, 187–8, 194–6, 206
affective
  actions 161, 163, 173, 175, 176, 194–6
  economies 163, 165
  evaluation 126, 189–92, 199
  expression 161, 165
  flow 162, 173, 175, 176, 196, 198–9, 207
  homophily 164, 170, 192
  practices 159, 164, 165, 170, 173, 176, 194, 207
  publics 162
  stance 99, 122, 126, 161
  turn 160
  values 169
affective connection, *see* connection
affiliation 59, 65–9, 72, 86, 90, 115
affinities 11
agency 13–14, 24, 30
alignment 66–8, 116–17, 126, 163, 192, 195
alternative family, *see* family
ambient co-presence, *see* co-presence
ambient virtual co-presence, *see* co-presence

anonymity 15, 50, 118, 209–10, 212

bisexual parent, *see* parents

care 12, 97, 99, 127, 147, 166–7, 174–8, 193–6, 198–9, 205–7
case studies 5, 43, 61–2, 65–6, 85–6, 107–8, 111–13, 137–8, 156–7, 159–60, 168, 170, 179–80, 185
Charmaz, K. 23–5, 39, 41, 43, 45–6
checking-in 5, 12, 34, 166, 186–7, 193–6, 207
chosen family, *see* family
coding
  for action 46–7
  focused 51–3
  initial 45–7
  theoretical 51–3
collective connection, *see* connection
collective venting 101–5
collectivization 66–8, 78, 99–100, 135
community
  of feeling 165
  online 115, 117, 125–7, 171, 176–7, 206–7
  parenting 8, 70, 81, 86–7, 91, 102, 109–10, 117, 125–7
  queer 160, 167–9, 171, 206–7
comparative analysis 24, 45–6
complaining 186–9, 191–2
connected
  knowing 107, 110
  parenting 1–5, 58–63, 95, 107, 134–5, 159–60, 200–8, 210–13
connection
  affectionate 188, 194
  affective 2–3, 11, 63, 95, 126, 159–60, 162–4, 166–9, 175–6, 188–9, 191–3, 196, 198–200, 202–4, 206–8
  collective 65–70, 79, 83–4, 97–100, 105–6, 113–14, 123, 202–6, 210

Index

constant   12–13, 89
epistemic   2, 77, 95, 107–11, 118, 126, 137–8, 147–9, 203, 206
family   6, 14, 199
intimate   19–20, 192, 194, 199, 201
peer-to-peer   69, 108, 205, 210, 213
physical   175–6
social   11–15
spiritual   169, 175–6
visual   187
connective action, *see* action
constructivist grounded theory, *see* grounded theory
co-presence   11, 12, 166, 182

data
collection   14, 24, 26, 39–40, 48–50, 103
selection   49, 62, 209
decontextualisation, *see* entextualization
deixis   78, 82, 84, 100, 104
digital
connection   12–14, 60, 65, 67–9, 116–17, 168, 177, 201, 205, 212
media   1–2, 4, 9–15, 40, 43–4, 48–50, 53, 62, 79, 94, 113–14, 117–18, 138–9, 165–6, 179–82, 184–6, 201–3, 209, 211–12
networks   1, 15, 43, 48–9, 51–8, 62, 71–5, 86, 89–90, 109–10, 112–17, 138–42, 167–70, 184, 201, 211–12
technologies   11, 15–16, 18, 29, 33–4, 166
discourse
and action   30–1, 62
analysis   9, 23, 25–6, 27–8, 30, 61–2, 162, *see also* mediated discourse analysis
identification   26
itineraries   33
as language   30–1
displaying family, *see* family
donor conception   8, 111, 137, 152
dyadic interaction   180, 184–5, 192, 199

emotion   3, 20, 31, 159–63, 167–77, 171, 184, 195–6, 199, 203
emotional

care   12, 166
expression   164–5, 169, 184
intimacy   12
reciprocity   69, 159, 163, 165, 170–1, 195
responses   68, 127, 195–6
sharing, *see* sharing
support   91, 166, 184
empathy   77, 91, 94, 164, 170, 187
endorsement   117–19
entextualization   35, 62, 108, 125, 141–2, 149–51, 156–7, 175–7, 194–6, 203–7, 209, *see also* micro-entextualisation
epistemic connection, *see* connection
ethics   18, 39–41, 44, 63, 171, 209–10
ethnography   28–9
experiential sharing, *see* sharing
expertise   14, 43, 47, 53–5, 60, 107–10, 113, 114, 121, 126, 128, 133, 135, 157, 203, 206

Facebook
groups   20, 37, 42, 49–50, 60, 63, 68, 72–3, 75, 85–6, 89, 91–2, 105, 112, 160, 170–1, 174, 184, 204–5
messenger   83
page   88, 171
posts   35, 49–50, 75, 89, 92
timeline   71
family
alternative   6–8, 14, 23, 205, 211–13
chosen   20, 177
display   6
extended   5, 52, 59, 167
given   177
heterosexual   6–7
idealised   6, 156
life   4–7, 9–10, 14, 41, 54, 89, 91–2, 109, 111–12, 152, 156, 203–4, 206, 208
migratory   159, 165
nuclear   20, 178
practices   1–7, 9–11, 18, 20–1, 23, 38–9, 59, 61–2, 70, 79, 83–5, 105, 154–6, 176, 178, 201–7
roles   155–6
sociology   4–6
fathers   152–3, 160, 164, 173

feeling rules   165, 195
focused coding, *see* coding
friendship   12–13, 72–3, 79, 83, 91, 113, 159, 169–70, 180–2, 200, 207

gay parent, *see* parents
gender   4, 7, 9, 18, 27, 62, 156
grounded theory   1, 18, 23–30, 37–9, 45, 47, 62–3, 208–9

hashtags   67, 115, 140–1, 144, 149, 154–5
home education   127, 133–4
homophily   57–9, 72, 86, 90–1, 192, *see also* affective, homophily
humour   93, 186, 188, 196–9
inductive research design   14, 24–6, 39–40, 43, 209

infant feeding   37, 62
influencers   142, 144, 165
informed
    consent   42, 50
    parents   109–11
    patients   109
initial coding, *see* coding
Instagram   115, 139–44, 149–50, 156, 205
instant messaging, *see* messaging
intensification
    of experience   142
    of parenting   142–3
interviews   14, 43–5, 92
intimacy   11–12, 43, 166, 170, 175, 177, 193–6, 199, 206–7

Jones, R.   31–7, 141, 188

kinship   6, 8–9, 126, 160, 166, 175, 181
knowledge
    construction   19, 108, 112, 205–6
    resources   10, 37, 77, 107, 149, 203, 206

media references   188–92
mediated
    action   1, 10–11, 23, 31–2, 201
    discourse analysis   4, 23, 30–3, 62–3, 159, 208–10
    technologies   4, 62

texts   1, 23
mediational means   14, 30–4, 185, 209, 212
memos   18, 24, 26–7, 39, 44
mentions   76, 88, 115, 117, 123, 140
messaging
    apps   70, 73–4, 114, 138, 167, 171, 183–4, 207, 211
    instant   72, 74, 86, 184
    mobile   2, 12–13, 74–5, 79, 114, 138, 167, 179, 180, 182–4, 191, 211
    private   114, 167
messenger   17, 19, 49–50, 62, 65–6, 70, 73–6, 79–83, 85, 167, 171, 183
Meta   19, 73, 89, 140, 183
metonymy   82–4, 149, 205
micro-entextualization   81–4, 99–100, 103–4, 205, *see also* entextualization
mobile
    messaging, *see* messaging
    phones   13, 41, 56, 74, 82, 89, 166, 183, 191–2
Morgan, D.   4–6
motherhood   8–9, 138, 142–4, 149, 151, 154–6, 159, 165, 203, 206, 208
mothering   9, 143, 163–4, 195, 203
mothers   8, 68, 75, 109–11, 138, 142–3, 150–1, 154–6, 163, 165, 186

network diagrams   54–8, 71–3, 79, 86–8, 92, 113–14, 168, 180–2
networked individuals   1, 4, 14
nexus of practice   3, 5, 20, 31–3, 200, 202, 204, 207, 210

online community, *see* community

parenting
    collectives   65, 69, 159, 163–5, 170–4, 177, 195, 205–6
    communities   160, 165
    practice   4, 37, 61, 79, 91–2, 102–3, 109, 156, 200–1
parents
    adoptive   2, 7–8, 60, 65–6, 70–3, 85–9, 95–7, 106–7, 112, 124–30, 132–4, 210–12
    bisexual   1, 3, 15–16, 41

gay 1, 3, 7, 15, 17, 167, 179–81
heterosexual 6–7, 15–17, 86, 112, 137–8, 182, 208
lesbian 1, 3, 15, 17, 41, 60, 159–60, 167
same-sex 6–7
single 8, 60, 65–6, 70–3, 86, 112, 146, 148, 154, 210
participant
  anonymity, *see* anonymity
  autonomy 40, 43, 48, 53–4, 118, 209–10
  recruitment 23, 41–3
polymedia 13, 15
practices 1–6, 9–12, 18–21, 26–34, 36–9, 48–9, 58–66, 68–70, 79–80, 85, 96–100, 116–18, 134–35, 159–66, 168–70, 175–9, 199–213
privacy 48–9, 115, 118, 167, 171, 180, 183, 212
professional support 8, 10, 70, 87–8, 94, 103, 114, 210

qualitative data analysis software 44–5
queer
  community, *see* community
  culture 172
  family 167, 169, 175, 204
  media 166
questionnaires 1, 42

recontextualisation, *see* entextualization
rejection 10, 117–20, 127, 168–9
relationality 12, 67
research design, *see* inductive research design
retweet 90, 115–16, 119–20, 124–7, 132–5, 203

safe spaces 89, 95, 169, 202
Scollon, R. 1, 3–4, 30–3, 62, 202, 210
self-representation 140–3
shared
  action 70, 78–9, 100, 105, 202
  experience 65–6, 68, 72, 75–6, 79, 81, 83–5, 94, 99–100, 104, 126–7, 134, 143, 203–4
  knowledge 77, 81–4, 95, 100, 137, 205

practice 65, 96, 100, 107
understanding 69, 98, 103–4, 164, 172, 174, 195
viewing 189–91
sharing
  emotional 160, 163–4, 170–1, 174, 195
  experiential 144–7, 152–5, 186–8, 196, 198
  info-relational 85, 92, 94–100
single parent, *see* parents
sites of engagement 4, 31–3
social
  action, *see* action
  networking sites 12, 70, 74, 109, 114, 138, 212
  networks 11, 14–15, 51, 58, 138, 140–1, 180, 184
  support 167, 204, 211
solidarity 65–6, 68–9, 79–80, 91, 95–7, 104–8, 123, 134–5, 164, 174, 195, 204–5, 210
staged dialogue 132, 134–5
support-seeking 94, 109
surrogacy 14, 17, 20, 42, 62, 160, 179, 180, 208
symbolic interactionism 24–5, 29–30, 32, 46

takedown thread 117–19, 127, 129, 132–4
technologies of entextualisation, *see* entextualization
texts 23, 26, 29–30, 33–6, 38–9, 61–2, 64–5, 81–3, 98–100, 161, 163, 172, 205, 208–9
theoretical codes, *see* coding
transcription 44–5
Twitter 15–17, 19, 41–2, 44, 49–50, 58, 90, 112–19, 126–7, 140–1, 184, 203–6

venting 85, 92–4, 101, 103–5, 186–7

WhatsApp 10, 15–17, 49–50, 62–3, 166–7, 179–80, 182–6, 188, 191–2, 197–9, 204–5, 207

www.ingramcontent.com/pod-product-compliance
Lightning Source LLC
Chambersburg PA
CBHW062148300426
44115CB00012BA/2041